An Outcast
Or, Virtue and Faith

by

F. Colburn Adams

An Outcast
or, virtue and faith
by F. Colburn Adams

ISBN: 978-93-64287-87-6

Published by

DOUBLE 9 BOOKS
2/13-B, Ansari Road
Daryaganj, New Delhi – 110002
info@double9books.com
www.double9books.com
Tel. 011-40042856

ABOUT THE AUTHOR

F. Colburn Adams (1836–1899) was an American author and journalist known for his work in literature and the press. Here's a detailed look at his life and contributions.: Among his notable works is "The Beautiful Wife," a novel published in the late 19th century, which reflects his interest in social issues and personal relationships. His works often dealt with themes of morality, social justice, and personal growth. Adams's writing frequently included social commentary, reflecting his interest in issues such as social justice and moral dilemmas. His novels often explored the complexities of human relationships and societal norms. His narrative style was characterized by its clarity and engagement, with a focus on character development and plot. Adams's work often combined elements of drama and satire, providing a nuanced view of the society he wrote about. F. Colburn Adams is remembered for his contributions to American literature and journalism during the 19th century. His works offer insights into the social and moral issues of his time, and his ability to address these issues with both depth and accessibility has earned him a place in literary history. While not as widely recognized as some of his contemporaries, Adams's work is appreciated for its thoughtful exploration of social themes and its contribution to the literature of the period. F. Colburn Adams's career as a journalist and author highlights his commitment to addressing important social issues through his writing. His novels and articles provide a window into the concerns and values of 19th-century American society.

CONTENTS

PREFACE

When reason and conscience are a man's true guides to what he undertakes, and he acts strictly in obedience to them, he has little to fear from what the unthinking may say. You cannot, I hold, mistake a man intent only on doing good. You may differ with him on the means he calls to his aid; but having formed a distinct plan, and carried it out in obedience to truth and right, it will be difficult to impugn the sincerity of his motives. For myself, I care not what weapon a man choose, so long as he wield it effectively, and in the cause of humanity and justice. We are a sensitive nation, prone to pass great moral evils over in silence rather than expose them boldly, or trace them to their true sources. I am not indifferent to the duty every writer owes to public opinion, nor the penalties he incurs in running counter to it. But fear of public opinion, it seems to me, has been productive of much evil, inasmuch as it prefers to let crime exist rather than engage in reforms. Taking this view of the matter, I hold fear of public opinion to be an evil much to be deplored. It aids in keeping out of sight that which should be exposed to public view, and is satisfied to pass unheeded the greatest of moral evils. Most writers touch these great moral evils with a timidity that amounts to fear, and in describing crimes of the greatest magnitude, do it so daintily as to divest their arguments of all force. The public cannot reasonably be expected to apply a remedy for an evil, unless the cause as well as the effect be exposed truthfully to its view. It is the knowledge of their existence and the magnitude of their influence upon society, which no false delicacy should keep out of sight, that nerves the good and generous to action. I am aware that in exciting this action, great care should be taken lest the young and weak-minded become fascinated with the gilding of the machinery called to the writer's aid. It is urged by many good people, who take somewhat narrow views of this subject, that in dealing with the mysteries of crime vice should only be described as an ugly dame with most repulsive features. I differ with those persons. It would be a violation of the truth to paint her thus, and few would read of her in such an unsightly dress. These persons do not, I think, take a sufficiently clear view of the grades into which the vicious of our community are divided, and their different modes of living. They found their opinions solely on the moral and physical condition of the most wretched and abject class, whose sufferings they would have us hold up to public view, a warning to those who stand hesitating on the brink between virtue and vice. I hold it better to expose the allurements first, and then paint vice in her natural colors—a dame so gay and fascinating that it is difficult not to become enamored of her. The ugly and repulsive dame would have few followers, and no need of writers to caution the unwary against her snares. And I cannot forget, that truth always carries the more forcible lesson. But we must paint the road to vice as well as the castle, if we would give effect to our warning. That road is too frequently strewn with the brightest of flowers, the thorns only discovering themselves when the sweetness of the flowers has departed. I have chosen, then, to describe things as they are. You, reader, must be the judge whether I have put too much gilding on the decorations.

I confess that the subject of this work was not congenial to my feelings. I love to deal with the bright and cheerful of life; to leave the dark and sorrowful to those whose love for them is stronger than mine. Nor am I insensible to the liabilities incurred by a writer who, having found favor with the public, ventures upon so delicate and hazardous an undertaking. It matters not how carefully and discreetly he perform the task, there will always be persons enough to question his sincerity and cast suspicion upon his motives. What, I have already been asked, was my motive for writing such a book as this? Why did I descend into the repulsive haunts of the wretched and the gilded palaces of the vicious for the material of a novel? My answer is in my book.

New York, *January 1st*, 1861.

CHAPTER I
CHARLESTON

This simple story commences on a November evening, in the autumn of 185-. Charleston and New York furnish me with the scenes and characters.

Our quaint old city has been in a disquiet mood for several weeks. Yellow fever has scourged us through the autumn, and we have again taken to scourging ourselves with secession fancies. The city has not looked up for a month. Fear had driven our best society into the North, into the mountains, into all the high places. Business men had nothing to do; stately old mansions were in the care of faithful slaves, and there was high carnival in the kitchen. Fear had shut up the churches, shut up the law-courts, shut up society generally. There was nothing for lawyers to do, and the buzzards found it lonely enough in the market-place. The clergy were to be found at fashionable watering-places, and politicians found comfort in cards and the country. Timid doctors had taken to their heels, and were not to be found. Book-keepers and bank-clerks were on Sullivan's Island. The poor suffered in the city, and the rich had not a thought to give them. Grave-looking men gathered into little knots, at street corners, and talked seriously of Death's banquet. Old negroes gathered about the kitchen-table, and terrified themselves with tales of death: timid ones could not be got to pass through streets where the scourge raged fiercest. Mounted guardsmen patrolled the lonely streets at night, their horses' hoofs sounding on the still air, like a solemn warning through a deserted city.

Sisters of Mercy, in deep, dark garments, moved noiselessly along the streets, by day and by night, searching out and ministering to the sick and the dying. Like brave sentinels, they never deserted their posts. The city government was in a state of torpor. The city government did not know what to do. The city government never did know what to do. Four hundred sick and dying lay languishing in the hospital. The city government was sorry for them, and resolved that Providence would be the best doctor. The dead gave place to the dying by dozens, and there has been high carnival down in the dead-yard. The quick succession of funeral trains has cast a shade of melancholy over the broad road that leads to it. Old women are vending pies and cakes at the gates, and little boys are sporting over the newly-made graves, that the wind has lashed into furrows. Rude coffins stand about in piles, and tipsy negroes are making the very air jubilant with the songs they bury the dead to.

A change has come over the scene now. There is no more singing down in the dead-yard. A bright sun is shedding its cheerful rays over the broad landscape, flowers deck the roadside, and the air comes balmy and invigorating. There has been frost down in the lowlands. A solitary stranger paces listlessly along the walks of the dead-yard, searching in vain for the grave of a departed friend. The scourge has left a sad void between friends living and friends gone to eternal rest. Familiar faces pass us on the street, only to remind us of familiar faces passed away forever. The city is astir again. Society is coming back to us. There is bustle in the churches, bustle in the law courts, bustle in the hotels, bustle along the streets, bustle everywhere. There is bustle at the steamboat landings, bustle at the railway stations, bustle in all our high places. Vehicles piled with trunks are hurrying along the streets; groups of well-dressed negroes are waiting their master's return at the landings, or searching among piles of trunks for the family baggage. Other groups are giving Mas'r and Missus such a cordial greeting. Society is out of an afternoon, on King street, airing its dignity. There is Mr. Midshipman Button, in his best uniform, inviting the admiration of the fair, and making such a bow to all distinguished persons. Midshipman Button, as he is commonly called, has come home to us, made known to us the pleasing fact that he is ready to command our "navy" for us, whenever we build it for him. There is Major Longstring, of the Infantry, as fine a man in his boots as woman would fancy, ready to fight any foe; and corporal Quod, of the same regiment, ready to shoulder his weapon and march at a moment. We have an immense admiration for all these heroes, just now; it is only equalled by their admiration of themselves. The buzzards, too, have assumed an unusual air of importance—are busy again in the market; and long-bearded politicians are back again, at their old business, getting us in a state of discontent with the Union and everybody in general.

There is a great opening of shutters among the old mansions. The music of the organ resounds in the churches, and we are again in search of the highest pinnacle to pin our dignity upon. Our best old families have been doing the North extensively, and come home to us resolved never to go North again. But it is fashionable to go North, and they will break this resolution when spring comes. Mamma, and Julia Matilda have brought home an immense stock of Northern millinery, all paid for with the hardest of Southern money, which papa declares the greatest evil the state suffers under. He has been down in the wilderness for the last ten years, searching in vain for a remedy. The North is the hungry dog at the door, and he will not be kicked away. So we have again mounted that same old hobby-horse. There was so much low-breeding at the North, landlords were so extortionate, vulgarity in fine clothes got in your way wherever you went, servants were so impertinent, and the trades people were so given to cheating. We would shake our garments of the North, if only some one would tell us how to do it becomingly.

Master Tom and Julia Matilda differ with the old folks on this great question of bidding adieu to the North. Tom had a "high old time generally," and is sorry the season closed so soon. Julia Matilda has been in a pensive mood ever since she returned. That fancy ball was so brilliant; those moonlight drives were so pleasant; those flirtations were carried on with such charming grace! A dozen little love affairs, like pleasant dreams, are touching her heart with their sweet remembrance. The more she contemplates them the sadder she becomes. There are no drives on the beach now, no moonlight rambles, no promenades down the great, gay verandah, no waltzing, no soul-stirring music, no tender love-tales told under the old oaks. But they brighten in her fancy, and she sighs for their return. She is a prisoner now, surrounded by luxury in the grim old mansion. Julia Matilda and Master Tom will return to the North when spring comes, and enjoy whatever there is to be enjoyed, though Major Longstring and Mr. Midshipman Button should get us safe out of the Union.

Go back with us, reader, not to the dead-yard, but to the quiet walks of Magnolia Cemetery, hard by. A broad avenue cuts through the centre, and stretches away to the west, down a gently undulating slope. Rows of tall pines stand on either side, their branches forming an arch overhead, and hung with long, trailing moss, moving and whispering mysteriously in the gentle wind. Solemn cypress trees mark the by-paths; delicate flowers bloom along their borders, and jessamine vines twine lovingly about the branches of palmetto and magnolia trees. An air of enchanting harmony pervades the spot; the dead could repose in no prettier shade. Exquisitely chiselled marbles decorate the resting-places of the rich; plain slabs mark those of the poor.

It is evening now. The shadows are deepening down the broad avenue, the wind sighs touchingly through the tall pines, and the sinking sun is shedding a deep purple hue over the broad landscape. A solitary mocking-bird has just tuned its last note, and sailed swiftly into the dark hedgerow, down in the dead-yard.

A young girl, whose fair oval face the sun of eighteen summers has warmed into exquisite beauty, sits musingly under a cypress tree. Her name is Anna Bonnard, and she is famous in all the city for her beauty, as well as the symmetry of her form. Her dress is snowy white, fastened at the neck with a blue ribbon, and the skirts flowing. Her face is like chiselled marble, her eyes soft, black, and piercing, and deep, dark tresses of silky hair fall down her shoulders to her waist. Youth, beauty, and innocence are written in every feature of that fair face, over which a pensive smile now plays, then deepens into sadness. Here she has sat for several minutes, her head resting lightly on her right hand, and her broad sun-hat in her left, looking intently at a newly sodded grave with a plain white slab, on which is inscribed, in black letters—"Poor Miranda." This is all that betrays the sleeper beneath.

"And this is where they have laid her," she says, with a sigh. "Poor Miranda! like me, she was lost to this world. The world only knew the worst of her." And the tears that steal from her eyes tell the tale of her affection. "Heaven will deal kindly with the outcast, for Heaven only knows her sorrows." She rises quickly from her seat, casts a glance over the avenue, then pats the sods with her hands, and strews cypress branches and flowers over the grave, saying, "This is the last of poor Miranda. Some good friend has laid her here, and we are separated forever. It was misfortune that made us friends." She turns slowly from the spot, and walks down the avenue towards the great gate leading to the city. A shadow crosses her path; she hesitates, and looks with an air of surprise as the tall figure of a man advances hastily, saying, "Welcome, sweet Anna—welcome home."

He extends his gloved hand, which she receives with evident reluctance. "Pray what brought you here, Mr. Snivel?" she inquires, fixing her eyes on him, suspiciously.

"If you would not take it impertinent, I might ask you the same question. No, I will not. It was your charms, sweetest Anna. Love can draw me—I am a worshipper at its fountain. And as for law,—you know I live by that."

Mr. Snivel is what may be called a light comedy lawyer; ready to enter the service of any friend in need. He is commonly called "Snivel the lawyer," although the profession regard him with suspicion, and society keeps him on its out skirts. He is, in a word, a sportsman of small game, ready to bring down any sort of bird that chances within reach of his fowling-piece. He is tall of figure and slender, a pink of fashion in dress, wears large diamonds, an eye-glass, and makes the most of a light, promising moustache. His face is small, sharp, and discolored with the sun, his eyes grey and restless, his hair fair, his mouth wide and characterless. Cunning and low intrigue are marked in every feature of his face; and you look in vain for the slightest evidence of a frank and manly nature.

"Only heard you were home an hour ago. Set right off in pursuit of you. Cannot say exactly what impelled me. Love, perhaps, as I said before." Mr. Snivel twirls his hat in the air, and condescends to say he feels in an exceedingly happy state of mind. "I knew you needed a protector, and came to offer myself as your escort. I take this occasion to say, that you have always seen me in the false light my enemies magnify me in."

"I have no need of your escort, Mr. Snivel; and your friendship I can dispense with, since, up to this time, it has only increased my trouble," she interposes, continuing down the avenue.

"We all need friends— —"

"True friends, you mean, Mr. Snivel."

"Well, then, have it so. You hold that all is false in men. I hold no such thing. Come, give me your confidence, Anna. Look on the bright side. Forget the past, and let the present serve. When you want a friend, or a job of law, call on me." Mr. Snivel adjusts his eye-glass, and again twirls his hat.

The fair girl shakes her head and says, "she hopes never to need either. But, tell me, Mr. Snivel, are you not the messenger of some one else?" she continues.

"Well, I confess," he replies, with a bow, "its partly so and partly not so. I came to put in one word for myself and two for the judge. Its no breach of confidence to say he loves you to distraction. At home in any court, you know, and stands well with the bar— —"

"Love for me! He can have no love for me. I am but an outcast, tossed on the sea of uncertainty; all bright to-day, all darkness to-morrow. Our life is a stream of excitement, down which we sail quickly to a miserable death. I know the doom, and feel the pang. But men do not love us, and the world never regrets us. Go, tell him to forget me."

"Forget you? not he. Sent me to say he would meet you to-night. You are at the house of Madame Flamingo, eh?"

"I am; and sorry am I that I am. Necessity has no choice."

"You have left Mulholland behind, eh? Never was a fit companion for you. Can say that without offence. He is a New York rough, you know. Charleston gentlemen have a holy dislike of such fellows."

"He has been good to me. Why should I forsake him for one who affects to love me to-day, and will loathe me to-morrow? He has been my only true friend. Heaven may smile on us some day, and give us enough to live a life of virtue and love. As for the mystery that separates me from my parents, that had better remain unsolved forever." As she says this, they pass out of the great gate, and are on the road to the city.

A darker scene is being enacted in a different part of the city. A grim old prison, its walls, like the state's dignity, tumbling down and going to decay; its roof black with vegetating moss, and in a state of dilapidation generally,—stands, and has stood for a century or more, on the western outskirts of the city. We have a strange veneration for this damp old prison, with its strange histories cut on its inner walls. It has been threatening to tumble down one of these days, and it does not say much for our civilization that we have let it stand. But the question is asked, and by grave senators, if we pull it down, what shall we do with our pick-pockets and poor debtors? We mix them nicely up here, and throw in a thief for a messmate. What right has a poor debtor to demand that the sovereign state of South Carolina make a distinction between poverty and crime? It pays fifteen cents a day for getting them all well starved; and there its humanity ends, as all state humanity should end.

The inner iron gate has just closed, and two sturdy constables have dragged into the corridor a man, or what liquor has left of a man, and left him prostrate and apparently insensible on the floor. "Seventh time we've bring'd him 'ere a thin two months. Had to get a cart, or Phin and me never'd a got him 'ere," says one of the men, drawing a long breath, and dusting the sleeves of his coat with his hands.

"An officer earns what money he gits a committin' such a cove," says the other, shaking his head, and looking down resentfully at the man on the floor. "Life'll go out on him like a kan'l one of these days." Officer continues moralizing on the bad results of liquor, and deliberately draws a commitment from his breast pocket. "Committed by Justice Snivel—breaking the peace at the house of Madame——" He cannot make out the name.

First officer interposes learnedly—"Madame Flamingo." "Sure enuf, he's been playin' his shines at the old woman's house again. Why, Master Jailer, Justice Snivel must a made fees enuf a this 'ere cove to make a man rich enough," continues Mr. Constable Phin.

"As unwelcome a guest as comes to this establishment," rejoins the corpulent old jailer, adjusting his spectacles, and reading the commitment, a big key hanging from the middle finger of his left hand. "Used to be sent up here by his mother, to be starved into reform. He is past reform. The poor-house is the place to send him to, 'tis."

"Well, take good care on him, Master Jailer, now you've got him. He comes of a good enough family," says the first officer.

"He's bin in this condition more nor a week—layin' down yonder, in Snug Harbor. Liquor's drived all the sense out on him," rejoins the second—and bidding the jailer good-morning, they retire.

The forlorn man still lies prostrate on the floor, his tattered garments and besotted face presenting a picture of the most abject wretchedness. The old jailer looks down upon him with an air of sympathy, and shakes his head.

"The doctor that can cure you doesn't live in this establishment," he says. The sound of a voice singing a song is heard, and the figure of a powerfully framed man, dressed in a red shirt and grey homespun trousers, advances, folds his arms deliberately, and contemplates with an air of contempt the prostrate man. His broad red face, flat nose, massive lips, and sharp grey eyes, his crispy red hair, bristling over a low narrow forehead, and two deep scars on the left side of his face, present a picture of repulsiveness not easily described. Silently and sullenly he contemplates the object before him for several minutes, then says:

"Dogs take me, Mister Jailer! but he's what I calls run to the dogs. That's what whisky's did for him."

"And what it will do for you one of these days," interrupts the jailer, admonishingly. "Up for disturbing the peace at Madame Flamingo's. Committed by Justice Snivel."

"Throwing stones by way of repentance, eh? Tom was, at one time, as good a customer as that house had. A man's welcome at that house when he's up in the world. He's sure a gittin' kicked out when he is down."

"He's here, and we must get him to a cell," says the jailer, setting his key down and preparing to lift the man on his feet.

"Look a here, Tom Swiggs,—in here again, eh?" resumes the man in the red shirt. "Looks as if you liked the institution. Nice son of a respectable mother, you is!" He stoops down and shakes the prostrate man violently.

The man opens his eyes, and casts a wild glance on the group of wan faces peering eagerly at him. "I am bad enough. You are no better than me," he whispers. "You are always here."

"Not always. I am a nine months' guest. In for cribbing voters. Let out when election day comes round, and paid well for my services. Sent up when election is over, and friends get few. No moral harm in cribbing voters. You wouldn't be worth cribbing, eh, Tom? There ain't no politician what do'nt take off his hat, and say—'Glad to see you, Mister Mingle,' just afore election." The man folds his arms and walks sullenly down the corridor, leaving the newcomer to his own reflections. There is a movement among the group looking on; and a man in the garb of a sailor advances, presses his way through, and seizing the prostrate by the hand, shakes it warmly and kindly. "Sorry to see you in here agin, Tom," he says, his bronzed face lighting up with the fires of a generous heart. "There's no man in this jail shall say a word agin Tom Swiggs. We have sailed shipmates in this old craft afore."

The man was a sailor, and the prisoner's called him Spunyarn, by way of shortness. Indeed, he had became so familiarized to the name, that he would answer to none other. His friendship for the inebriate was of the most sincere kind. He would watch over him, and nurse him into sobriety, with the care and tenderness of a brother. "Tom was good to me, when he had it;" he says, with an air of sympathy. "And here goes for lendin' a hand to a shipmate in distress." He takes one arm and the jailer the other, and together they support the inebriate to his cell. "Set me down for a steady boarder, and have done with it," the forlorn man mutters, as they lay him gently upon the hard cot. "Down for steady board, jailer—that's it."

"Steady, steady now," rejoins the old sailor, as the inebriate tosses his arms over his head. "You see, there's a heavy ground swell on just now, and a chap what don't mind his helm is sure to get his spars shivered." He addresses the the jailer, who stands looking with an air of commiseration on the prostrate man. "Take in head-sail—furl top-gallant-sails—reef topsails—haul aft main-sheet—put her helm hard down—bring her to the wind, and there let her lay until it comes clear weather." The man writhes and turns his body uneasily. "There, there," continues the old sailor, soothingly; "steady, steady,—keep her away a little, then let her luff into a sound sleep. Old Spunyarn's the boy what'll stand watch." A few minutes more and the man is in a deep, sound sleep, the old sailor keeping watch over him so kindly, so like a true friend.

CHAPTER II
THE HOUSE OF A VERY DISTINGUISHED LADY

The mansion of Madame Flamingo stands stately in Berresford street. An air of mystery hangs over it by day, and it is there young Charleston holds high carnival at night. It is a very distinguished house, and Madame Flamingo assures us she is a very distinguished lady, who means to make her peace with heaven before she dies, and bestow largely on the priests, who have promised to make her comfortable while on the road through purgatory. The house is in high favor with young Charleston, and old Charleston looks in now and then. Our city fathers have great sympathy for it, and protect it with their presence. Verily it is a great gate on the road to ruin, and thousands pass heedlessly through its decorated walks, quickly reaching the dark end.

It is evening, and thin fleecy clouds flit along the heavens. The gas sheds a pale light over the streets, and shadowy figures pass and repass us as we turn into the narrow street leading to the house of the old hostess. We have reached the great arched door, and stand in the shadow of a gas-light, playing over its trap, its network of iron, and its bright, silver plate. We pause and contemplate the massive walls, as the thought flashes upon us—How mighty is vice, that it has got such a mansion dedicated to its uses! Even stranger thoughts than these flit through the mind as we hesitate, and touch the bell timidly. Now, we have excited your curiosity, and shall not turn until we have shown you what there is within.

We hear the bell faintly tinkle—now voices in loud conversation break upon the ear—then all is silent. Our anxiety increases, and keeps increasing, until a heavy footstep is heard advancing up the hall. Now there is a whispering within—then a spring clicks, and a small square panel opens and is filled with a broad fat face, with deep blue eyes and a profusion of small brown curls, all framed in a frosty cap-border. It is the old hostess, done up in her best book muslin, and so well preserved.

"Gentlemen, or ain't ye gentlemen?" inquires the old hostess, in a low voice. "This is a respectable house, I'd have you remember. Gentlemen what ain't gentlemen don't git no show in this house—no they don't." She looks curiously at us, and pauses for a reply. The display of a kid glove and a few assuring words gain us admittance into the great hall, where a scene of barbaric splendor excites curious emotions. "There ain't nothin' but gentlemen gets into this house—they don't! and when they are in they behaves like gentlemen," says the hostess, bowing gracefully, and closing the door after us.

The time prints of sixty summers have furrowed the old hostess' brow, and yet she seems not more than forty—is short of figure, and weighs two hundred. Soft Persian carpets cover the floor, lounges, in carved walnut and satin, stand along the sides; marble busts on pedestals, and full-length figures of statesmen and warriors are interspersed at short intervals; and the ceiling is frescoed in uncouth and fierce-looking figures. Flowers hang from niches in the cornice; a marble group, representing St. George and the dragon, stands at the foot of a broad circular stairs; tall mirrors reflect and magnify each object, and over all the gas from three chandeliers sheds a bewitching light. Such is the gaudy scene that excites the fancy, but leaves our admiration unmoved.

"This is a castle, and a commonwealth, gentlemen. Cost me a deal of money; might get ruined if gentlemen forgot how to conduct themselves. Ladies like me don't get much credit for the good they do. Gentlemen will be introduced into the parlor when they are ready," says the old hostess, stepping briskly round us, and watching our every movement; we are new-comers, and her gaudy tabernacle is novel to us.

"Have educated a dozen young men to the law, and made gentlemen of a dozen more, excellent young men—fit for any society. Don't square my accounts with the world, as the world squares its account with me," she continues, with that air which vice affects while pleading its own cause. She cannot shield the war of conscience that is waging in her heart; but, unlike most of those engaged in her unnatural trade, there is nothing in her face to indicate a heart naturally inclined to evil. It is indeed bright with smiles, and you see only the picture of a being sailing calmly down the smooth sea of peace and contentment. Her dress is of black glossy satin, a cape of fine point lace covers her broad shoulders, and bright blue cap-ribbons stream down her back.

"Listen," says the old hostess—"there's a full house to-night. Both parlors are full. All people of good society!" she continues, patronizingly. "Them what likes dancin' dances in the left-hand parlor. Them what prefers to sit and converse, converses in the right-hand parlor. Some converses about religion, some converses about politics—(by way of lettin' you know my position, I may say that I go for secession, out and out)—some converses about law, some converses about beauty. There isn't a lady in this house as can't converse on anything." Madame places her ear to the door, and thrusts her fat jewelled fingers under her embroidered apron.

"This is my best parlor, gentlemen," she resumes; "only gentlemen of deportment are admitted—I might add, them what takes wine, and, if they does get a little in liquor, never loses their dignity." Madame bows, and the door of her best parlor swings open, discovering a scene of still greater splendor.

"Gentlemen as can't enjoy themselves in my house, don't know how to enjoy anything. Them is all gentlemen you see, and them is all ladies you see," says the hostess, as we advance timidly into the room, the air of which is sickly of perfumes. The foot falls upon the softest of carpets; quaint shadows, from stained-glass windows are flitting and dancing on the frescoed ceiling; curtains of finest brocade, enveloped in lace, fall cloud-like down the windows. The borderings are of amber-colored satin, and heavy cornices, over which eagles in gilt are perched, surmount the whole. Pictures no artist need be ashamed of decorate the walls, groups in bronze and Parian, stand on pedestals between the windows, and there is a regal air about the furniture, which is of the most elaborate workmanship. But the living figures moving to and fro, some in uncouth dresses and some scarce dressed at all, and all reflected in the great mirrors, excite the deepest interest. Truly it is here that vice has arrayed itself in fascinating splendors, and the young and the old have met to pay it tribute. The reckless youth meets the man high in power here. The grave exchange salutations with the gay. Here the merchant too often meets his clerk, and the father his son. And before this promiscuous throng women in bright but scanty drapery, and wan faces, flaunt their charms.

Sitting on a sofa, is the fair young girl we saw at the cemetery. By her side is a man of venerable presence, endeavoring to engage her in conversation. Her face is shadowed in a pensive smile;—she listens to what falls from the lips of her companion, shakes her head negatively, and watches the movements of a slender, fair-haired young man, who saunters alone on the opposite side of the room. He has a deep interest in the fair girl, and at every turn casts a look of hate and scorn at her companion, who is no less a person than Judge Sleepyhorn, of this history.

"Hain't no better wine nowhere, than's got in this house," ejaculates the old hostess, calling our attention to a massive side-board, covered with cut-glass of various kinds. "A gentleman what's a gentleman may get a little tipsy, providin' he do it on wine as is kept in this house, and carry himself square." Madame motions patronizingly with her hand, bows condescendingly, and says, "Two bottles I think you ordered, gentlemen— what gentlemen generally call for."

Having bowed assent, and glad to get off so cheaply, Manfredo, a slave in bright livery, is directed to bring it in.

Mr. Snivel enters, to the great delight of the old hostess and various friends of the house. "Mr. Snivel is the spirit of this house," resumes the old hostess, by way of introduction; "a gentleman of distinction in the law." She turns to Mr. Snivel inquiringly. "You sent that ruffin, Tom Swiggs, up for me to-day?"

"Lord bless you, yes—gave him two months for contemplation. Get well starved at fifteen cents a day——"

"Sorry for the fellow," interrupts the old hostess, sympathizingly. "That's what comes a drinkin' bad liquor. Tom used to be a first-rate friend of this house—spent heaps of money, and we all liked him so. Tried hard to make a man of Tom. Couldn't do it." Madame shakes her head in sadness. "Devil got into him, somehow. Ran down, as young men will when they gets in the way. I does my part to save them, God knows." A tear almost steals into Madame's eyes. "When Tom used to come here, looking so down, I'd give him a few dollars, and get him to go somewhere else. Had to keep up the dignity of the house, you know. A man as takes his liquor as Tom does ain't fit company for my house."

Mr. Snivel says: "As good advice, which I am bound to give his mother, I shall say she'd better give him steady lodgings in jail." He turns and recognizes his friend, the judge, and advances towards him. As he does so, Anna rises quickly to her feet, and with a look of contempt, addressing the judge, says, "Never, never. You deceived me once, you never shall again. You ask me to separate myself from him. No, never, never." And as she turns to walk away the judge seizes her by the hand, and retains her. "You must not go yet," he says.

"She shall go!" exclaims the fair young man, who has been watching their movements. "Do you know me? I am the George Mulholland you are plotting to send to the whipping-post,—to accomplish your vile purposes. No, sir, I am not the man you took me for, as I would show you were it not for your grey hairs." He releases her from the judge's grasp, and stands menacing that high old functionary with his finger. "I care not for your power. Take this girl from me, and you pay the penalty with your life. We are equals here. Release poor Langdon from prison, and go pay penance over the grave of his poor wife. It's the least you can do. You ruined her—you can't deny it." Concluding, he clasps the girl in his arms, to the surprise of all present, and rushes with her out of the house.

The house of Madame Flamingo is in a very distinguished state of commotion. Men sensitive of their reputations, and fearing the presence of the police, have mysteriously disappeared. Madame is in a fainting condition, and several of her heroic damsels have gone screaming out of the parlor, and have not been seen since.

Matters have quieted down now. Mr. Snivel consoles the judge for the loss of dignity he has suffered, Madame did not quite faint, and there is peace in the house.

Manfredo, his countenance sullen, brings in the wine. Manfredo is in bad temper to-night. He uncorks the bottles and lets the wine foam over the table, the sight of which sends Madame into a state of distress.

"This is all I gets for putting such good livery on you!" she says, pushing him aside with great force. "That's thirty-nine for you in the morning, well-laid on. You may prepare for it. Might have known better (Madame modifies her voice) than buy a nigger of a clergyman!" She commences filling the glasses herself, again addressing Manfredo, the slave: "Don't do no good to indulge you. This is the way you pay me for lettin' you go to church of a Sunday. Can't give a nigger religion without his gettin' a big devil in him at the same time."

Manfredo passes the wine to her guests, in sullen silence, and they drink to the prosperity of the house.

And now it is past midnight; the music in the next parlor has ceased, St. Michael's clock has struck the hour of one, and business is at an end in the house of the old hostess. A few languid-looking guests still remain, the old hostess is weary with the fatigues of the night, and even the gas seems to burn dimmer. The judge and Mr. Snivel are the last to take their departure, and bid the hostess good-night. "I could not call the fellow out," says the judge, as they wend their way into King street. "I can only effect my purpose by getting him into my power. To do that you must give me your assistance."

"Remain silent on that point," returns the other. "You have only to leave its management to me. Nothing is easier than to get such a fellow into the power of the law."

On turning into King street they encounter a small, youthful looking man, hatless and coatless, his figure clearly defined in the shadows of the gas-light, engaged in a desperate combat with the lamp-post. "Now, Sir, defend yourself, and do it like a man, for you have the reputation of being a craven coward," says the man, cutting and thrusting furiously at the lamp-post; Snivel and Sleepyhorn pause, and look on astonished. "Truly the poor man's mad," says Sleepyhorn, touching his companion on the arm—"uncommonly mad for the season."

Mr. Snivel whispers, "Not so mad. Only courageously tight." "Gentlemen!" says the man, reproachfully, "I am neither mad nor drunk." Here he strikes an attitude of defence, cutting one, two, and three with his small sword. "I am Mister Midshipman Button—no madman, not a bit of it. As brave a man as South Carolina ever sent into the world. A man of pluck, Sir, and genuine, at that." Again he turns and makes several thrusts at the lamp-post, demanding that it surrender and get down on its knees, in abject obedience to superior prowess.

"Button, Button, my dear fellow, is it you? What strange freak is this?" inquires Mr. Snivel, extending his hand, which the little energetic man refuses to take.

"Mister Midshipman Button, if you please, gentlemen," replies the man, with an air of offended dignity. "I'm a gentleman, a man of honor, and what's more, a Carolinian bred and born, or born and bred—cut it as you like it." He makes several powerful blows at the lamp-post, and succeeds only in breaking his sword.

"Poor man," says the judge, kindly, "he is in need of friends to take care of him, and advise him properly. He has not far to travel before he gets into the mad-house."

The man overhears his remarks, and with a vehement gesture and flourish of his broken sword, says, "Do you not see, gentlemen, what work I have made of this Northern aggressor, this huge enemy bringing oppression to our very doors?" He turns and addresses the lamp-post in a tone of superiority. "Surrender like a man, and confess yourself vanquished, Northern aggressor that you are! You see, gentlemen, I have gained a victory—let all his bowels out. Honor all belongs to my native state—I shall resign it all to her." Here the man begins to talk in so wild a strain, and to make so many demands of his imaginary enemy, that they called a passing guardsman, who, seeing his strange condition, replaced his hat, and assisted them in getting him to a place of safety for the night, when sleep and time would restore him to a sound state of mind.

CHAPTER III
IN WHICH THE READER IS PRESENTED
WITH A VARIED PICTURE

Tom has passed a restless night in jail. He has dreamed of bottled snakes, with eyes wickedly glaring at him; of fiery-tailed serpents coiling all over him; of devils in shapes he has no language to describe; of the waltz of death, in which he danced at the mansion of Madame Flamingo; and of his mother, (a name ever dear in his thoughts,) who banished him to this region of vice, for what she esteemed a moral infirmity. Further on in his dream he saw a vision, a horrible vision, which was no less than a dispute for his person between Madame Flamingo, a bishop, and the devil. But Madame Flamingo and the devil, who seemed to enjoy each other's company exceedingly, got the better of the bishop, who was scrupulous of his dignity, and not a little anxious about being seen in such society. And from the horrors of this dream he wakes, surprised to find himself watched over by a kind friend—a young, comely-featured man, in whom he recognizes the earnest theologian, as he is plumed by the prisoners, whom he daily visits in his mission of good. There was something so frank and gentle in this young man's demeanor—something so manly and radiant in his countenance—something so disinterested and holy in his mission of love—something so opposite to the coldness of the great world without—something so serene and elevated in his youth, that even the most inveterate criminal awaited his coming with emotions of joy, and gave a ready ear to his kindly advice. Indeed, the prisoners called him their child; and he seemed not dainty of their approach, but took them each by the hand, sat at their side, addressed them as should one brother address another;—yea, he made them to feel that what was their interest it was his joy to promote.

The young theologian took him a seat close by the side of the dreaming inebriate; and as he woke convulsively, and turned towards him his distorted face, viewing with wild stare each object that met his sight, the young man met his recognition with a smile and a warm grasp of the hand. "I am sorry you find me here again—yes, I am."

"Better men, perhaps, have been here—"

"I am ashamed of it, though; it isn't as it should be, you see," interrupts Tom.

"Never mind—(the young man checks himself)—I was going to say there is a chance for you yet; and there is a chance; and you must struggle; and I will help you to struggle; and your friends—"

Tom interrupts by saying, "I've no friends."

"I will help you to struggle, and to overcome the destroyer. Never think you are friendless, for then you are a certain victim in the hands of the ruthless enemy—"

"Well, well," pauses Tom, casting a half-suspicious look at the young man, "I forgot. There's you, and him they call old Spunyarn, are friends, after all. You'll excuse me, but I didn't think of that;" and a feeling of satisfaction seemed to have come over him. "How grateful to have friends when a body's in a place of this kind," he mutters incoherently, as the tears gush from his distended eyes, and childlike he grasps the hand of the young man.

"Be comforted with the knowledge that you have friends, Tom. One all-important thing is wanted, and you are a man again."

"As to that!" interrupts Tom, doubtingly, and laying his begrimed hand on his burning forehead, while he alternately frets and frisks his fingers through his matted hair.

"Have no doubts, Tom—doubts are dangerous."

"Well, say what it is, and I'll try what I can do. But you won't think I'm so bad as I seem, and'll forgive me? I know what you think of me, and that's what mortifies me; you think I'm an overdone specimen of our chivalry—you do!"

"You must banish from your mind these despairing thoughts," replies the young man, laying his right hand approvingly on Tom's head. "First, Tom," he pursues, "be to yourself a friend; second, forget the error of your mother, and forgive her sending you here; and third, cut the house of Madame Flamingo, in which our chivalry are sure to get a shattering. To be honest in temptation, Tom, is one of the noblest attributes of our nature; and to be capable of forming and maintaining a resolution to shake off the thraldom of vice, and to place oneself in the serener atmosphere of good society, is equally worthy of the highest commendation."

Tom received this in silence, and seemed hesitating between what he conceived an imperative demand and the natural inclination of his passions.

"Give me your hand, and with it your honor—I know you yet retain the latent spark—and promise me you will lock up the cup—"

"You'll give a body a furlough, by the way of blowing off the fuddle he has on hand?"

"I do not withhold from you any discretionary indulgence that may bring relief—"

Tom interrupts by saying, "My mother, you know!"

"I will see her, and plead with her on your behalf; and if she have a mother's feelings I can overcome her prejudice."

Tom says, despondingly, he has no home to go to. It's no use seeing his mother; she's all dignity, and won't let it up an inch. "If I could only persuade her—" Tom pauses here and shakes his head.

"Pledge me your honor you'll from this day form a resolution to reform, Tom; and if I do not draw from your mother a reconciliation, I will seek a home for you elsewhere."

"Well, there can't be much harm in an effort, at all events; and here's my hand, in sincerity. But it won't do to shut down until I get over this bit of a fog I'm now in." With childlike simplicity, Tom gives his hand to the young man, who, as old Spunyarn enters the cell to, as he says, get the latitude of his friend's nerves, departs in search of Mrs. Swiggs.

Mrs. Swiggs is the stately old member of a crispy old family, that, like numerous other families in the State, seem to have outlived two chivalrous generations, fed upon aristocracy, and are dying out contemplating their own greatness. Indeed, the Swiggs family, while it lived and enjoyed the glory of its name, was very like the Barnwell family of this day, who, one by one, die off with the very pardonable and very harmless belief that the world never can get along without the aid of South Carolina, it being the parthenon from which the outside world gets all its greatness. Her leading and very warlike newspapers, (the people of these United States ought to know, if they do not already,) it was true, were editorialized, as it was politely called in the little State-militant, by a species of unreputationized Jew and Yankee; but this you should know—if you do not already, gentle reader—that it is only because such employments are regarded by the lofty-minded chivalry as of too vulgar a nature to claim a place in their attention.

The clock of old Saint Michaels, a clock so tenacious of its dignity as to go only when it pleases, and so aristocratic in its habits as not to go at all in rainy weather;—a clock held in great esteem by the "very first families," has just struck eleven. The young, pale-faced missionary inquiringly hesitates before a small, two-story building of wood, located on the upper side of Church street, and so crabbed in appearance that you might, without endangering your reputation, have sworn it had incorporated in its framework a portion of that chronic disease for which the State has gained for itself an unenviable reputation. Jutting out of the black, moss-vegetating roof, is an old-maidish looking window, with a dowdy white curtain spitefully tucked up at the side. The mischievous young negroes have pecked half the bricks out of the foundation, and with them made curious grottoes on the pavement. Disordered and unpainted clapboards spread over the dingy front, which is set off with two upper and two lower windows, all blockaded with infirm, green shutters. Then there is a snuffy door, high and narrow (like the State's notions), and reached by six venerable steps and a stoop, carefully guarded with a pine hand-rail, fashionably painted in blue, and looking as dainty as the State's white glove. This, reader, is the abode of the testy but extremely dignified Mrs. Swiggs. If you would know how much dignity can be crowded into the smallest space, you have only to look in here and be told (she closely patterns after the State in all things!) that fifty-five summers of her crispy life have been spent here, reading Milton's Paradise Lost and contemplating the greatness of her departed family.

The old steps creak and complain as the young man ascends them, holding nervously on at the blue hand-rail, and reaching in due time the stoop, the strength of which he successively tests with his right foot, and stands contemplating the snuffy door. A knocker painted in villanous green—a lion-headed knocker, of grave deportment, looking as savage as lion can well do in this chivalrous atmosphere, looks admonitiously at him. "Well!" he sighs as he raises it, "there's no knowing what sort of a reception I may get." He has raised the monster's head and given three gentle taps. Suddenly a frisking and whispering, shutting of doors and tripping of feet, is heard within; and after a lapse of several minutes the door swings carefully open, and the dilapidated figure of an old negro woman, lean, shrunken, and black as Egyptian darkness—with serious face and hanging lip, the picture of piety and starvation, gruffly asks who he is and what he wants?

Having requested an interview with her mistress, this decrepit specimen of human infirmity half closes the door against him and doddles back. A slight whispering, and Mrs. Swiggs is heard to say—"show him into the best parlor." And into the best parlor, and into the august presence of Mrs. Swiggs is he ushered. The best parlor is a little, dingy room, low of ceiling, and skirted with a sombre-colored surbase, above which is papering, the original color of which it would be difficult to discover. A listen carpet, much faded and patched, spreads over the floor, the walls are hung with several small engravings, much valued for their age and associations, but so crooked as to give one the idea of the house having withstood a storm at sea; and the furniture is made up of a few venerable mahogany chairs, a small side-table, on which stands, much disordered, several well-worn books and papers, two patch-covered foot-stools, a straight-backed rocking-chair, in which the august woman rocks her straighter self, and a great tin cage, from between the bars of which an intelligent parrot chatters—"my lady, my lady, my lady!" There is a cavernous air about the place, which gives out a sickly odor, exciting the suggestion that it might at some time have served as a receptacle for those second-hand coffins the State buries its poor in.

"Well! who are you? And what do you want? You have brought letters, I s'pose?" a sharp, squeaking voice, speaks rapidly.

The young man, without waiting for an invitation to sit down, takes nervously a seat at the side-table, saying he has come on a mission of love.

"Love! love! eh? Young man—know that you have got into the wrong house!" Mrs. Swiggs shakes her head, squeaking out with great animation.

There she sits, Milton's "Paradise Lost" in her witch-like fingers, herself lean enough for the leanest of witches, and seeming to have either shrunk away from the faded black silk dress in which she is clad, or passed through half a century of starvation merely to bolster up her dignity. A sharp, hatchet-face, sallow and corrugated; two wicked gray eyes, set deep in bony sockets; a long, irregular nose, midway of which is adjusted a pair of broad, brass-framed spectacles; a sunken, purse-drawn mouth, with two discolored teeth protruding from her upper lip; a high, narrow forehead, resembling somewhat crumpled parchment; a dash of dry, brown hair relieving the ponderous border of her steeple-crowned cap, which she seems to have thrown on her head in a hurry; a moth-eaten, red shawl thrown spitefully over her shoulders, disclosing a sinewy and sassafras-colored neck above, and the small end of a gold chain in front, and, reader, you have the august Mrs. Swiggs, looking as if she diets on chivalry and sour krout. She is indeed a nice embodiment of several of those qualities which the State clings tenaciously to, and calls its own, for she lives on the labor of eleven aged negroes, five of whom are cripples.

The young man smiles, as Mrs. Swiggs increases the velocity of her rocking, lays her right hand on the table, rests her left on her Milton, and continues to reiterate that he has got into the wrong house.

"I have no letter, Madam—"

"I never receive people without letters—never!" again she interrupts, testily.

"But you see, Madam—"

"No I don't. I don't see anything about it!" again she interposes, adjusting her spectacles, and scanning him anxiously from head to foot. "Ah, yes (she twitches her head), I see what you are—"

"I was going to say, if you please, Madam, that my mission may serve as a passport—"

"I'm of a good family, you must know, young man. You could have learned that of anybody before seeking this sort of an introduction. Any of our first families could have told you about me. You must go your way, young man!" And she twitches her head, and pulls closer about her lean shoulders the old red shawl.

"I (if you will permit me, Madam) am not ignorant of the very high standing of your famous family—" Madam interposes by saying, every muscle of her frigid face unmoved the while, she is glad he knows something, "having read of them in a celebrated work by one of our more celebrated genealogists—"

"But you should have brought a letter from the Bishop! and upon that based your claims to a favorable reception. Then you have read of Sir Sunderland Swiggs, my ancestor? Ah! he was such a Baron, and owned such estates in the days of Elizabeth. But you should have brought a letter, young man." Mrs. Swiggs replies rapidly, alternately raising and lowering her squeaking voice, twitching her head, and grasping tighter her Milton.

"Those are his arms and crest." She points with her Milton to a singular hieroglyphic, in a wiry black frame, resting on the marble-painted mantelpiece. "He was very distinguished in his time; and such an excellent Christian." She shakes her head and wipes the tears from her spectacles, as her face, which had before seemed carved in wormwood, slightly relaxes the hardness of its muscles.

"I remember having seen favorable mention of Sir Sunderland's name in the book I refer to—"

She again interposes. The young man watches her emotions with a penetrating eye, conscious that he has touched a chord in which all the milk of kindness is not dried up.

"It's a true copy of the family arms. Everybody has got to having arms now-a-days. (She points to the indescribable scrawl over the mantelpiece.) It was got through Herald King, of London, who they say keeps her Majesty's slippers and the great seal of State. We were very exact, you see. Yes, sir—we were very exact. Our vulgar people, you see—I mean such as have got up by trade, and that sort of thing—went to a vast expense in sending to England a man of great learning and much aforethought, to ransack heraldry court and trace out their families. Well, he went, lived very expensively, spent several years abroad, and being very clever in his way, returned, bringing them all pedigrees of the very best kind. With only two exceptions, he traced them all down into noble blood. These two, the cunning fellow had it, came of martyrs. And to have come of the blood of martyrs, when all the others, as was shown, came of noble blood, so displeased—the most ingenious (the old lady shakes her head regrettingly) can't please everybody—the living members of these families, that they refused to pay the poor man for his researches, so he was forced to resort to a suit at law. And to this day (I don't say it disparagingly of them!) both families stubbornly refuse to accept the pedigree. They are both rich grocers, you see! and on this account we were very particular about ours."

The young man thought it well not to interrupt the old woman's display of weakness, inasmuch as it might produce a favorable change in her feelings.

"And now, young man, what mission have you besides love?" she inquires, adding an encouraging look through her spectacles.

"I am come to intercede—"

"You needn't talk of interceding with me; no you needn't! I've nothing to intercede about"—she twitches her head spitefully.

"In behalf of your son."

"There—there! I knew there was some mischief. You're a Catholic! I knew it. Never saw one of your black-coated flock about that there wasn't mischief brewing—never! I can't read my Milton in peace for you—"

"But your son is in prison, Madam, among criminals, and subject to the influence of their habits—"

"Precisely where I put him—where he won't disgrace the family; yes, where he ought to be, and where he shall rot, for all me. Now, go your way, young man; and read your Bible at home, and keep out of prisons; and don't be trying to make Jesuits of hardened scamps like that Tom of mine."

"I am a Christian: I would like to extend a Christian's hand to your son. I may replace him on the holy pedestal he has fallen from—"

"You are very aggravating, young man. Do you live in South Carolina?"

The young man says he does. He is proud of the State that can boast so many excellent families.

"I am glad of that," she says, looking querulously over her spectacles, as she twitches her chin, and increases the velocity of her rocking. "I wonder how folks can live out of it."

"As to that, Madam, permit me to say, I am happy to see and appreciate your patriotism; but if you will grant me an order of release—"

"I won't hear a word now! You're very aggravating, young man—very! He has disgraced the family; I have put him where he is seven times; he shall rot were he is! He never shall disgrace the family again. Think of Sir Sunderland Swiggs, and then think of him, and see what a pretty level the family has come to! That's the place for him, I have told him a dozen times how I wished him gone. The quicker he is out of the way, the better for the name of the family."

The young man waits the end of this colloquy with a smile on his countenance. "I have no doubt I can work your son's reform—perhaps make him an honor to the family—"

"He honor the family!" she interrupts, twitches the shawl about her shoulders, and permits herself to get into a state of general excitement. "I should like to see one who has disgraced the family as much as he has think of honoring it—"

"Through kindness and forbearance, Madam, a great deal may be done," the young man replies.

"Now, you are very provoking, young man—very. Let other people alone; go your way home, and study your Bible." And with this the old lady calls Rebecca, the decrepit slave who opened the door, and directs her to show the young man out. "There now!" she says testily, turning to the marked page of her Milton.

The young man contemplates her for a few moments, but, having no alternative, leaves reluctantly.

On reaching the stoop he encounters the tall, handsome figure of a man, whose face is radiant with smiles, and his features ornamented with neatly-combed Saxon hair and beard, and who taps the old negress under the chin playfully, as she says, "Missus will be right glad to see you, Mr. Snivel—that she will." And he bustles his way laughing into the presence of the old lady, as if he had news of great importance for her.

CHAPTER IV
A FEW REFLECTIONS ON THE CURE OF VICE

Disappointed, and not a little chagrined, at the failure of his mission, the young man muses over the next best course to pursue. He has the inebriate's welfare at heart; he knows there is no state of degradation so low that the victim cannot, under proper care, be reclaimed from it; and he feels duty calling loudly to him not to stand trembling on the brink, but to enter the abode of the victim, and struggle to make clean the polluted. Vice, he says to himself, is not entailed in the heart; and if you would modify and correct the feelings inclined to evil, you must first feed the body, then stimulate the ambition; and when you have got the ambition right, seek a knowledge of the heart, and apply to it those mild and judicious remedies which soften its action, and give life to new thoughts and a higher state of existence. Once create the vine of moral rectitude, and its branches will soon get where they can take care of themselves. But to give the vine creation in poor soil, your watching must exhibit forbearance, and your care a delicate hand. The stubbornly-inclined nature, when coupled with ignorance, is that in which vice takes deepest root, as it is, when educated, that against which vice is least effectual. To think of changing the natural inclination of such natures with punishment, or harsh correctives, is as useless as would be an attempt to stop the ebbing and flowing of the tide. You must nurture the feelings, he thought, create a susceptibility, get the heart right, by holding out the value of a better state of things, and make the head to feel that you are sincere in your work of love; and, above all, you must not forget the stomach, for if that go empty crime will surely creep into the head. You cannot correct moral infirmity by confining the victim of it among criminals, for no greater punishment can be inflicted on the feelings of man; and punishment destroys rather than encourages the latent susceptibility of our better nature. In nine cases out of ten, improper punishment makes the hardened criminals with which your prisons are filled, destroying forever that spark of ambition which might have been fostered into a means to higher ends.

And as the young man thus muses, there recurs to his mind the picture of old Absalom McArthur, a curious old man, but excessively kind, and always ready to do "a bit of a good turn for one in need," as he would say when a needy friend sought his assistance. McArthur is a dealer in curiosities, is a venerable curiosity himself, and has always something on hand to meet the wants of a community much given to antiquity and broken reputations.

The young theologian will seek this good old man. He feels that time will work a favorable revolution in the feelings of Tom's mother; and to be prepared for that happy event he will plead a shelter for him under McArthur's roof.

And now, generous reader, we will, with your permission, permit him to go on his errand of mercy, while we go back and see how Tom prospers at the old prison. You, we well know, have not much love of prisons. But unless we do now and then enter them, our conceptions of how much misery man can inflict upon man will be small indeed.

The man of sailor-like deportment, and whom the prisoners salute with the sobriquet of "Old Spunyarn," entered, you will please remember, the cell, as the young theologian left in search of Mrs. Swiggs, "I thought I'd just haul my tacks aboard, run up a bit, and see what sort of weather you were making, Tom," says he, touching clumsily his small-brimmed, plait hat, as he recognizes the young man, whom he salutes in that style so frank and characteristic of the craft. "He's a bit better, sir—isn't he?" inquires Spunyarn, his broad, honest face, well browned and whiskered, warming with a glow of satisfaction.

Receiving an answer in the affirmative, he replies he is right glad of it, not liking to see a shipmate in a drift. And he gives his quid a lurch aside, throws his hat carelessly upon the floor, shrugs his shoulders, and as he styles it, nimbly brings himself to a mooring, at Tom's side. "It's a hard comforter, this state. I don't begrudge your mother the satisfaction she gets of sending you here. In her eyes, ye see, yeer fit only to make fees out on, for them ar lawyer chaps. They'd keep puttin' a body in an' out here during his natural life, just for the sake of gettin', the fees. They don't care for such things as you and I. We hain't no rights; and if we had, why we hain't no power. This carry in' too much head sail, Tom, won't do—'twon't!" Spunyarn shakes his head reprovingly, fusses over Tom, turns him over on his wales, as he has it, and finally gets him on his beam's ends, a besotted wreck unable to carry his canvas. "Lost yeer reckoning eh, Tom?" he continues as that bewildered individual stares vacantly at him. The inebriate contorts painfully his face, presses and presses his hands to his burning forehead, and says they are firing a salute in his head, using his brains for ammunition.

"Well, now Tom, seein' as how I'm a friend of yourn—"

"Friend of mine?" interrupts Tom, shaking his head, and peering through his fingers mistrustfully.

"And this is a hard lee shore you've beached upon; I'll lend ye a hand to get in the head sail, and get the craft trimmed up a little. A dash of the same brine will help keep the ballast right, then a skysail-yard breakfast must be carefully stowed away, in order to give a firmness to the timbers, and on the strength of these two blocks for shoring up the hull, you must begin little by little, and keep on brightening up until you have got the craft all right again. And when you have got her right you must keep her right. I say, Tom!—it won't do. You must reef down, or the devil'll seize the helm in one of these blows, and run you into a port too warm for pea-jackets." For a moment, Spunyarn seems half inclined to grasp Tom by his collarless coat and shake the hydrophobia, as he calls it, out of him; then, as if incited by a second thought, he draws from his shirt-bosom a large, wooden comb, and humming a tune commences combing and fussing over Tom's hair, which stands erect over his head like marlinspikes. At length he gets a craft-like set upon his foretop, and turning his head first to the right, then to the left, as a child does a doll, he views him with an air of exultation. "I tell you what it is, Tom," he continues, relieving him of the old coat, "the bright begins to come! There's three points of weather made already."

"God bless you, Spunyarn," replies Tom, evidently touched by the frankness and generosity of the old sailor. Indeed there was something so whole-hearted about old Spunyarn, that he was held in universal esteem by every one in jail, with the single exception of Milman Mingle, the vote-cribber.

"Just think of yourself, Tom—don't mind me," pursues the sailor as Tom squeezes firmly his hand. "You've had a hard enough time of it—" Tom interrupts by saying, as he lays his hands upon his sides, he is sore from head to foot.

"Don't wonder," returns the sailor. "It's a great State, this South Carolina. It seems swarming with poor and powerless folks. Everybody has power to put everybody in jail, where the State gives a body two dog's-hair and rope-yarn blankets to lay upon, and grants the sheriff, Mr. Hardscrable, full license to starve us, and put the thirty cents a day it provides for our living into his breeches pockets. Say what you will about it, old fellow, it's a brief way of doing a little profit in the business of starvation. I don't say this with any ill-will to the State that regards its powerless and destitute with such criminal contempt—I don't." And he brings water, gets Tom upon his feet, forces him into a clean shirt, and regards him in the light of a child whose reformation he is determined on perfecting. He sees that in the fallen man which implies a hope of ultimate usefulness, notwithstanding the sullen silence, the gloomy frown on his knitted brow, and the general air of despair that pervades the external man.

"There!" he exclaims, having improved the personal of the inebriate, and folding his arms as he steps back apace to have a better view of his pupil—"now, don't think of being triced up in this dreary vault. Be cheerful, brace up your resolution—never let the devil think you know he is trying to put the last seal on your fate—never!" Having slipped the black kerchief from his own neck, he secures it about Tom's, adjusts the shark's bone at the throat, and mounts the braid hat upon his head with a hearty blow on the crown. "Look at yourself! They'd mistake you for a captain of the foretop," he pursues, and good-naturedly he lays his broad, browned hands upon Tom's shoulders, and forces him up to a triangular bit of glass secured with three tacks to the wall.

Tom's hands wander down his sides as he contemplates himself in the glass, saying: "I look a shade up, I reckon! And I feel—I have to thank you for it, Spunyarn—something different all over me. God bless you! I won't forget you. But I'm hungry; that's all that ails me now.

"I may thank my mother—"

"Thank yourself, Tom," interposes the sailor.

"For all this. She has driven me to this; yes, she has made my soul dead with despair!" And he bursts into a wild, fierce laugh. A moment's pause, and he says, in a subdued voice, "I'm a slave, a fool, a wanderer in search of his own distress."

The kind-hearted sailor seats his pupil upon a board bench, and proceeds down stairs, where, with the bribe of a glass of whiskey, he induces the negro cook to prepare for Tom a bowl of coffee and a biscuit. In truth, we must confess, that Spunyarn was so exceedingly liberal of his friendship that he would at times appropriate to himself the personal effects of his neighbors. But we must do him justice by saying that this was only when a friend in need claimed his attention. And this generous propensity he the more frequently exercised upon the effects—whiskey, cold ham, crackers and cheese—of the vote-cribber, whom he regards as a sort of cold-hearted land-lubber, whose political friends outside were not what they should be. If the vote-cribber's aristocratic friends (and South Carolina politicians were much given to dignity and bad whiskey) sent him luxuries that tantalized the appetites of poverty-oppressed debtors, and poor prisoners starving on a pound of bread a-day, Spunyarn held this a legitimate plea for holding in utter contempt the right to such gifts. And what was more singular of this man was, that he always knew the latitude and longitude of the vote-cribber's bottle, and what amount of water was necessary to keep up the gauge he had reduced in supplying his flask.

And now that Tom's almost hopeless condition presents a warrantable excuse, (the vote-cribber has this moment passed into the cell to take a cursory glance at Tom,) Spunyarn slips nimbly into the vote-cribber's cell, withdraws a brick from the old chimney, and seizing the black neck of a blacker bottle, drags it forth, holds it in the shadow of the doorway, squints exultingly at the contents, shrugs his stalwart shoulders, and empties a third of the liquid, which he replaces with water from a bucket near by, into his tin-topped flask. This done, he ingeniously replaces the bottle, slides the flask suspiciously into his bosom, saying, "It'll taste just as strong to a vote-cribber," and seeks that greasy potentate, the prison cook. This dignitary has always laid something aside for Spunyarn; he knows Spunyarn has something laid aside for him, which makes the condition mutual.

"A new loafer let loose on the world!" says the vote-cribber, entering the domain of the inebriate with a look of fierce scorn. "The State is pestered to death with such things as you. What do they send you here for?—disturbing the quiet and respectability of the prison! You're only fit to enrich the bone-yard—hardly that; perhaps only for lawyers to get fees of. The State'll starve you, old Hardscrabble'll make a few dollars out of your feed—but what of that? We don't want you here." There was something so sullen and mysterious in the coarse features of this stalwart man—something so revolting in his profession, though it was esteemed necessary to the elevation of men seeking political popularity—something so at variance with common sense in the punishment meted out to him who followed it, as to create a deep interest in his history, notwithstanding his coldness towards the inebriate. And yet you sought in vain for one congenial or redeeming trait in the character of this man.

"I always find you here; you're a fixture, I take it—"

The vote-cribber interrupts the inebriate—"Better have said a patriot!"

"Well," returns the inebriate, "a patriot then; have it as you like it. I'm not over-sensitive of the distinction." The fallen man drops his head into his hands, stabbed with remorse, while the vote-cribber folds his brawny arms leisurely, paces to and fro before him, and scans him with his keen, gray eyes, after the manner of one mutely contemplating an imprisoned animal.

"You need not give yourself so much concern about me—"

"I was only thinking over in my head what a good subject to crib, a week or two before fall election, you'd be. You've a vote?"

Tom good-naturedly says he has. He always throws it for the "old Charleston" party, being sure of a release, as are some dozen caged birds, just before election.

"I have declared eternal hatred against that party; never pays its cribbers!" Mingle scornfully retorts; and having lighted his pipe, continues his pacing. "As for this jail," he mutters to himself, "I've no great respect for it; but there is a wide difference between a man who they put in here for sinning against himself, and one who only violates a law of the State, passed in opposition to popular opinion. However, you seem brightened up a few pegs, and, only let whiskey alone, you may be something yet. Keep up an acquaintance with the pump, and be civil to respectable prisoners, that's all."

This admonition of the vote-cribber had a deeper effect on the feelings of the inebriate than was indicated by his outward manner. He had committed no crime, and yet he found himself among criminals of every kind; and what was worse, they affected to look down upon him. Had he reached a state of degradation so low that even the felon loathed his presence? Was he an outcast, stripped of every means of reform—of making himself a man? Oh no! The knife of the destroyer had plunged deep—disappointment had tortured his brain—he was drawn deeper into the pool of misery by the fatal fascinations of the house of Madame Flamingo, where, shunned by society, he had sought relief—but there was yet one spark of pride lingering in his heart. That spark the vote-cribber had touched; and with that spark Tom resolved to kindle for himself a new existence. He had pledged his honor to the young theologian; he would not violate it.

The old sailor, with elated feelings, and bearing in his hands a bowl of coffee and two slices of toasted bread, is accosted by several suspicious-looking prisoners, who have assembled in the corridor for the purpose of scenting fresh air, with sundry questions concerning the state of his pupil's health.

"He has had a rough night," the sailor answers, "but is now a bit calm. In truth, he only wants a bit of good steering to get him into smooth weather again." Thus satisfying the inquirers, he hurries up stairs as the vote-cribber hurries down, and setting his offering on the window-sill, draws from his bosom the concealed flask. "There, Tom!" he says, with childlike satisfaction, holding the flask before him—"only two pulls. To-morrow reef down to one; and the day after swear a dissolution of copartnership, for this chap (he points to the whiskey) is too mighty for you."

Tom hesitates, as if questioning the quality of the drug he is about to administer.

"Only two!" interrupts the sailor. "It will reduce the ground-swell a bit." The outcast places the flask to his lips, and having drank with contorted face passes it back with a sigh, and extends his right hand. "My honor is nothing to the world, Spunyarn, but it is yet something to me; and by it I swear (here he grasps tighter the hand of the old sailor, as a tear moistens his suffused cheeks) never to touch the poison again. It has grappled me like a fierce animal I could not shake off; it has made me the scoffed of felons—I will cease to be its victim; and having gained the victory, be hereafter a friend to myself."

"God bless you—may you never want a friend, Tom—and may He give you strength to keep the resolution. That's my wish." And the old sailor shook Tom's hand fervently, in pledge of his sincerity.

CHAPTER V
IN WHICH MR. SNIVEL, COMMONLY CALLED THE ACCOMMODATION MAN, IS INTRODUCED, AND WHAT TAKES PLACE BETWEEN HIM AND MRS. SWIGGS

Reader! have you ever witnessed how cleverly one of our mob-politicians can, through the all-soothing medium of a mint-julep, transpose himself from a mass of passion and bad English into a child of perfect equanimity? If not, perhaps you have witnessed in our halls of Congress the sudden transition through which some of our Carolina members pass from a state of stupidity to a state of pugnacity? (We refer only to those members who do their own "stumping," and as a natural consequence, get into Congress through abuse of the North, bad whiskey, and a profusion of promises to dissolve the Union.) And if you have, you may form some idea of the suddenness with which Lady Swiggs, as she delights in having her friends call her, transposes herself from the incarnation of a viper into a creature of gentleness, on hearing announced the name of Mr. Soloman Snivel.

"What!—my old friend! I wish I had words to say how glad I am to see you, Lady Swiggs!" exclaims a tall, well-proportioned and handsome-limbed man, to whose figure a fashionable claret-colored frock coat, white vest, neatly-fitting dark-brown trowsers, highly-polished boots, a cluster of diamonds set in an avalanche of corded shirt-bosom, and carelessly-tied green cravat, lend a respectability better imagined than described. A certain reckless dash about him, not common to a refined gentleman, forces us to set him down as one of those individuals who hold an uncertain position in society; and though they may now and then mingle with men of refinement, have their more legitimate sphere in a fashionable world of doubtful character.

"Why!—Mr. Snivel. Is it you?" responds the old woman, reciprocating his warm shake of the hand, and getting her hard face into a smile.

"I am so glad—But (Mr. Snivel interrupts himself) never mind that!"

"You have some important news?" hastily inquires Mrs. Swiggs, laying a bit of muslin carefully between the pages of her Milton, and returning it to the table, saying she has just been grievously provoked by one of that black-coated flock who go about the city in search of lambs. They always remind her of light-houses pointing the road to the dominions of the gentleman in black.

"Something very important!" parenthesises Soloman—"very." And he shakes his head, touches her significantly on the arm with his orange-colored glove,—he smiles insidiously.

"Pray be seated, Mr. Snivel. Rebecca!—bring Mr. Snivel the rocking-chair."

"You see, my good Madam, there's such a rumor about town this morning! (Soloman again taps her on the arm with his glove.) The cat has got out of the bag—it's all up with the St. Cecilia!—"

"Do, Rebecca, make haste with the rocking-chair!" eagerly interrupts the old woman, addressing herself to the negress, who fusses her way into the room with a great old-fashioned rocking-chair. "I am so sensitive of the character of that society," she continues with a sigh, and wipes and rubs her spectacles, gets up and views herself in the glass, frills over her cap border, and becomes very generally anxious. Mrs. Swiggs is herself again. She nervously adjusts the venerable red shawl about her shoulders, draws the newly-introduced arm-chair near her own, ("I'm not so old, but am getting a little deaf," she says), and begs her visitor will be seated.

Mr. Soloman, having paced twice or thrice up and down the little room, contemplating himself in the glass at each turn, now touching his neatly-trimmed Saxon mustache and whiskers, then frisking his fingers through his candy-colored hair, brings his dignity into the chair.

"I said it was all up with the St. Cecilia—"

"Yes!" interrupts Mrs. Swiggs, her eyes glistening like balls of fire, her lower jaw falling with the weight of anxiety, and fretting rapidly her bony hands.

Soloman suddenly pauses, says that was a glorious bottle of old Madeira with which he enjoyed her hospitality on his last visit. The flavor of it is yet fresh in his mouth.

"Thank you—thank you! Mr. Soloman. I've a few more left. But pray lose no time in disclosing to me what hath befallen the St. Cecilia."

"Well then—but what I say must be in confidence. (The old woman says it never shall get beyond her lips—never!) An Englishman of goodly looks, fashion, and money—and, what is more in favor with our first families, a Sir attached to his name, being of handsome person and accomplished manners, and travelling and living after the manner of a nobleman, (some of our first families are simple enough to identify a Baronet with nobility!) was foully set upon by the fairest and most marriageable belles of the St. Cecilia. If he had possessed a dozen hearts, he could have had good markets for them all. There was such a getting up of attentions! Our fashionable mothers did their very best in arraying the many accomplishments of their consignable daughters, setting forth in the most foreign but not over-refined phraseology, their extensive travels abroad—"

"Yes!" interrupts Mrs. Swiggs, nervously—"I know how they do it. It's a pardonable weakness." And she reaches out her hand and takes to her lap her inseparable Milton.

"And the many marked attentions—offers, in fact—they have received at the hands of Counts and Earls, with names so unpronounceable that they have outlived memory—"

"Perhaps I have them in my book of autographs!" interrupts the credulous old woman, making an effort to rise and proceed to an antique side-board covered with grotesque-looking papers.

Mr. Soloman urbanely touches her on the arm—begs she will keep her seat. The names only apply to things of the past. He proceeds, "Well—being a dashing fellow, as I have said—he played his game charmingly. Now he flirted with this one, and then with that one, and finally with the whole society, not excepting the very flirtable married ladies;—that is, I mean those whose husbands were simple enough to let him. Mothers were in a great flutter generally, and not a day passed but there was a dispute as to which of their daughters he would link his fortunes with and raise to that state so desirable in the eyes of our very republican first families—the State-Militant of nobility—"

"I think none the worse of 'em for that," says the old woman, twitching her wizard-like head in confirmation of her assertion. "My word for it, Mr. Soloman, to get up in the world, and to be above the common herd, is the grand ambition of our people; and our State has got the grand position it now holds before the world through the influence of this ambition."

"True!—you are right there, my dear friend. You may remember, I have always said you had the penetration of a statesman, (Mrs. Swiggs makes a curt bow, as a great gray cat springs into her lap and curls himself down on her Milton;) and, as I was going on to say of this dashing Baronet, he played our damsels about in agony, as an old sportsman does a covey of ducks, wounding more in the head than in the heart, and finally creating no end of a demand for matrimony. To-day, all the town was positive, he would marry the beautiful Miss Boggs; to-morrow it was not so certain that he would not marry the brilliant and all-accomplished Miss Noggs; and the next day he was certain of marrying the talented and very wealthy heiress, Miss Robbs. Mrs. Stepfast, highly esteemed in fashionable society, and the very best gossip-monger in the city, had confidentially spread it all over the neighborhood that Mr. Stepfast told her the young Baronet told him (and he verily believed he was head and ears in love with her!) Miss Robbs was the most lovely creature he had seen since he left Belgravia. And then he went into a perfect rhapsody of excitement while praising the poetry of her motion, the grace with which she performed the smallest offices of the drawing-room, her queenly figure, her round, alabaster arms, her smooth, tapering hands, (so chastely set off with two small diamonds, and so unlike the butchers' wives of this day, who bedazzle themselves all the day long with cheap jewelry,)—the beautiful swell of her marble bust, the sweet smile ever playing over her thoughtful face, the regularity of her Grecian features, and those great, languishing eyes, constantly flashing with the light of irresistible love. Quoth ye! according to what Mr. Stepfast told Mrs. Stepfast, the young Baronet would, with the ideal of a real poet, as was he, have gone on recounting her charms until sundown, had not Mr. Stepfast invited him to a quiet family dinner. And to confirm what Mr. Stepfast said, Miss Robbs had been seen by Mrs. Windspin looking in at Mrs. Stebbins', the fashionable dress-maker, while the young Baronet had twice been at Spears', in King Street, to select a diamond necklace of great value, which he left subject to the taste of Miss Robbs. And putting them two and them two together there was something in it!"

"I am truly glad it's nothing worse. There has been so much scandal got up by vulgar people against our St. Cecilia."

"Worse, Madam?" interpolates our hero, ere she has time to conclude her sentence, "the worst is to come yet."

"And I'm a member of the society!" Mrs. Swiggs replies with a languishing sigh, mistaking the head of the cat for her Milton, and apologizing for her error as that venerable animal, having got well squeezed, sputters and springs from her grasp, shaking his head, "elected solely on the respectability of my family."

Rather a collapsed member, by the way, Mr. Soloman thinks, contemplating her facetiously.

"Kindly proceed—proceed," she says, twitching at her cap strings, as if impatient to get the sequel.

"Well, as to that, being a member of the St. Cecilia myself, you see, and always—(I go in for a man keeping up in the world)—maintaining a high position among its most distinguished members, who, I assure you, respect me far above my real merits, (Mrs. Swiggs says we won't say anything about that now!) and honor me with all its secrets, I may, even in your presence, be permitted to say, that I never heard a member who didn't speak in high praise of you and the family of which you are so excellent a representative."

"Thank you—thank you. O thank you, Mr. Soloman!" she rejoins.

"Why, Madam, I feel all my veneration getting into my head at once when I refer to the name of Sir Sunderland Swiggs."

"But pray what came of the young Baronet?"

"Oh!—as to him, why, you see, he was what we call—it isn't a polite word, I confess—a humbug."

"A Baronet a humbug!" she exclaims, fretting her hands and commencing to rock herself in the chair.

"Well, as to that, as I was going on to say, after he had beat the bush all around among the young birds, leaving several of them wounded on the ground—you understand this sort of thing—he took to the older ones, and set them polishing up their feathers. And having set several very respectable families by the ears, and created a terrible flutter among a number of married dames—he was an adept in this sort of diplomacy, you see—it was discovered that one very distinguished Mrs. Constance, leader of fashion to the St. Cecilia, (and on that account on no very good terms with the vulgar world, that was forever getting up scandal to hurl at the society that would not permit it to soil, with its common muslin, the fragrant atmosphere of its satin and tulle), had been carrying on a villanous intrigue—yes, Madam! villanous intrigue! I said discovered: the fact was, this gallant Baronet, with one servant and no establishment, was feted and fooled for a month, until he came to the very natural and sensible conclusion, that we were all snobbs— yes, snobbs of the very worst kind. But there was no one who fawned over and flattered the vanity of this vain man more than the husband of Mrs. Constance. This poor man idolized his wife, whom he regarded as the very diamond light of purity, nor ever mistrusted that the Baronet's attentions were bestowed with any other than the best of motives. Indeed, he held it extremely condescending on the part of the Baronet to thus honor the family with his presence.

"And the Baronet, you see, with that folly so characteristic of Baronets, was so flushed with his success in this little intrigue with Madame Constance—the affair was too good for him to keep!—that he went all over town showing her letters. Such nice letters as they were—brim full of repentance, love, and appointments. The Baronet read them to Mr. Barrows, laughing mischievously, and saying what a fool the woman must be. Mr. Barrows couldn't keep it from Mrs. Barrows, Mrs. Barrows let the cat out of the bag to Mrs. Simpson, and Mrs. Simpson would let Mr. Simpson have no peace till he got on the soft side of the Baronet, and, what was not a difficult matter, got two of the letters for her to have a peep into. Mrs. Simpson having feasted her eyes on the two Mr. Simpson got of the Baronet, and being exceedingly fond of such wares as they contained, must needs— albeit, in strict confidence—whisper it to Mrs. Fountain, who was a very fashionable lady, but unfortunately had a head very like a fountain, with the exception that it ejected out double the amount it took in. Mrs. Fountain—as anybody might have known—let it get all over town. And then the vulgar herd took it up, as if it were assafœtida, only needing a little stirring up, and hurled it back at the St. Cecilia, the character of which it would damage without a pang of remorse.

"Then the thing got to Constance's ears; and getting into a terrible passion, poor Constance swore nothing would satisfy him but the Baronet's life. But the Baronet—"

"A sorry Baronet was he—not a bit like my dear ancestor, Sir Sunderland," Mrs. Swiggs interposes.

"Not a bit, Madam," bows our hero. "Like a sensible gentleman, as I was about to say, finding it getting too hot for him, packed up his alls, and in the company of his unpaid servant, left for parts westward of this. I had a suspicion the fellow was not what he should be; and I made it known to my select friends of the St. Cecilia, who generally pooh-poohed me. A nobleman, they said, should receive every attention. And to show that he wasn't what he should be, when he got to Augusta his servant sued him for his wages; and having nothing but his chivalry, which the servant very sensibly declined to accept for payment, he came out like a man, and declared himself nothing but a poor player.

"But this neither satisfied Constance nor stayed the drifting current of slander—"

"Oh! I am so glad it was no worse," Mrs. Swiggs interrupts again.

"True!" Mr. Soloman responds, laughing heartily, as he taps her on the arm. "It might have been worse, though. Well, I am, as you know, always ready to do a bit of a good turn for a friend in need, and pitying poor Constance as I did, I suggested a committee of four most respectable gentlemen, and myself, to investigate the matter. The thing struck Constance favorably, you see. So we got ourselves together, agreed to consider ourselves a Congress, talked over the affairs of the nation, carried a vote to dissolve the Union, drank sundry bottles of Champagne, (I longed for a taste of your old Madeira, Mrs. Swiggs,) and brought in a verdict that pleased Mrs. Constance wonderfully—and so it ought. We were, after the most careful examination, satisfied that the reports prejudicial to the character and standing of Mrs. Constance had no foundation in truth, being the base fabrications of evil-minded persons, who sought, while injuring an innocent lady, to damage the reputation of the St. Cecilia Society. Mr. Constance was highly pleased with the finding; and finally it proved the sovereign balm that healed all their wounds. Of course, the Knight, having departed, was spared his blood."

Here Mr. Soloman makes a pause. Mrs. Swiggs, with a sigh, says, "Is that all?"

"Quite enough for once, my good Madam," Mr. Soloman bows in return.

"Oh! I am so glad the St. Cecilia is yet spared to us. You said, you know, it was all up with it—"

"Up? up?—so it is! That is, it won't break it up, you know. Why—oh, I see where the mistake is—it isn't all over, you know, seeing how the society can live through a score of nine-months scandals. But the thing's in every vulgar fellow's lips—that is the worst of it."

Mrs. Swiggs relishes this bit of gossip as if it were a dainty morsel; and calling Rebecca, she commands her to forthwith proceed into the cellar and bring a bottle of the old Madeira—she has only five left—for Mr. Soloman. And to Mr. Soloman's great delight, the old negress hastily obeys the summons; brings forth a mass of cobweb and dust, from which a venerable black bottle is disinterred, uncorked, and presented to the guest, who drinks the health of Mrs. Swiggs in sundry well-filled glasses, which he declares choice, adding, that it always reminds him of the age and dignity of the family. Like the State, dignity is Mrs. Swiggs' weakness—her besetting sin. Mr. Soloman, having found the key to this vain woman's generosity, turns it when it suits his own convenience.

"By-the-bye," he suddenly exclaims, "you've got Tom locked up again."

"As safe as he ever was, I warrant ye!" Mrs. Swiggs replies, resuming her Milton and rocking-chair.

"Upon my faith I agree with you. Never let him get out, for he is sure to disgrace the family when he does—"

"I've said he shall rot there, and he shall rot! He never shall get out to disgrace the family—no, not if I live to be as gray as Methuselah, I warrant you!" And Mr. Soloman, having made his compliments to the sixth glass, draws from his breast pocket a legal-looking paper, which he passes to Mrs. Swiggs, as she ejaculates, "Oh! I am glad you thought of that."

Mr. Soloman, watching intently the changes of her face, says, "You will observe, Madam, I have mentioned the cripples. There are five of them. We are good friends, you see; and it is always better to be precise in those things. It preserves friendship. This is merely a bit of a good turn I do for you." Mr. Soloman bows, makes an approving motion with his hands, and lays at her disposal on the table, a small roll of bills. "You will find two hundred dollars there," he adds, modulating his voice. "You will find it all right; I got it for you of Keepum. We do a little in that way; he is very exact, you see—"

"Honor is the best security between people of our standing," she rejoins, taking up a pen and signing the instrument, which her guest deposits snugly in his pocket, and takes his departure for the house of Madame Flamingo.

CHAPTER VI
CONTAINING SUNDRY MATTERS
APPERTAINING TO THIS HISTORY

If, generous reader, you had lived in Charleston, we would take it for granted that you need no further enlightening on any of our very select societies, especially the St. Cecilia; but you may not have enjoyed a residence so distinguished, rendering unnecessary a few explanatory remarks. You must know that we not only esteem ourselves the quintessence of refinement, as we have an undisputed right to do, but regard the world outside as exceedingly stupid in not knowing as much of us as we profess to know of ourselves. Abroad, we wonder we are not at once recognized as Carolinians; at home, we let the vulgar world know who we are. Indeed, we regard the outside world—of these States we mean—very much in that light which the Greeks of old were wont to view the Romans in. Did we but stop here, the weakness might be pardonable. But we lay claim to Grecian refinement of manners, while pluming all our mob-politicians Roman orators. There is a profanity about this we confess not to like; not that danger can befall it, but because it hath about it that which reminds us of the oyster found in the shell of gold. Condescending, then, to believe there exists outside of our State a few persons silly enough to read books, we will take it for granted, reader, that you are one of them, straightway proceeding with you to the St. Cecilia.

You have been a fashionable traveller in Europe? You say—yes! rummaged all the feudal castles of England, sought out the resting places of her kings, heard some one say "that is poet's corner," as we passed into Westminster Abbey, thought they couldn't be much to have such a corner,—"went to look" where Byron was buried, moistened the marble with a tear ere we were conscious of it, and saw open to us the gulf of death as we contemplated how greedy graveyard worms were banqueting on his greatness. A world of strange fancies came over us as we mused on England's poets. And we dined with several Dukes and a great many more Earls, declining no end of invitations of commoners. Very well! we reply, adding a sigh. And on your return to your home, that you may not be behind the fashion, you compare disparagingly everything that meets your eye. Nothing comes up to what you saw in Europe. A servant doesn't know how to be a servant here; and were we to see the opera at Covent Garden, we would be sure to stare our eyes out. It is become habitual to introduce your conversation with, "when I was in Europe." And you know you never write a letter that you don't in some way bring in the distinguished persons you met abroad. There is something (no matter what it is) that forcibly reminds you of what occurred at the table of my Lady Clarendon, with whom you twice had the pleasure and rare honor of dining. And by implication, you always give us a sort of lavender-water description of the very excellent persons you met there, and what they were kind enough to say of America, and how they complimented you, and made you the centre and all-absorbing object of attraction—in a word, a truly wonderful person. And you will not fail, now that it is become fashionable, to extol with fulsome breath the greatness of every European despot it hath been your good fortune to get a bow from. And you are just vain enough to forever keep this before your up-country cousins. You say, too, that you have looked in at Almacks. Almacks! alas! departed greatness. With the rise of the Casino hath it lain its aristocratic head in the dust.

Well!—the St. Cecilia you must know (its counterparts are to be found in all our great cities) is a miniature Almacks—a sort of leach-cloth, through which certain very respectable individuals must pass ere they can become the elite of our fashionable world. To become a member of the St. Cecilia—to enjoy its recherché assemblies—to luxuriate in the delicate perfumes of its votaries, is the besetting sin of a great many otherwise very sensible people. And to avenge their disappointment at not being admitted to its precious precincts, they are sure to be found in the front rank of scandal-mongers when anything in their line is up with a member. And it is seldom something is not up, for the society would seem to live and get lusty in an atmosphere of perpetual scandal. Any amount of duels have come of it; it hath made rich no end of milliners; it hath made bankrupt husbands by the dozen; it hath been the theatre of several distinguished romances; it hath witnessed the first throbbings of sundry hearts, since made happy in wedlock; it hath been the *shibolath* of sins that shall be nameless here. The reigning belles are all members (provided they belong to our first families) of the St. Cecilia, as is also the prettiest and most popular unmarried parson. And the parson being excellent material for scandal, Mother Rumor is sure to have a dash at him. Nor does this very busy old lady seem over-delicate about which of the belles she associates with the parson, so long as the scandal be fashionable enough to afford her a good traffic.

An Outcast Or, Virtue and Faith | 49

There is continually coming along some unknown but very distinguished foreigner, whom the society adopts as its own, flutters over, and smothers with attentions, and drops only when it is discovered he is an escaped convict. This, in deference to the reputation of the St. Cecilia, we acknowledge has only happened twice. It has been said with much truth that the St. Cecilia's worst sin, like the sins of its sister societies of New York, is a passion for smothering with the satin and Honiton of its assemblies a certain supercilious species of snobby Englishmen, who come over here, as they have it (gun and fishing-rod in hand), merely to get right into the woods where they can have plenty of bear-hunting, confidently believing New York a forest inhabited by such animals. As for our squaws, as Mr. Tom Toddleworth would say, (we shall speak more at length of Tom!) why! they have no very bad opinion of them, seeing that they belong to a race of semi-barbarians, whose sayings they delight to note down. Having no society at home, this species of gentry the more readily find themselves in high favor with ours. They are always Oxonians, as the sons of green grocers and fishmongers are sure to be when they come over here (so Mr. Toddleworth has it, and he is good authority), and we being an exceedingly impressible people, they kindly condescend to instruct us in all the high arts, now and then correcting our very bad English. They are clever fellows generally, being sure to get on the kind side of credulous mothers with very impressible-headed daughters.

There was, however, always a distinguished member of the St. Cecilia society who let out all that took place at its assemblies. The vulgar always knew what General danced with the lovely Miss A., and how they looked, and what they said to each other; how many jewels Miss A. wore, and the material her dress was made of; they knew who polkaed with the accomplished Miss B., and how like a duchess she bore herself; they had the exact name of the colonel who dashed along so like a knight with the graceful and much-admired Mrs. D., whose husband was abroad serving his country; what gallant captain of dragoons (captains of infantry were looked upon as not what they might be) promenaded so imperiously with the vivacious Miss E.; and what distinguished foreigner sat all night in the corner holding a suspicious and very improper conversation with Miss F., whose skirts never were free of scandal, and who had twice got the pretty parson into difficulty with his church. Hence there was a perpetual outgoing of scandal on the one side, and pelting of dirt on the other.

When Mr. Soloman sought the presence of Mrs. Swiggs and told her it was all up with the St. Cecilia, and when that august member of the society was so happily disappointed by his concluding with leaving it an undamaged reputation, the whole story was not let out. In truth the society was at that moment in a state of indignation, and its reputation as well-nigh the last stage of disgrace as it were possible to bring it without being entirely absorbed. The Baronet, who enjoyed a good joke, and was not over-scrupulous in measuring the latitude of our credulity, had, it seems, in addition to the little affair with Mrs. Constance, been imprudent enough to introduce at one of the assemblies of the St. Cecilia, a lady of exceedingly fair but frail import: this loveliest of creatures—this angel of fallen fame— this jewel, so much sought after in her own casket—this child of gentleness and beauty, before whom a dozen gallant knights were paying homage, and claiming her hand for the next waltz, turned out to be none other than the Anna Bonard we have described at the house of Madame Flamingo. The discovery sent the whole assembly into a fainting fit, and caused such a fluttering in the camp of fashion. Reader! you may rest assured back-doors and smelling-bottles were in great demand.

The Baronet had introduced her as his cousin; just arrived, he said, in the care of her father—the cousin whose beauty he had so often referred to. So complete was her toilet and disguise, that none but the most intimate associate could have detected the fraud. Do you ask us who was the betrayer, reader? We answer,—

One whose highest ambition did seem that of getting her from her paramour, George Mullholland. It was Judge Sleepyhorn. Reader! you will remember him—the venerable, snowy-haired man, sitting on the lounge at the house of Madame Flamingo, and on whom George Mullholland swore to have revenge. The judge of a criminal court, the admonisher of the erring, the sentencer of felons, the *habitue* of the house of Madame Flamingo—no libertine in disguise could be more scrupulous of his standing in society, or so sensitive of the opinion held of him by the virtuous fair, than was this daylight guardian of public morals.

The Baronet got himself nicely out of the affair, and Mr. Soloman Snivel, commonly called Mr. Soloman, the accommodation man, is at the house of Madame Flamingo, endeavoring to effect a reconciliation between the Judge and George Mullholland.

CHAPTER VII
IN WHICH IS SEEN A
COMMINGLING OF CITIZENS

Night has thrown her mantle over the city. There is a great gathering of denizens at the house of Madame Flamingo. She has a *bal-masque* to-night. Her door is beset with richly-caparisoned equipages. The town is on tip-toe to be there; we reluctantly follow it. An hundred gaudily-decorated drinking saloon are filled with gaudier-dressed men. In loudest accent rings the question—"Do you go to Madame Flamingo's to-night?" Gentlemen of the genteel world, in shining broadcloth, touch glasses and answer—"yes!" It is a wonderful city—this of ours. Vice knows no restraint, poverty hath no friends here. We bow before the shrine of midnight revelry; we bring licentiousness to our homes, but we turn a deaf ear to the cries of poverty, and we gloat over the sale of men.

The sickly gas-light throws a sicklier glare over the narrow, unpaved streets. The city is on a frolic, a thing not uncommon with it. Lithe and portly-figured men, bearing dominos in their hands, saunter along the sidewalk, now dangling ponderous watch-chains, then flaunting highly-perfumed cambrics—all puffing the fumes of choice cigars. If accosted by a grave wayfarer—they are going to the opera! They are dressed in the style of opera-goers. And the road to the opera seems the same as that leading to the house of the old hostess. A gaily-equipped carriage approaches. We hear the loud, coarse laughing of those it so buoyantly bears, then there comes full to view the glare of yellow silks and red satins, and doubtful jewels—worn by denizens from whose faded brows the laurel wreath hath fallen. How shrunken with the sorrow of their wretched lives, and yet how sportive they seem! The pale gas-light throws a spectre-like hue over their paler features; the artificial crimson with which they would adorn the withered cheek refuses to lend a charm to features wan and ghastly. The very air is sickly with the odor of their cosmetics. And with flaunting cambrics they bend over carriage sides, salute each and every pedestrian, and receive in return answers unsuited to refined ears. They pass into the dim vista, but we see with the aid of that flickering gas, the shadow of that polluting hand which hastens life into death.

Old Mr. McArthur, who sits smoking his long pipe in the door of his crazy-looking curiosity shop, (he has just parted company with the young theologian, having assured him he would find a place to stow Tom Swiggs in,) wonders where the fashionable world of Charleston can be going? It is going to the house of the Flamingo. The St. Cecilia were to have had a ball to-night; scandal and the greater attractions here have closed its doors.

A long line of carriages files past the door of the old hostess. An incessant tripping of feet, delicately encased in bright-colored slippers; an ominous fluttering of gaudy silks and satins; an inciting glare of borrowed jewelry, mingling with second-hand lace; an heterogeneous gleaming of bare, brawny arms, and distended busts, all lend a sort of barbaric splendor to that mysterious group floating, as it were, into a hall in one blaze of light. A soft carpet, overlain with brown linen, is spread from the curbstone into the hall. Two well-developed policemen guard the entrance, take tickets of those who pass in, and then exchange smiles of recognition with venerable looking gentlemen in masks. The hostess, a clever "business man" in her way, has made the admission fee one dollar. Having paid the authorities ten dollars, and honored every Alderman with a complimentary ticket, who has a better right? No one has a nicer regard for the Board of Aldermen than Madame Flamingo; no one can reciprocate this regard more condescendingly than the honorable Board of Aldermen do. Having got herself arrayed in a dress of sky-blue satin, that ever and anon streams, cloud-like, behind her, and a lace cap of approved fashion, with pink strings nicely bordered in gimp, and a rich Honiton cape, jauntily thrown over her shoulders, and secured under the chin with a great cluster of blazing diamonds, and rows of unpolished pearls at her wrists, which are immersed in crimped ruffles, she doddles up and down the hall in a state of general excitement. A corpulent colored man, dressed in the garb of a beadle, — a large staff in his right hand, a cocked hat on his head, and broad white stripes down his flowing coat, stands midway between the parlor doors. He is fussy enough, and stupid enough, for a Paddington beadle. Now Madame Flamingo looks scornfully at him, scolds him, pushes him aside; he is only a slave she purchased for the purpose; she commands that he gracefully touch his hat (she snatches it from his head, and having elevated it over her own, performs the delicate motion she would have him imitate) to every visitor. The least neglect of duty will incur (she tells him in language he cannot mistake) the penalty of thirty-nine well laid on in the morning. In another minute her fat, chubby-face glows with smiles, her whole soul seems lighted up with childlike enthusiasm; she has a warm welcome for each new comer, retorts saliently upon her old friends, and says—"you know how welcome you all are!" Then she curtsies with such becoming grace. "The house, you know, gentlemen, is a commonwealth to-night." Ah! she recognizes the tall, comely figure of Mr. Soloman, the accommodation man. He did not spring from among the bevy of coat-takers, and hood-retainers, at the extreme end of the great hall, nor from among the heap of promiscuous garments piled in one corner; and yet he is here, looking as if some magic process had brought him from a mysterious labyrinth. "Couldn't get along without me, you see. It's an ambition with me to befriend everybody. If I can do a bit of a good turn for a friend, so much the better!" And he grasps the old hostess by the hand with a self-satisfaction he rather improves by tapping her encouragingly on the shoulder. "You'll make a right good thing of this!—a clear thousand, eh?"

"The fates have so ordained it," smiles naively the old woman.

"Of course the fates could not ordain otherwise—"

"As to that, Mr. Soloman, I sometimes think the gods are with me, and then again I think they are against me. The witches—they have done my fortune a dozen times or more—always predict evil (I consult them whenever a sad fit comes over me), but witches are not to be depended upon! I am sure I think what a fool I am for consulting them at all." She espies, for her trade of sin hath made keen her eye, the venerable figure of Judge Sleepyhorn advancing up the hall, masked. "Couldn't get along without you," she lisps, tripping towards him, and greeting him with the familiarity of an intimate friend. "I'm rather aristocratic, you'll say!—and I confess I am, though a democrat in principle!" And Madame Flamingo confirms what she says with two very dignified nods. As the Judge passes silently in she pats him encouragingly on the back, saying,—"There ain't no one in this house what'll hurt a hair on your head." The Judge heeds not what she says.

"My honor for it, Madame, but I think your guests highly favored, altogether! Fine weather, and the prospect of a *bal-masque* of Pompeian splendor. The old Judge, eh?"

"The gods smile—the gods smile, Mr. Soloman!" interrupts the hostess, bowing and swaying her head in rapid succession.

"The gods have their eye on him to-night—he's a marked man! A jolly old cove of a Judge, he is! Cares no more about rules and precedents, on the bench, than he does for the rights and precedents some persons profess to have in this house. A high old blade to administer justice, eh?"

"But, you see, Mr. Soloman," the hostess interrupts, a gracious bow keeping time with the motion of her hand, "he is such an aristocratic prop in the character of my house."

"I rather like that, I confess, Madame. You have grown rich off the aristocracy. Now, don't get into a state of excitement!" says Mr. Soloman, fingering his long Saxon beard, and eyeing her mischievously. She sees a bevy of richly-dressed persons advancing up the hall in high glee. Indeed her house is rapidly filling to the fourth story. And yet they come! she says. "The gods are in for a time. I love to make the gods happy."

Mr. Soloman has lain his hand upon her arm retentively.

"It is not that the aristocracy and such good persons as the Judge spend so much here. But they give *eclat* to the house, and *eclat* is money. That's it, sir! Gold is the deity of *our* pantheon! Bless you (the hostess evinces the enthusiasm of a politician), what better evidence of the reputation of my house than is before you, do you want? I've shut up the great Italian opera, with its three squalling prima donnas, which in turn has shut up the poor, silly *Empresario* as they call him; and the St. Cecilia I have just used up. I'm a team in my way, you see;—run all these fashionable oppositions right into bankruptcy." Never were words spoken with more truth. Want of patronage found all places of rational amusement closed. Societies for intellectual improvement, one after another, died of poverty. Fashionable lectures had attendance only when fashionable lecturers came from the North; and the Northman was sure to regard our taste through the standard of what he saw before him.

The house of the hostess triumphs, and is corpulent of wealth and splendor. To-morrow she will feed with the rich crumbs that fall from her table the starving poor. And although she holds poor virtue in utter contempt, feeding the poor she regards a large score on the passport to a better world. A great marble stairway winds its way upward at the farther end of the hall, and near it are two small balconies, one on each side, presenting barricades of millinery surmounted with the picturesque faces of some two dozen denizens, who keep up an incessant gabbling, interspersed here and there with jeers directed at Mr. Soloman. "Who is he seeking to accommodate to-night?" they inquire, laughing merrily.

The house is full, the hostess has not space for one friend more; she commands the policemen to close doors. An Alderman is the only exception to her *fiat*. "You see," she says, addressing herself to a courtly individual who has just saluted her with urbane deportment, "I must preserve the *otium cum dignitate* of my (did I get it right?) standing in society. I don't always get these Latin sayings right. Our Congressmen don't. And, you see, like them, I ain't a Latin scholar, and may be excused for any little slips. Politics and larnin' don't get along well together. Speaking of politics, I confess I rather belong to the Commander and Quabblebum school—I do!"

At this moment (a tuning of instruments is heard in the dancing-hall) the tall figure of the accommodation man is seen, in company of the venerable Judge, passing hurriedly into a room on the right of the winding stairs before described. "Judge!" he exclaims, closing the door quickly after him, "you will be discovered and exposed. I am not surprised at your passion for her, nor the means by which you seek to destroy the relations existing between her and George Mullholland. It is an evidence of taste in you. But she is proud to a fault, and, this I say in friendship, you so wounded her feelings, when you betrayed her to the St. Cecilia, that she has sworn to have revenge on you. George Mullholland, too, has sworn to have your life.

"I tell you what it is, Judge, (the accommodation man assumes the air of a bank director,) I have just conceived—you will admit I have an inventive mind!—a plot that will carry you clean through the whole affair. Your ambition is divided between a passion for this charming creature and the good opinion of better society. The resolution to retain the good opinion of society is doing noble battle in your heart; but it is the weaker vessel, and it always will be so with a man of your mould, inasmuch as such resolutions are backed up by the less fierce elements of our nature. Put this down as an established principle. Well, then, I will take upon myself the betrayal. I will plead you ignorant of the charge, procure her forgiveness, and reconcile the matter with this Mullholland. It's worth an hundred or more, eh?"

The venerable man smiles, shakes his head as if heedless of the admonition, and again covers his face with his domino.

The accommodation man, calling him by his judicial title, says he will yet repent the refusal!

It is ten o'clock. The gentleman slightly colored, who represents a fussy beadle, makes a flourish with his great staff. The doors of the dancing hall are thrown open. Like the rushing of the gulf stream there floods in a motley procession of painted females and masked men—the former in dresses as varied in hue as the fires of remorse burning out their unuttered thoughts. Two and two they jeer and crowd their way along into the spacious hall, the walls of which are frescoed in extravagant mythological designs, the roof painted in fret work, and the cornices interspersed with seraphs in stucco and gilt. The lights of two massive chandeliers throw a bewitching refulgence over a scene at once picturesque and mysterious; and from four tall mirrors secured between the windows, is reflected the forms and movements of the masquers.

Reader! you have nothing in this democratic country with which to successfully compare it. And to seek a comparison in the old world, where vice, as in this city of chivalry, hath a license, serves not our office.

Madame Flamingo, flanked right and left by twelve colored gentlemen, who, their collars decorated with white and pink rosettes, officiate as masters of ceremony, and form a crescent in front of the thronging procession, steps gradually backward, curtsying and bowing, and spreading her hands to her guests, after the manner of my Lord Chamberlain.

Eight colored musicians, (everything is colored here,) perched on a raised platform covered with maroon-colored plush, at the signal of a lusty-tongued call-master, strike up a march, to which the motley throng attempt to keep time. It is martial enough; and discordant enough for anything but keeping time to.

The plush-covered benches filing along the sides and ends of the hall are eagerly sought after and occupied by a strange mixture of lookers on in Vienna. Here the hoary-headed father sits beside a newly-initiated youth who is receiving his first lesson of dissipation. There the grave and chivalric planter sports with the nice young man, who is cultivating a beard and his way into the by-ways. A little further on the suspicious looking gambler sits freely conversing with the man whom a degrading public opinion has raised to the dignity of the judicial bench. Yonder is seen the man who has eaten his way into fashionable society, (and by fashionable society very much caressed in return,) the bosom companion of the man whose crimes have made him an outcast.

Generous reader! contemplate this grotesque assembly; study the object Madame Flamingo has in gathering it to her fold. Does it not present the accessories to wrong doing? Does it not show that the wrong-doer and the criminally inclined, too often receive encouragement by the example of those whoso duty it is to protect society? The spread of crime, alas! for the profession, is too often regarded by the lawyer as rather a desirable means of increasing his trade.

Quadrille follows quadrille, the waltz succeeds the schottish, the scene presents one bewildering maze of flaunting gossamers and girating bodies, now floating sylph-like into the foreground, then whirling seductively into the shadowy vista, where the joyous laugh dies out in the din of voices. The excitement has seized upon the head and heart of the young,—the child who stood trembling between the first and second downward step finds her reeling brain a captive in this snare set to seal her ruin.

Now the music ceases, the lusty-tongued call-master stands surveying what he is pleased to call the oriental splendor of this grotesque assembly. He doesn't know who wouldn't patronize such a house! It suddenly forms in platoon, and marshalled by slightly-colored masters of ceremony, promenades in an oblong figure.

An Outcast Or, Virtue and Faith | 57

Here, leaning modestly on the arm of a tall figure in military uniform, and advancing slowly up the hall, is a girl of some sixteen summers. Her finely-rounded form is in harmony with the ravishing vivacity of her face, which is beautifully oval. Seen by the glaring gas-light her complexion is singularly clear and pale. But that freshness which had gained her many an admirer, and which gave such a charm to the roundness of early youth, we look for in vain. And yet there is a softness and delicacy about her well-cut and womanly features—a childlike sweetness in her smile—a glow of thoughtfulness in those great, flashing black eyes—an expression of melancholy in which at short intervals we read her thoughts—an incessant playing of those long dark eyelashes, that clothes her charms with an irresistible, a soul-inspiring seductiveness. Her dress, of moire antique, is chasteness itself; her bust exquisite symmetry; it heaves as softly as if touched by some gentle zephyr. From an Haidean brow falls and floats undulating over her marble-like shoulders, the massive folds of her glossy black hair. Nature had indeed been lavish of her gifts on this fair creature, to whose charms no painter could give a touch more fascinating. This girl, whose elastic step and erect carriage contrasts strangely with the languid forms about her, is Anna Bonard, the neglected, the betrayed. There passes and repasses her, now contemplating her with a curious stare, then muttering inaudibly, a man of portly figure, in mask and cowl. He touches with a delicate hand his watch-guard, we see two sharp, lecherous eyes peering through the domino; he folds his arms and pauses a few seconds, as if to survey the metal of her companion, then crosses and recrosses her path. Presently his singular demeanor attracts her attention, a curl of sarcasm is seen on her lip, her brow darkens, her dark orbs flash as of fire,—all the heart-burnings of a soul stung with shame are seen to quicken and make ghastly those features that but a moment before shone lambent as summer lightning. He pauses as with a look of withering scorn she scans him from head to foot, raises covertly her left hand, tossing carelessly her glossy hair on her shoulder, and with lightning quickness snatches with her right the domino from his face. "Hypocrite!" she exclaims, dashing it to the ground, and with her foot placed defiantly upon the domino, assumes a tragic attitude, her right arm extended, and the forefinger of her hand pointing in his face, "Ah!" she continues, in biting accents, "it is against the perfidy of such as you. I have struggled. Your false face, like your heart, needed a disguise. But I have dragged it away, that you may be judged as you are. This is my satisfaction for your betrayal. Oh that I could have deeper revenge!" She has unmasked Judge Sleepyhorn, who stands before the anxious gaze of an hundred night revellers, pressing eagerly to the scene of confusion. Madame Flamingo's house, as you may judge, is much out in its dignity, and in a general uproar. There was something touching—something that the graver head might ponder over, in the words of this unfortunate girl—"I have struggled!" A heedless and gold-getting world seldom enters upon the mystery of its meaning. But it hath a meaning deep and powerful in its appeal to society—one that might serve the good of a commonwealth did society stoop and take it by the hand.

So sudden was the motion with which this girl snatched the mask from the face of the Judge, (he stood as if appalled,) that, ere he had gained his self-possession, she drew from her girdle a pearl-hilted stiletto, and in attempting to ward off the dreadful lunge, he struck it from her hand, and into her own bosom. The weapon fell gory to the floor—the blood trickled down her bodice—a cry of "murder" resounded through the hall! The administrator of justice rushed out of the door as the unhappy girl swooned in the arms of her partner. A scene so confused and wild that it bewilders the brain, now ensued. Madame Flamingo calls loudly for Mr. Soloman; and as the reputation of her house is uppermost in her thoughts, she atones for its imperiled condition by fainting in the arms of a grave old gentleman, who was beating a hasty retreat, and whose respectability she may compromise through this uncalled-for act.

A young man of slender form, and pale, sandy features, makes his way through the crowd, clasps Anna affectionately in his arms, imprints a kiss on her pallid brow, and bears her out of the hall.

By the aid of hartshorn and a few dashes of cold water, the old hostess is pleased to come to, as we say, and set about putting her house in order. Mr. Soloman, to the great joy of those who did not deem it prudent to make their escape, steps in to negotiate for the peace of the house and the restoration of order. "It is all the result of a mistake," he says laughingly, and good-naturedly, patting every one he meets on the shoulder. "A little bit of jealousy on the part of the girl. It all had its origin in an error that can be easily rectified. In a word, there's much ado about nothing in the whole of it. Little affairs of this kind are incident to fashionable society all over the world! The lady being only scratched, is more frightened than hurt. Nobody is killed; and if there were, why killings are become so fashionable, that if the killed be not a gentleman, nobody thinks anything of it," he continues. And Mr. Soloman being an excellent diplomatist, does, with the aid of the hostess, her twelve masters of ceremony, her beadle, and two policemen, forthwith bring the house to a more orderly condition. But night has rolled into the page of the past, the gray dawn of morning is peeping in at the half-closed windows, the lights burning in the chandeliers shed a pale glow over the wearied features of those who drag, as it were, their languid bodies to the stifled music of unwilling slaves. And while daylight seems modestly contending with the vulgar glare within, there appears among the pale revellers a paler ghost, who, having stalked thrice up and down the hall, preserving the frigidity and ghostliness of the tomb, answering not the questions that are put to him, and otherwise deporting himself as becometh a ghost of good metal, is being taken for a demon of wicked import. Now he pauses at the end of the hall, faces with spectre-like stare the alarmed group at the opposite end, rests his left elbow on his scythe-staff, and having set his glass on the floor, points to its running sands warningly with his right forefinger. Not a muscle does he move. "Truly a ghost!" exclaims one. "A ghost would have vanished before this," whispers another. "Speak to him," a third responds, as the musicians are seen to pale and leave their benches. Madame Flamingo, pale and weary, is first to rush for the door, shrieking as his ghostship turns his grim face upon her. Shriek follows shriek, the lights are put out, the gray dawn plays upon and makes doubly frightful the spectre. A Pandemonium of shriekings and beseechings is succeeded by a stillness as of the tomb. Our ghost is victor.

CHAPTER VIII
WHAT TAKES PLACE BETWEEN GEORGE MULLHOLLAND AND MR. SNIVEL

The man who kissed and bore away the prostrate girl was George Mullholland.

"Oh! George—George!" she whispers imploringly, as her eyes meet his; and turning upon the couch of her chamber, where he hath lain her, awakes to consciousness, and finds him watching over her with a lover's solicitude. "I was not cold because I loved you less—oh no! It was to propitiate my ambition—to be free of the bondage of this house—to purge myself of the past—to better my future!" And she lays her pale, nervous hand gently on his arm—then grasps his hand and presses it fervently to her lips.

Though placed beyond the pale of society—though envied by one extreme and shunned by the other—she finds George her only true friend. He parts and smooths gently over her polished shoulders her dishevelled hair; he watches over her with the tenderness of a brother; he quenches and wipes away the blood oozing from her wounded breast; he kisses and kisses her flushed cheek, and bathes her Ion-like brow. He forgives all. His heart would speak if his tongue had words to represent it. He would the past were buried—the thought of having wronged him forgotten. She recognizes in his solicitude for her the sincerity of his heart. It touches like sweet music the tenderest chords of her own; and like gushing fountains her great black eyes fill with tears. She buries her face in her hands, crying, "Never, never, George, (I swear it before the God I have wronged, but whose forgiveness I still pray,) will I again forget my obligation to you! I care not how high in station he who seeks me maybe. Ambitious!—I was misled. His money lured me away, but he betrayed me in the face of his promises. Henceforth I have nothing for this deceptive world; I receive of it nothing but betrayal—"

"The world wants nothing more of either of us," interrupts George.

More wounded in her feelings than in her flesh, she sobs and wrings her hands like one in despair.

"You have ambition. I am too poor to serve your ambition!"

That word, too "poor," is more than her already distracted brain can bear up under. It brings back the terrible picture of their past history; it goads and agonizes her very soul. She throws her arms frantically about his neck; presses him to her bosom; kisses him with the fervor of a child. Having pledged his forgiveness with a kiss, and sealed it by calling in a witness too often profaned on such occasions, George calms her feelings as best he can; then he smooths with a gentle hand the folds of her uplifted dress, and with them curtains the satin slippers that so delicately encase her small feet. This done, he spreads over her the richly-lined India morning-gown presented to her a few days ago by the Judge, who, as she says, so wantonly betrayed her, and on whom she sought revenge. Like a Delian maid, surrounded with Oriental luxury, and reclining on satin and velvet, she flings her flowing hair over her shoulders, nestles her weary head in the embroidered cushion, and with the hand of her only true friend firmly grasped in her own, soothes away into a calm sleep—that sovereign but too transient balm for sorrowing hearts.

Our scene changes. The ghost hath taken himself to the graveyard; the morning dawns soft and sunny on what we harmlessly style the sunny city of the sunny South. Madame Flamingo hath resolved to nail another horse-shoe over her door. She will propitiate (so she hath it) the god of ghosts.

George Mullholland, having neither visible means of gaining a livelihood nor a settled home, may be seen in a solitary box at Baker's, (a coffee-house at the corner of Meeting and Market streets,) eating an humble breakfast. About him there is a forlornness that the quick eye never fails to discover in the manners of the homeless man. "Cleverly done," he says, laying down the *Mercury* newspaper, in which it is set forth that "the St. Cecilia, in consequence of an affliction in the family of one of its principal members, postponed its assembly last night. The theatre, in consequence of a misunderstanding between the manager and his people, was also closed. The lecture on comparative anatomy, by Professor Bones, which was to have been delivered at Hibernian Hall, is, in consequence of the indisposition of the learned Professor, put off to Tuesday evening next, when he will have, as he deserves, an overflowing house. Tickets, as before, may be had at all the music and bookstores." The said facetious journal was silent on the superior attractions at the house of the old hostess; nor did it deem it prudent to let drop a word on the misunderstanding between the patrons of the drama and the said theatrical manager, inasmuch as it was one of those that are sure to give rise to a very serious misunderstanding between that functionary and his poor people.

In another column the short but potent line met his eye: "An overflowing and exceedingly fashionable house greeted the Negro Minstrels last night. First-rate talent never goes begging in our city." George sips his coffee and smiles. Wonderfully clever these editors are, he thinks. They have nice apologies for public taste always on hand; set the country by the ears now and then; and amuse themselves with carrying on the most prudent description of wars.

His own isolated condition, however, is uppermost in his mind. Poverty and wretchedness stare him in the face on one side; chivalry, on the other, has no bows for him while daylight lasts. Instinct whispers in his ear—where one exists the other is sure to be.

To the end that this young man will perform a somewhat important part in the by-ways of this history, some further description of him may be necessary. George Mullholland stands some five feet nine, is wiry-limbed, and slender and erect of person. Of light complexion, his features, are sharp and irregular, his face narrow and freckled, his forehead small and retreating, his hair sandy and short-cropped. Add to these two small, dull, gray eyes, and you have features not easily described. Nevertheless, there are moments when his countenance wears an expression of mildness—one in which the quick eye may read a character more inoffensive than intrusive. A swallow-tail blue coat, of ample skirts, and brass buttons; a bright-colored waistcoat, opening an avalanche of shirt-bosom, blossoming with cheap jewelry; a broad, rolling shirt-collar, tied carelessly with a blue ribbon; a steeple-crowned hat, set on the side of his head with a challenging air; and a pair of broadly-striped and puckered trowsers, reaching well over a small-toed and highly-glazed boot, constitutes his dress. For the exact set of those two last-named articles of his wardrobe he maintains a scrupulous regard. We are compelled to acknowledge George an importation from New York, where he would be the more readily recognized by that vulgar epithet, too frequently used by the self-styled refined—"a swell."

Life with George is a mere drift of uncertainty. As for aims and ends, why he sees the safer thing in having nothing to do with them. Mr. Tom Toddleworth once advised this course, and Tom was esteemed good authority in such matters. Like many others, his character is made up of those yielding qualities which the teachings of good men may elevate to usefulness, or bad men corrupt by their examples. There is a stage in the early youth of such persons when we find their minds singularly susceptible, and ready to give rapid growth to all the vices of depraved men; while they are equally apt in receiving good, if good men but take the trouble to care for them, and inculcate lessons of morality.

Not having a recognized home, we may add, in resuming our story, that George makes Baker's his accustomed haunt during the day, as do also numerous others of his class—a class recognized and made use of by men in the higher walks of life only at night.

"Ah! ha, ha! into a tight place this time, George," laughs out Mr. Soloman, the accommodation man, as he hastens into the room, seats himself in the box with George, and seizes his hand with the earnestness of a true friend. Mr. Soloman can deport himself on all occasions with becoming good nature. "It's got out, you see."

"What has got out?" interrupts George, maintaining a careless indifference.

"Come now! none of that, old fellow."

"If I understood you—"

"That affair last night," pursues Mr. Soloman, his delicate fingers wandering into his more delicately-combed beard. "It'll go hard with you. He's a stubborn old cove, that Sleepyhorn; administers the law as Cæsar was wont to. Yesterday he sent seven to the whipping-post; to-day he hangs two 'niggers' and a white man. There is a consolation in getting rid of the white. I say this because no one loses a dollar by it."

George, continuing to masticate his bread, says it has nothing to do with him. He may hang the town.

"If I can do you a bit of a good turn, why here's your man. But you must not talk that way—you must not, George, I assure you!" Mr. Soloman assumes great seriousness of countenance, and again, in a friendly way, takes George by the hand. "That poignard, George, was yours. It was picked up by myself when it fell from your hand—"

"My hand! my hand!" George quietly interposes, his countenance paling, and his eyes wandering in excitement.

"Now don't attempt to disguise the matter, you know! Come out on the square—own up! Jealousy plays the devil with one now and then. I know—I have had a touch of it; had many a little love affair in my time—"

George again interrupts by inquiring to what he is coming.

"To the attempt (the accommodation man assumes an air of sternness) you made last night on the life of that unhappy girl. It is needless," he adds, "to plead ignorance. The Judge has the poignard; and what's more, there are four witnesses ready to testify. It'll go hard with you, my boy." He shakes his head warningly.

"I swear before God and man I am as innocent as ignorant of the charge. The poignard I confess is mine; but I had no part in the act of last night, save to carry the prostrate girl—the girl I dearly love—away. This I can prove by her own lips."

Mr. Soloman, with an air of legal profundity, says: "This is all very well in its way, George, but it won't stand in law. The law is what you have got to get at. And when you have got at it, you must get round it; and then you must twist it and work it every which way—only be careful not to turn its points against yourself; that, you know, is the way we lawyers do the thing. You'll think we're a sharp lot; and we have to be sharp, as times are."

"It is not surprising," replies George, as if waking from a fit of abstraction, "that she should have sought revenge of one who so basely betrayed her at the St. Cecilia—"

"There, there!" Mr. Soloman interrupts, changing entirely the expression of his countenance, "the whole thing is out! I said there was an unexplained mystery somewhere. It was not the Judge, but me who betrayed her to the assembly. Bless you, (he smiles, and crooking his finger, beckons a servant, whom he orders to bring a julep,) I was bound to do it, being the guardian of the Society's dignity, which office I have held for years. But you don't mean to have it that the girl attempted—(he suddenly corrects himself)—Ah, that won't do, George. Present my compliments to Anna—I wouldn't for the world do aught to hurt her feelings, you know that—and say I am ready to get on my knees to her to confess myself a penitent for having injured her feelings. Yes, I am ready to do anything that will procure her forgiveness. I plead guilty. But she must in return forgive the Judge. He is hard in law matters—that is, we of the law consider him so—now and then; but laying that aside, he is one of the best old fellows in the world, loves Anna to distraction; nor has he the worst opinion in the world of you, George. Fact is, I have several times heard him refer to you in terms of praise. As I said before, being the man to do you a bit of a good turn, take my advice as a friend. The Judge has got you in his grasp, according to every established principle of law; and having four good and competent witnesses, (You have no voice in law, and Anna's won't stand before a jury,) will send you up for a twelve-months' residence in Mount Rascal."

It will be almost needless here to add, that Mr. Soloman had, in an interview with the Judge, arranged, in consideration of a goodly fee, to assume the responsibility of the betrayal at the St. Cecilia; and also to bring about a reconciliation between him and the girl he so passionately sought.

Keep out of the way a few days, and everything will blow over and come right. I will procure you the Judge's friendship—yes, his money, if you want. More than that, I will acknowledge my guilt to Anna; and being as generous of heart as she is beautiful, she will, having discovered the mistake, forgive me and make amends to the Judge for her foolish act.

It is almost superfluous to add, that the apparent sincerity with which the accommodation man pleaded, had its effect on the weak-minded man. He loved dearly the girl, but poverty hung like a leaden cloud over him. Poverty stripped him of the means of gratifying her ambition; poverty held him fast locked in its blighting chains; poverty forbid his rescuing her from the condition necessity had imposed upon her; poverty was goading him into crime; and through crime only did he see the means of securing to himself the cherished object of his love.

"I am not dead to your friendship, but I am too sad at heart to make any pledge that involves Anna, at this moment. We met in wretchedness, came up in neglect and crime, sealed our love with the hard seal of suffering. Oh! what a history of misery my heart could unfold, if it had but a tongue!" George replies, in subdued accents, as a tear courses down his cheek.

Extending his hand, with an air of encouragement, Mr. Soloman says nothing in the world would so much interest him as a history of the relations existing between George and Anna. Their tastes, aims, and very natures, are different. To him their connection is clothed in mystery.

CHAPTER IX
IN WHICH A GLEAM OF LIGHT IS SHED ON THE HISTORY OF ANNA BONARD

A bottle of wine, and the mild, persuasive manner of Mr. Snivel, so completely won over George's confidence, that, like one of that class always too ready to give out their heart-achings at the touch of sympathy, and too easily betrayed through misplaced confidence, he commences relating his history. That of Anna is identified with it. "We will together proceed to New York, for it is there, among haunts of vice and depravity—"

"In depth of degradation they have no counterpart on our globe," Mr. Soloman interrupts, filling his glass.

"We came up together—knew each other, but not ourselves. That was our dark age." George pauses for a moment.

"Bless you," again interrupts Mr. Soloman, tipping his glass very politely, "I never—that is, when I hear our people who get themselves laced into narrow-stringed Calvinism, and long-founded foreign missions, talk—think much could have come of the dark ages. I speak after the manner of an attorney, when I say this. We hear a deal of the dark ages, the crimes of the dark ages, the dark idolatry of darker Africa. My word for it, and it's something, if they had anything darker in Sodom; if they had in Babylon a state of degradation more hardened of crime; if in Egypt there existed a benightedness more stubbornly opposed to the laws of God—than is to be found in that New York; that city of merchant princes with princely palaces; that modern Pompeii into which a mighty commerce teems its mightier gold, where a coarse throng revel in coarser luxury, where a thousand gaudy churches rear heavenward their gaudier steeples, then I have no pity for Sodom, not a tear to shed over fallen Babylon, and very little love for Egypt." Mr. Snivel concludes, saying—"proceed, young man."

"Of my mother I know nothing. My father (I mean the man I called father, but who they said was not my father, though he was the only one that cared anything for me) was Tom English, who used to live here and there with me about the Points. He was always looking in at Paddy Pie's, in Orange street, and Paddy Pie got all his money, and then Paddy Pie and him quarrelled, and we were turned out of Paddy Pie's house. So we used to lodge here and there, in the cellars about the Points, in 'Cut Throat Alley,' or 'Cow Bay,' or 'Murderer's Alley,' or in 'The House of the Nine Nations,' or wherever we could get a sixpenny rag to lay down upon. Nobody but English seemed to care for me, and English cared for nobody but me. And English got thick with Mrs. McCarty and her three daughters—they kept the Rookery in 'Cow Bay,' which we used to get to up a long pair of stairs outside, and which God knows I never want to think of again,—where sometimes fourteen or fifteen of us, men and women, used to sleep in a little room Mrs. McCarty paid eight dollars a month for. And Mr. Crown, who always seemed a cross sort of man, and was agent for all the houses on the Points I thought, used to say she had it too cheap. And English got to thinking a good deal of Mrs. McCarty, and Mrs. McCarty's daughters got to thinking a good deal of him. And Boatswain Bill, who lived at the house of the 'Nine Nations'—the house they said had a bottomless pit—and English used to fight a deal about the Miss McCartys, and Bill one night threw English over the high stoop, down upon the pavement, and broke his arms. They said it was a wonder it hadn't a broken his neck. Fighting Mary (Mary didn't go by that name then) came up and took English's part, and whipped Boatswain Bill, and said she'd whip the whole house of the 'Nine Nations' if it had spunk enough in it to come on. But no one dare have a set-to with Mary. Mary used to drink a deal of gin, and say—'this gin and the devil'll get us all one of these days. I wonder if Mr. Crown'll sell bad gin to his highness when he gets him?' Well, Bill was sent up for six months, so the McCartys had peace in the house, and Mrs. McCarty got him little things, and did for English until his arms got well. Then he got a little money, (I don't know how he got it,) and Paddy Pie made good friends with him, and got him from the Rookery, and then all his money. I used to think all the money in the Points found its way either to the house of Paddy Pie, or the Bottomless Pit at the house of the 'Nine Nations,' and all the clothes to the sign of the 'Three Martyrs,' which the man with the eagle face kept round the corner.

"English used to say in one of his troubled fits, 'I'd like to be a respectable man, and get out of this, if there was a chance, and do something for you, George. There's no chance, you see.' And when we went into Broadway, which we did now and then, and saw what another world it was, and how rich everything looked, English used to shake his head and say, 'they don't know how we live, George.'

"Paddy Pie soon quarrelled with English, and being penniless again we had to shift for ourselves. English didn't like to go back to Mrs. McCarty, so we used to sleep at Mrs. Sullivan's cellar in 'Cut Throat Alley.' And Mrs. Sullivan's cellar was only about twelve feet by twenty, and high enough to stand up in, and wet enough for anything, and so overrun with rats and vermin that we couldn't sleep. There were nine rag-beds in the cellar, which as many as twenty-three would sometimes sleep on, or, if they were not too tipsy, try to sleep on. And folks used to come into the cellar at night, and be found dead in the morning. This made such a fuss in the neighborhood (there was always a fuss when Old Bones, the coroner, was about), and frightened so many, that Mrs. Sullivan couldn't get lodgers for weeks. She used to nail no end of horse-shoes over the door to keep out the ghosts of them that died last. But it was a long while before her lodgers got courage enough to come back. Then we went to the house of the Blazers, in 'Cow Bay,' and used to lodge there with Yellow Bill. They said Bill was a thief by profession; but I wasn't old enough to be a judge. Little Lizza Rock, the nondescript, as people called her, used to live at the Blazers. Poor Lizza had a hard time of it, and used to sigh and say she wished she was dead. Nobody thought of her, she said, and she was nothing because she was deformed, and a cripple. She was about four feet high, had a face like a bull-dog, and a swollen chest, and a hunchback, a deformed leg, and went with a crutch. She never combed her hair, and what few rags she had on her back hung in filth. What few shillings she got were sure to find their way either into Bill's pocket, or send her tipsy into the 'Bottomless Pit' of the house of the 'Nine Nations.' There was in the Bottomless Pit a never-ending stream of gin that sent everybody to the Tombs, and from the Tombs to the grave. But Lizza was good to me, and used to take care of me, and steal little things for me from old Dan Sullivan, who begged in Broadway, and let Yellow Bill get his money, by getting him tipsy. And I got to liking Lizza, for we both seemed to have no one in the world who cared for us but English. And there was always some trouble between the Blazers and the people at the house of the 'Nine Nations.'

"Well, English was hard to do for some time, and through necessity, which he said a deal about, we were driven out of every place we had sought shelter in. And English did something they sent him up for a twelve-month for, and I was left to get on as I could. I was took in by 'Hard-Fisted Sall,' who always wore a knuckle-duster, and used to knock everybody down she met, and threatened a dozen times to whip Mr. Fitzgerald, the detective, and used to rob every one she took in tow, and said if she could only knock down and rob the whole pumpkin-headed corporation she should die easy, for then she would know she had done a good thing for the public, whose money they were squandering without once thinking how the condition of such wretches as herself could be bettered.

"English died before he had been up two months. And death reconciled the little difficulty between him and the McCartys; and old Mrs. McCarty's liking for him came back, and she went crying to the Bellevue and begged them, saying she was his mother, to let her take his body away and bury it. They let her have it, and she brought it away to the rookery, in a red coffin, and got a clean sheet of the Blazers, and hung it up beside the coffin, and set four candles on a table, and a little cross between them, and then borrowed a Bible with a cross on it, and laid it upon the coffin. Then they sent for me. I cried and kissed poor English, for poor English was the only father I knew, and he was good to me. I never shall forget what I saw in that little room that night. I found a dozen friends and the McCartys there, forming a half-circle of curious and demoniacal faces, peering over the body of English, whose face, I thought, formed the only repose in the picture. There were two small pictures—one of the Saviour, and the other of Kossuth—hung at the head and feet of the corpse; and the light shed a lurid paleness over the living and the dead. And detective Fitzgerald and another gentleman looked in.

"'Who's here to-night?' says Fitzgerald, in a friendly sort of way.

"'God love ye, Mr. Fitzgerald, poor English is gone! Indeed, then, it was the will of the Lord, and He's taken him from us—poor English!' says Mrs. McCarty. And Fitzgerald, and the gentleman with him, entered the den, and they shuddered and sat down at the sight of the face in the coffin. 'Sit down, Mr. Fitzgerald, do!—and may the Lord love ye! There was a deal of good in poor English. He's gone—so he is!' said Mrs. McCarty, begging them to sit down, and excuse the disordered state of her few rags. She had a hard struggle to live, God knows. They took off their hats, and sat a few minutes in solemn silence. The rags moved at the gentleman's side, which made him move towards the door. 'What is there, my good woman?' he inquired. 'She's a blessed child, Mr. Fitzgerald knows that same:' says Mrs. McCarty, turning down the rags and revealing the wasted features of her youngest girl, a child eleven years old, sinking in death. 'God knows she'll be better in heaven, and herself won't be long out of it,' Mrs. McCarty twice repeated, maintaining a singular indifference to the hand of death, already upon the child. The gentleman left some money to buy candles for poor English, and with Mr. Fitzgerald took himself away.

"Near midnight, the tall black figure of solemn-faced Father Flaherty stalked in. He was not pleased with the McCartys, but went to the side of the dying child, fondled her little wasted hand in his own, and whispered a prayer for her soul. Never shall I forget how innocently she looked in his face while he parted the little ringlets that curled over her brow, and told her she would soon have a better home in a better world. Then he turned to poor English, and the cross, and the candles, and the pictures, and the living faces that gave such a ghastliness to the picture. Mrs. McCarty brought him a basin of water, over which he muttered, and made it holy. Then he again muttered some unintelligible sentences, and sprinkled the water over the dying child, over the body of poor English, and over the living—warning Mrs. McCarty and her daughters, as he pointed to the coffin. Then he knelt down, and they all knelt down, and he prayed for the soul of poor English, and left. What holy water then was left, Mrs. McCarty placed near the door, to keep the ghosts out.

"The neighbors at the Blazers took a look in, and a few friends at the house of the 'Nine Nations' took a look in, and 'Fighting Mary,' of Murderer's Alley, took a look in, and before Father Flaherty had got well out of 'Cow Bay,' it got to be thought a trifle of a wake would console Mrs. McCarty's distracted feelings. 'Hard-fisted Sall' came to take a last look at poor English; and she said she would spend her last shilling over poor English, and having one, it would get a drop, and a drop dropped into the right place would do Mrs. McCarty a deal of good.

"And Mrs. McCarty agreed that it wouldn't be amiss, and putting with Sall's shilling the money that was to get the candles, I was sent to the 'Bottomless Pit' at the house of the 'Nine Nations,' where Mr. Crown had a score with the old woman, and fetched away a quart of his gin, which they said was getting the whole of them. The McCartys took a drop, and the girls took a drop, and the neighbors took a drop, and they all kept taking drops, and the drops got the better of them all. One of the Miss McCartys got to having words with 'Fighting Mary,' about an old affair in which poor English was concerned, and the words got to blows, when Mr. Flanegan at the Blazers stepped in to make peace. But the whole house got into a fight, and the lights were put out, the corpse knocked over, and the child (it was found dead in the morning) suffocated with the weight of bodies felled in the melee. The noise and cries of murder brought the police rushing in, and most of them were dragged off to the Station; and the next day being Sunday, I wandered homeless and friendless into Sheriff street. Poor English was taken in charge by the officers. They kept him over Monday to see if any one would come up and claim him. No one came for him; no one knew more of him than that he went by the name of English; no one ever heard him say where he came from—he never said a word about my mother, or whether he had a relation in the world. He was carted off to Potter's Field and buried. That was the last of poor English.

"We seldom got much to eat in the Points, and I had not tasted food for twenty-four hours. I sat down on the steps of a German grocery, and was soon ordered away by the keeper. Then I wandered into a place they called Nightmare's Alley, where three old wooden buildings with broken-down verandas stood, and were inhabited principally by butchers. I sat down on the steps of one, and thought if I only had a mother, or some one to care for me, and give me something to eat, how happy I should be. And I cried. And a great red-faced man came out of the house, and took me in, and gave me something to eat. His name was Mike Mullholland, and he was good to me, and I liked him, and took his name. And he lived with a repulsive looking woman, in a little room he paid ten dollars a month for. He had two big dogs, and worked at day work, in a slaughter-house in Staunton street. The dogs were known in the neighborhood as Mullholland's dogs, and with them I used to sleep on the rags of carpet spread for us in the room with Mullholland and his wife, who I got to calling mother. This is how I took the name of Mullholland. I was glad to leave the Points, and felt as if I had a home. But there was a 'Bottomless Pit' in Sheriff street, and though not so bad as the one at the house of the 'Nine Nations,' it gave out a deal of gin that the Mullhollands had a liking for. I was continually going for it, and the Mullhollands were continually drinking it; and the whole neighborhood liked it, and in 'Nightmare's Alley' the undertaker found a profitable business.

"In the morning I went with the dogs to the slaughter-house, and there fed them, and took care of the fighting cocks, and brought gin for the men who worked there. In the afternoon I joined the newsboys, as ragged and neglected as myself, gambled for cents, and watched the policemen, whom we called the Charleys. I lived with Mullholland two years, and saw and felt enough to make hardened any one of my age. One morning there came a loud knocking at the door, which was followed by the entrance of two officers. The dogs had got out and bitten a child, and the officers, knowing who owned them, had come to arrest Mullholland. We were all surprised, for the officers recognized in Mullholland and the woman two old offenders. And while they were dragged off to the Tombs, I was left to prey upon the world as best I could. Again homeless, I wandered about with urchins as ragged and destitute as myself. It seemed to me that everybody viewed me as an object of suspicion, for I sought in vain for employment that would give me bread and clothing. I wanted to be honest, and would have lived honest; but I could not make people believe me honest. And when I told who I was, and where I sheltered myself, I was ordered away. Everybody judged me by the filthy shreds on my back; nobody had anything for me to do.

"I applied at a grocer's, to sweep his store and go errands. When I told him where I had lived, he shook his head and ordered me away. Knowing I could fill a place not unknown to me, I applied at a butcher's in Mott street; but he pointed his knife—which left a wound in my feelings—and ordered me away. And I was ordered away wherever I went. The doors of the Chatham theatre looked too fine for me. My ragged condition rebuked me wherever I went, and for more than a week I slept under a cart that stood in Mott street. Then Tom Farley found me, and took me with him to his cellar, in Elizabeth street, where we had what I thought a good bed of shavings. Tom sold *Heralds*, gambled for cents, and shared with me, and we got along. Then Tom stole a dog, and the dog got us into a deal of trouble, which ended with getting us both into the Tombs, where Tom was locked up. I was again adrift, as we used to call it, and thought of poor Tom a deal. Every one I met seemed higher up in the world than I was. But I got into Centre Market, carried baskets, and did what I could to earn a shilling, and slept in Tom's bed, where there was some nights fifteen and twenty like myself.

"One morning, while waiting a job, my feet and hands benumbed with the cold, a beautiful lady slipped a shilling into my hand and passed on. To one penniless and hungry, it seemed a deal of money. Necessity had almost driven me to the sign of the 'Three Martyrs,' to see what the man of the eagle face would give me on my cap, for they said the man at the 'Three Martyrs' lent money on rags such as I had. I followed the woman, for there was something so good in the act that I could not resist it. She entered a fine house in Leonard street.

"You must now go with me into the den of Hag Zogbaum, in 'Scorpion Cove;' and 'Scorpion Cove' is in Pell street. Necessity next drove me there. It is early spring, we will suppose; and being in the Bowery, we find the streets in its vicinity reeking with putrid matter, hurling pestilence into the dark dwellings of the unknown poor, and making thankful the coffin-maker, who in turn thanks a nonundertaking corporation for the rich harvest. The muck is everywhere deep enough for hogs and fat aldermen to wallow in, and would serve well the purposes of a supper-eating corporation, whose chief business it was to fatten turtles and make Presidents.

"We have got through the muck of the mucky Bowery. Let us turn to the left as we ascend the hill from Chatham street, and into a narrow, winding way, called Doyer's street. Dutch Sophy, then, as now, sits in all the good nature of her short, fat figure, serving her customers with ices, at three cents. Her cunning black eyes and cheerful, ruddy face, enhance the air of pertness that has made her a favorite with her customers. We will pass the little wooden shop, where Mr. Saunders makes boots of the latest style, and where old lapstone, with curious framed spectacles tied over his bleared eyes, has for the last forty years been seen at the window trimming welts, and mending every one's sole but his own; we will pass the four story wooden house that the landlord never paints—that has the little square windows, and the little square door, and the two little iron hand rails that curl so crabbedly at the ends, and guard four crabbeder steps that give ingress and egress to its swarm of poor but honest tenants; we will pass the shop where a short, stylish sign tells us Mr. Robertson makes bedsteads; and the little, slanting house a line of yellow letters on a square of black tin tells us is a select school for young ladies, and the bright, dainty looking house with the green shutters, where lives Mr. Vredenburg the carpenter, who, the neighbors say, has got up in the world, and paints his house to show that he feels above poor folks—and find we have reached the sooty and gin-reeking grocery of Mr. Korner, who sells the *devil's elixir* to the sootier devils that swarm the cellars of his neighbors. The faded blue letters, on a strip of wood nailed to the bricks over his door, tell us he is a dealer in 'Imported and other liquors.' Next door to Mr. Korner's tipsy looking grocery lives Mr. Muffin, the coffin-maker, who has a large business with the disciples who look in at Korner's. Mrs. Downey, a decent sort of body, who lives up the alley, and takes sixpenny lodgers by the dozen, may be seen in great tribulation with her pet pig, who, every day, much to the annoyance of Mr. Korner, manages to get out, and into the pool of decaying matter opposite his door, where he is sure to get stuck, and with his natural propensity, squeals lustily for assistance. Mrs. Downey, as is her habit, gets distracted; and having well abused Mr. Korner for his interference in a matter that can only concern herself and the animal, ventures to her knees in the mire, and having seized her darling pig by the two ears, does, with the assistance of a policeman, who kindly takes him by the tail, extricate his porkship, to the great joy of herself. The animal scampers, grunting, up the alley, as Mr. Korner, in his shirt sleeves, throws his broom after him, and the policeman surlily says he wishes it was the street commissioner.

"We have made the circle of Doyer's street, and find it fortified on Pell street, with two decrepit wooden buildings, that the demand for the 'devil's elixir,' has converted into Dutch groceries, their exteriors presenting the appearance of having withstood a storm of dilapidated clapboards, broken shutters, red herrings, and onions. Mr. Voss looks suspiciously through the broken shutters of his Gibraltar, at his neighbor of the opposite Gibraltar, and is heard to say of his wares that they are none of the best, and that while he sells sixpence a pint less, the article is a shilling a pint better. And there the two Gibraltars stand, apparently infirm, hurling their unerring missiles, and making wreck of everything in the neighborhood.

"We have turned down Pell street toward Mott, and on the north side a light-colored sign, representing a smith in the act of shoeing a horse, attracts the eye, and tells us the old cavern-like building over which it swings, is where Mr. Mooney does smithwork and shoeing. And a little further on, a dash of yellow and white paint on a little sign-board at the entrance of an alley, guarded on one side by a broken-down shed, and on the other, by a three-story, narrow, brick building (from the windows of which trail long water-stains, and from the broken panes a dozen curious black heads, of as many curious eyed negroes protrude), tells us somewhat indefinitely, that Mister Mills, white-washer and wall-colorer, may be found in the neighborhood, which, judging from outward appearances, stands much in need of this good man's services. Just keep your eye on the sign of the white-washer and wall-colorer, and passing up the sickly alley it tells you Mister Mills maybe found in, you will find yourself (having picked your way over putrid matter, and placed your perfumed cambric where it will protect your lungs from the inhalation of pestilential air,) in the cozy area of 'Scorpion Cove.' Scorpion Cove is bounded at one end by a two-story wooden house, with two decayed and broken verandas in front, and rickety steps leading here and there to suspicious looking passages, into which, and out of which a never-ending platoon of the rising generation crawl and toddle, keep up a cheap serenade, and like rats, scamper away at the sight of a stranger; and on the other, by the back of the brick house with the negro-headed front. At the sides are two broken-down board fences, and forming a sort of network across the cove, are an innumerable quantity of unoccupied clothes-lines, which would seem only to serve the mischievous propensities of young negroes and the rats. There is any quantity of rubbish in 'Scorpion Cove,' and any amount of disease-breeding cesspools; but the corporation never heard of 'Scorpion Cove,' and wouldn't look into it if it had. If you ask me how it came to be called 'Scorpion Cove,' I will tell you. The brick house at one end was occupied by negroes; and the progeny of these negroes swarmed over the cove, and were called scorpions. The old house of the verandas at the other end, and which had an air of being propped up after a shock of paralysis, was inhabited by twenty or more families, of the Teutonic race, whose numerous progeny, called the hedge-hogs, were more than a match for the scorpions, and with that jealousy of each other which animates these races did the scorpions and hedge-hogs get at war. In the morning the scorpions would crawl up through holes in the cellar, through broken windows, through the trap-doors, down the long stairway that wound from the second and third stories over the broken pavilion, and from nobody could tell where—for they came, it seems, from every rat-hole, and with rolling white eyes, marshalled themselves for battle. The hedge-hogs mustering in similar strength, and springing up from no one could tell where, would set upon the scorpions, and after a goodly amount of wallowing in the mire, pulling hair and wool, scratching faces and pommeling noses, the scorpions being alternately the victors and vanquished, the war would end at the appearance of Hag Zogbaum, who, with her broom, would cause the scorpions to beat a hasty retreat. The hedge-hogs generally came off victorious, for they were the stronger race. But the old hedge-hogs got much shattered in time by the broadsides of the two Gibraltars, which sent them broadside on into the Tombs. And this passion of the elder hedge-hogs for getting into the Tombs, caused by degrees a curtailing of the younger hedge-hogs. And this falling off in the forces of the foe, singularly inspirited the scorpions, who mustered courage, and after a series of savage battles, in which there was a notorious amount of wool-pulling, gained the day. And this is how 'Scorpion Cove' got its name.

"Hag Zogbaum lived in the cellar of the house with the verandas; and old Dan Sullivan and the rats had possession of the garret. In the cellar of this woman, whose trade was the fostering of crime in children as destitute as myself, there was a bar and a back cellar, where as many as twenty boys and girls slept on straw and were educated in vice. She took me into her nursery, and I was glad to get there, for I had no other place to go.

"In the morning we were sent out to pilfer, to deceive the credulous, and to decoy others to the den. Some were instructed by Hag Zogbaum to affect deaf and dumb, to plead the starving condition of our parents, to, in a word, enlist the sympathies of the credulous with an hundred different stories. We were all stimulated by a premium being held out to the most successful. Some were sent out to steal pieces of iron, brass, copper, and old junk; and these Hag Zogbaum would sell or give to the man who kept the junk-shop in Stanton street, known as the rookery at the corner. (This man lived with Hag Zogbaum.) We returned at night with our booty, and received our wages in gin or beer. The unsuccessful were set down as victims of bad luck. Now and then the old woman would call us a miserable lot of wretches she was pestered to take care of. At one time there were in this den of wretchedness fifteen girls from seven to eleven years old, and seven boys under eleven—all being initiated into the by-ways of vice and crime. Among the girls were Italians, Germans, Irish, and—shall I say it?—Americans! It was curious to see what means the old hag would resort to for the purpose of improving their features after they had arrived at a certain age. She had a purpose in this; and that purpose sprang from that traffic in depravity caused by the demands of a depraved society, a theme on her lips continually."

CHAPTER X
A CONTINUATION OF GEORGE MULLHOLLAND'S HISTORY

"Having served well the offices of felons and impostors, Hag Zogbaum would instruct her girls in the mysteries of licentiousness. When they reached a certain age, their personal appearance was improved, and one by one they were passed into the hands of splendidly-dressed ladies, as we then took them to be, who paid a sum for them to Hag Zogbaum, and took them away; and that was the last we saw of them. They had no desire to remain in their miserable abode, and were only too glad to get away from it. In most cases they were homeless and neglected orphans; and knowing no better condition, fell easy victims to the snares set for them.

"It was in this dark, cavern-like den—in this mysterious caldron of precocious depravity, rioting unheeded in the very centre of a great city, whose boasted wealth and civilization it might put to shame, if indeed it were capable of shame, I first met the child of beauty, Anna Bonard. Yes!—the Anna Bonard you now see at the house of Madame Flamingo. At that time she was but seven years old—a child of uncommon beauty and aptness, of delicate but well-proportioned features, of middle stature, and a face that care might have made charming beyond comparison. But vice hardens, corrodes, and gives a false hue to the features. Anna said she was an orphan. How far this was true I know not. A mystery shrouded the way in which she fell into the hands of Hag Zogbaum. Hag Zogbaum said she got her of an apple-woman; and the apple-woman kept a stand in West street, but never would disclose how she came by Anna. And Mr. Tom Toddleworth, who was the chronicle of the Points, and used to look into 'Scorpion Cove' now and then, and inquire about Anna, as if he had a sort of interest in her, they said knew all about her. But if he did, he always kept it a secret between himself and Hag Zogbaum.

"She was always of a melancholy turn, used to say life was but a burden to her—that she could see nothing in the future that did not seem dark and tortuous. The lot into which she was cast of necessity others might have mistaken for that which she had chosen. It was not. The hard hand of necessity had forced her into this quicksand of death; the indifference of a naturally generous community, robbed her of the light of intelligence, and left her a helpless victim in the hands of this cultivator of vice. How could she, orphan as she was called, and unencouraged, come to be a noble and generous-hearted woman? No one offered her the means to come up and ornament her sex; but tyrannical society neither forgets her misfortunes nor forgives her errors. Once seal the death-warrant of a woman's errors, and you have none to come forward and cancel it; the tomb only removes the seal. Anna took a liking to me, and was kind to me, and looked to me to protect her. And I loved her, and our love grew up, and strengthened; and being alike neglected in the world, our condition served as the strongest means of cementing our attachment.

"Hag Zogbaum then sent Anna away to the house up the alley, in Elizabeth street, where she sent most of her girls when they had reached the age of eleven and twelve. Hag Zogbaum had many places for her female pupils. The very best looking always went a while to the house in the alley; the next best looking were sure to find their way into the hands of Miss Brown, in Little Water street, and Miss Brown, they said, sold them to the fairies of the South, who dressed them in velvet and gold; and the 'scrubs,' as the old woman used to call the rest, got, by some mysterious process, into the hands of Paddy Pie and Tim Branahan, who kept shantees in Orange street.

"Anna had been away some time, and Mr. Tom Toddleworth had several times been seen to look in and inquire for her. Mr. Toddleworth said he had a ripping bid for her. At that time I was ignorant of its meaning. Harry Rooney and me were sent to the house in Elizabeth street, one morning, to bring Anna and another girl home. The house was large, and had an air of neatness about it that contrasted strangely with the den in 'Scorpion Cove.' We rang the bell and inquired for the girls, who, after waiting nearly an hour, were sent down to us, clean and neatly dressed. In Anna the change was so great, that though I had loved her, and thought of her day and night during her absence, I scarce recognized her. So glad did she seem to see me that she burst into tears, flung her arms about my neck, and kissed me with the fondness of a sister. Then she recounted with childlike enthusiasm the kind treatment she had received at the house of Madame Harding (for such it was called), between whom and Hag Zogbaum there was carried on a species of business I am not inclined to designate here. Two kind and splendidly-dressed ladies, Anna said, called to see them nearly every day, and were going to take them away, that they might live like fairies all the rest of their lives.

"When we got home, two ladies were waiting at the den. It was not the first time we had seen them at the den. Anna recognized them as the ladies she had seen at Madame Harding's. One was the woman who so kindly gave me the shilling in the market, when I was cold and hungry. A lengthy whispering took place between Hag Zogbaum and the ladies, and we were ordered into the back cellar. I knew the whispering was about Anna; and watching through the boards I heard the Hag say Anna was fourteen and nothing less, and saw one of the ladies draw from her purse numerous pieces of gold, which were slipped into her hand. In a few minutes more I saw poor little Anna follow her up the steps that led into 'Scorpion Cove.' When we were released Hag was serving ragged and dejected-looking men with gin and beer. Anna, she said when I inquired, had gone to a good home in the country. I loved her ardently, and being lonesome was not content with the statement of the old woman. I could not read, but had begun to think for myself, and something told me all was not right. For weeks and months I watched at the house in Leonard street, into which I had followed the woman who gave me the shilling. But I neither saw her nor the woman. Elegant carriages, and elegantly-dressed men drove to and from the door, and passed in and out of the house, and the house seemed to have a deal of fashionable customers, and that was all I knew of it then.

"As I watched one night, a gentleman came out of the house, took me by the arm and shook me, said I was a loitering vagrant, that he had seen me before, and having a suspicious look he would order the watch to lock me up. He inquired where my home was; and when I told him it was in 'Scorpion Cove,' he replied he didn't know where that was. I told him it wasn't much of a home, and he said I ought to have a better one. It was all very well to say so; but with me the case was different. That night I met Tom Farley, who was glad to see me, and told how he got out of the lock-up, and what he thought of the lock-up, and the jolly old Judge who sent him to the lock-up, and who he saw in the lock-up, and what mischief was concocted in the lock-up, and what he got to eat in the lock-up, and how the lock-up wasn't so bad a place after all.

"The fact was I was inclined to think the lock-up not so bad a place to get into, seeing how they gave people something good to eat, and clothes to wear. Tom and me went into business together. We sold *Heralds* and Sunday papers, and made a good thing of it, and shared our earnings, and got enough to eat and some clothes. I took up my stand in Centre Market, and Tom took up his at Peck Slip. At night we would meet, count our earnings, and give them to Mr. Crogan, who kept the cellar in Water street, where we slept. I left Hag Zogbaum, who we got to calling the wizard. She got all we could earn or pilfer, and we got nothing for our backs but a few rags, and unwholesome fish and beer for our bellies. I thought of Anna day and night; I hoped to meet in Centre Market the woman who took her away.

"I said no one ever looked in at the den in 'Scorpion Cove,' but there was a kind little man, with sharp black eyes, and black hair, and an earnest olive-colored face, and an earnester manner about him, who used to look in now and then, talk kindly to us, and tell us he wished he had a home for us all, and was rich enough to give us all enough to eat. He hated Hag Zogbaum, and Hag Zogbaum hated him; but we all liked him because he was kind to us, and used to shake his head, and say he would do something for us yet. Hag Zogbaum said he was always meddling with other people's business. At other times a man would come along and throw tracts in at the gate of the alley. We were ignorant of what they were intended for, and used to try to sell them at the Gibraltars. Nobody wanted them, and nobody could read at the den, so Hag Zogbaum lighted the fire with them, and that was the end of them.

"Well, I sold papers for nearly two years, and learned to read a little by so doing, and got up in the world a little; and being what was called smart, attracted the attention of a printer in Nassau street, who took me into his office, and did well by me. My mind was bent on getting a trade. I knew I could do well for myself with a trade to lean upon. Two years I worked faithfully at the printer's, was approaching manhood, and with the facilities it afforded me had not failed to improve my mind and get a tolerable good knowledge of the trade. But the image of Anna, and the singular manner in which she disappeared, made me unhappy.

"On my return from dinner one day I met in Broadway the lady who took Anna away. The past and its trials flashed across my brain, and I turned and followed her—found that her home was changed to Mercer street, and this accounted for my fruitless watching in Leonard street.

"The love of Anna, that had left its embers smouldering in my bosom, quickened, and seemed to burn with redoubled ardor. It was my first and only love; the sufferings of our childhood had made it lasting. My very emotion rose to action as I saw the woman I knew took her away. My anxiety to know her fate had no bounds. Dressing myself up as respectably as it was possible with my means, I took advantage of a dark and stormy night in the month of November to call at the house in Mercer street, into which I had traced the lady. I rung the bell; a sumptuously-dressed woman came to the door, which opened into a gorgeously-decorated hall. She looked at me with an inquiring eye and disdainful frown, inquired who I was and what I wanted. I confess I was nervous, for the dazzling splendor of the mansion produced in me a feeling of awe rather than admiration. I made known my mission as best I could; the woman said no such person had ever resided there. In that moment of disappointment I felt like casting myself away in despair. The associations of Scorpion Cove, of the house of the Nine Nations, of the Rookery, of Paddy Pie's—or any other den in that desert of death that engulphs the Points, seemed holding out a solace for the melancholy that weighed me down. But when I got back into Broadway my resolution gained strength, and with it I wept over the folly of my thoughts.

"Led by curiosity, and the air of comfort pervading the well-furnished room, and the piously-disposed appearance of the persons who passed in and out, I had several times looked in at the house of the 'Foreign Missions,' as we used to call it. A man with a good-natured face used to sit in the chair, and a wise-looking little man in spectacles (the Secretary) used to sit a bit below him, and a dozen or two well-disposed persons of both sexes, with sharp and anxious countenances, used to sit round in a half circle, listening. The wise-looking man in the spectacles would, on motion of some one present, read a long report, which was generally made up of a list of donations and expenditures for getting up a scheme to evangelize the world, and get Mr. Singleton Spyke off to Antioch. It seemed to me as if a deal of time and money was expended on Mr. Singleton Spyke, and yet Mr. Spyke never got off to Antioch. When the man of the spectacles got through reading the long paper, and the good-natured man in the chair got through explaining that the heavy amount of twenty-odd thousand dollars had been judiciously expended for the salary of officers of the society, and the getting Brothers Spurn and Witherspoon off to enlighten the heathen, Brother Singleton Spyke's mission would come up. Every one agreed that there ought to be no delay in getting Brother Spyke off to Antioch; but a small deficiency always stood in the way. And Brother Spyke seemed spiked to this deficiency; for notwithstanding Mrs. Slocum, who was reckoned the strongest-minded woman, and best business-man of the society, always made speeches in favor of Brother Spyke and his mission (a special one), he never got off to Antioch.

"Feeling forlorn, smarting under disappointment, and undecided where to go after I left the house in Mercer street, I looked in at the house of the 'Foreign Missions.' Mrs. Slocum, as I had many times before seen her, was warmly contesting a question concerning Brother Spyke, with the good-natured man in the chair. It was wrong, she said, so much money should be expended, and Brother Spyke not got off to Antioch. So leaving them debating Mr. Spyke's mission to Antioch, I proceeded back to the house in Mercer street, and inquired for the landlady of the house. The landlady, the woman that opened the door said, was engaged. The door was shut in my face, and I turned away more wounded in my feelings than before. Day and night I contemplated some plan by which to ascertain Anna's place of abode, her pursuit in life, her wants. When we parted she could neither write nor read: I had taken writing lessons, by which I could communicate tolerably well, while my occupation afforded me the means of improvement. A few weeks passed (I continued to watch the house), and I recognized her one afternoon, by her black, floating hair, sitting at a second-story window of the house in Mercer street, her back toward me. The sight was like electricity on my feelings; a transport of joy bore away my thoughts. I gazed, and continued to gaze upon the object, throwing, as it were, new passion into my soul. But it turned, and there was a changed face, a face more lovely, looking eagerly into a book. Looking eagerly into a book did not betray one who could not read. But there was that in my heart that prompted me to look on the favorable side of the doubt—to try a different expedient in gaining admittance to the house. When night came, I assumed a dress those who look on mechanics as vulgar people, would have said became a gentleman; and approaching the house, gained easy admittance. As I was about entering the great parlors, a familiar but somewhat changed voice at the top of the circling stairs that led from the hall caught my ear. I paused, listened, became entranced with suspense. Again it resounded—again my heart throbbed with joy. It was Anna's voice, so soft and musical. The woman who opened the door turned from me, and attempted to hush it. But Anna seemed indifferent to the admonition, for she tripped buoyantly down stairs, accompanying a gentleman to the door. I stood before her, a changed person. Her recognition of me was instantaneous. Her color changed, her lips quivered, her eyes filled with tears, her very soul seemed fired with emotions she had no power to resist. 'George Mullholland!' she exclaimed, throwing her arms about my neck, kissing me, and burying her head in my bosom, and giving vent to her feelings in tears and quickened sobs—'how I have thought of you, watched for you, and hoped for the day when we would meet again and be happy. Oh, George! George! how changed everything seems since we parted! It seems a long age, and yet our sufferings, and the fondness for each other that was created in that suffering, freshens in the mind. Dear, good George — my protector!' she continued, clinging to me convulsively. I took her in my arms (the scene created no little excitement in the house) and bore her away to her chamber, which was chastely furnished, displaying a correct taste, and otherwise suited to a princess. Having gained her presence of mind, and become calm, she commenced relating what had occurred since we parted at Scorpion Cove. I need not relate it at length here, for it was similar in character to what might be told by a thousand others if they were not powerless. For months she had been confined to the house, her love of dress indulged to the furthest extent, her mind polluted and initiated into the mysteries of refined licentiousness, her personal appearance scrupulously regarded, and made to serve the object of which she was a victim in the hands of the hostess, who made her the worse than slave to a banker of great respectability in Wall street. This good man and father was well down in the vale of years, had a mansion on Fifth Avenue, and an interesting and much-beloved family. He was, in addition, a prominent member of the commercial community; but his example to those more ready to imitate the errors of men in high positions, than to improve by the examples of the virtuous poor, was not what it should be. Though a child of neglect, and schooled to licentiousness under the very eye of a generous community, her natural sensibility recoiled at the thought that she was a mere object of prey to the passions of one she could not love.

"She resolved to remain in this condition no longer, and escaped to Savannah with a young man whose acquaintance she had made at the house in Mercer street. For a time they lived at a respectable hotel, as husband and wife. But her antecedents got out, and they got notice to leave. The same fate met them in Charleston, to which city they removed. Her antecedents seemed to follow her wherever she went, like haunting spirits seeking her betrayal. She was homeless; and without a home there was nothing open to her but that vortex of licentiousness the world seemed pointing her to. Back she went to the house in Mercer street—was glad to get back; was at least free from the finger of scorn. Henceforward she associated with various friends, who sought her because of her transcendent charms. She had cultivated a natural intelligence, and her manners were such as might have become one in better society. But her heart's desire was to leave the house. I took her from it; and for a time I was happy to find that the contaminating weeds of vice had not overgrown the more sensitive buds of virtue.

"I provided a small tenement in Centre street, such as my means would afford, and we started in the world, resolved to live respectably. But what had maintained me respectably was now found inadequate to the support of us both. Life in a house of sumptuous vice had rendered Anna incapable of adapting herself to the extreme of economy now forced upon us. Anna was taken sick; I was compelled to neglect my work, and was discharged. Discontent, embarrassment, and poverty resulted. I struggled to live for six months; but my prospects, my hopes of gaining an honest living, were gone. I had no money to join the society, and the trade being dull, could get nothing to do. Fate seemed driving us to the last stage of distress. One by one our few pieces of furniture, our clothing, and the few bits of jewelry Anna had presented her at the house in Mercer street, found their way to the sign of the Three Martyrs. The man of the eagle face would always lend something on them, and that something relieved us for the time. I many times thought, as I passed the house of the Foreign Missions in Centre street, where there was such an air of comfort, that if Mrs. Abijah Slocum, and the good-natured man who sat in the chair, and the wise little man in the spectacles, would condescend to look in at our little place, and instead of always talking about getting Mr. Singleton Spyke off to Antioch, take pity on our destitution, what a relief it would be. It would have made more hearts happy than Mr. Spyke, notwithstanding the high end of his mission, could have softened in ten years at Antioch.

"Necessity, not inclination, forced Anna back into the house in Mercer street, when I became her friend, her transient protector. Her hand was as ready to bestow as her heart was warm and generous. She gave me money, and was kind to me; but the degraded character of my position caused me to despond, to yield myself a victim to insidious vice, to become the associate of men whose only occupation was that of gambling and 'roping-in' unsuspecting persons. I was not long in becoming an efficient in the arts these men practiced on the unwary. We used to meet at the 'Subterranean,' in Church street, and there concoct our mode of operations. And from this centre went forth, daily, men who lived by gambling, larceny, picking pockets, counterfeiting, and passing counterfeit money. I kept Anna ignorant of my associations. Nevertheless I was forced to get money, for I found her affections becoming perverted. At times her manner towards me was cold, and I sought to change it with money.

"While thus pursuing a life so precarious and exciting, I used to look in at the 'Empire,' in Broadway, to see whom I could 'spot,' as we called it at the 'Subterranean.' And it was here I met poor Tom Swiggs, distracted and giving himself up to drink, in the fruitless search after the girl of his love, from whom he had been separated, as he said, by his mother. He had loved the girl, and the girl returned his love with all the sincerity and ardor of her soul. But she was poor, and of poor parents. And as such people were reckoned nothing in Charleston, his mother locked him up in jail, and she was got out of the way. Tom opened his heart to me, said foul means had been resorted to, and the girl had thrown herself away, because, while he was held in close confinement, falsehoods had been used to make her believe he had abandoned her. To have her an outcast on his account, to have her leading the life of an abandoned woman, and that with the more galling belief that he had forsaken her, was more than he could bear, and he was sinking under the burden. Instead of making him an object of my criminal profession, his story so touched my feelings that I became his protector, saw him to his lodgings in Green street, and ultimately got him on board a vessel bound to Charleston.

"Not many weeks after this, I, being moneyless, was the principal of a plot by which nearly a thousand dollars was got of the old man in Wall street, who had been Anna's friend; and fearing it might get out, I induced her to accompany me to Charleston, where she believed I had a prospect of bettering my condition, quitting my uncertain mode of living, and becoming a respectable man. Together we put up at the Charleston Hotel. But necessity again forced me to reveal to her my circumstances, and the real cause of my leaving New York. Her hopes of shaking off the taint of her former life seemed blasted; but she bore the shock with resignation, and removed with me to the house of Madame Flamingo, where we for a time lived privately. But the Judge sought her out, followed her with the zeal of a knight, and promised, if she would forsake me, to be her protector; to provide for her and maintain her like a lady during her life. What progress he has made in carrying out his promise you have seen. The English baronet imposed her upon the St. Cecilia, and the Judge was the first to betray her."

CHAPTER XI
IN WHICH THE READER IS INTRODUCED
TO MR. ABSALOM McARTHUR

You must know, reader, that King street is our Boulevard of fashion; and though not the handsomest street in the world, nor the widest, nor the best paved, nor the most celebrated for fine edifices, we so cherish its age and dignity that we would not for the world change its provincial name, or molest one of the hundred old tottering buildings that daily threaten a dissolution upon its pavement, or permit a wench of doubtful blood to show her head on the "north sidewalk" during promenade hours. We are, you see, curiously nice in matters of color, and we should be. You may not comprehend the necessity for this scrupulous regard to caste; others do not, so you are not to blame for your ignorance of the customs of an atmosphere you have only breathed through novels written by steam. We don't (and you wouldn't) like to have our wives meet our slightly-colored mistresses. And we are sure you would not like to have your highly-educated and much-admired daughters meet those cream-colored material evidences of your folly—called by Northern "fanatics" their half-sisters! You would not! And your wives, like sensible women, as our wives and daughters are, would, if by accident they did meet them, never let you have a bit of sleep until you sent them to old Graspum's flesh-market, had them sold, and the money put safely into their hands. We do these things just as you would; and our wives being philosophers, and very fashionable withal, put the money so got into fine dresses, and a few weeks' stay at some very select watering-place in the North. If your wife be very accomplished, (like ours,) and your daughters much admired for their beauty, (like ours,) they will do as ours did—put wisely the cash got for their detestable relatives into a journey of inspection over Europe. So, you see, we keep our fashionable side of King street; and woe be to the shady mortal that pollutes its bricks!

Mr. Absalom McArthur lives on the unfashionable side of this street, in a one-story wooden building, with a cottage roof, covered with thick, black moss, and having two great bow windows, and a very lean door, painted black, in front. It is a rummy old house to look at, for the great bow windows are always ornamented with old hats, which Mr. McArthur makes supply the place of glass; and the house itself, notwithstanding it keeps up the dignity of a circular window over the door, reminds one of that valiant and very notorious characteristic of the State, for it has, during the last twenty or more years, threatened (but never done it) to tumble upon the unfashionable pavement, just in like manner as the State has threatened (but never done it!) to tumble itself out of our unfashionable Union. We are a great people, you see; but having the impediment of the Union in the way of displaying our might, always stand ready to do what we never intended to do. We speak in that same good-natured sense and metaphor used by our politicians, (who are become very distinguished in the refined arts of fighting and whiskey-drinking,) when they call for a rope to put about the neck of every man not sufficiently stupid to acknowledge himself a secessionist. We imagine ourselves the gigantic and sublime theatre of chivalry, as we have a right to do; we raise up heroes of war and statesmanship, compared with whom your Napoleons, Mirabeaus, and Marats—yes, even your much-abused Roman orators and Athenian philosophers, sink into mere insignificance. Nor are we bad imitators of that art displayed by the Roman soldiers, when they entered the Forum and drenched it with Senatorial blood! Pardon this digression, reader.

Of a summer morning you will see McArthur, the old Provincialist, as he is called, arranging in his great bow windows an innumerable variety of antique relics, none but a Mrs. Toodles could conceive a want for—such as broken pots, dog-irons, fenders, saws, toasters, stew-pans, old muskets, boxing-gloves and foils, and sundry other odds and ends too numerous to mention. At evening he sits in his door, a clever picture of a by-gone age, on a venerable old sofa, supported on legs tapering into feet of lion's paws, and carved in mahogany, all tacked over with brass-headed nails. Here the old man sits, and sits, and sits, reading the "Heroes of the Revolution," (the only book he ever reads,) and seemingly ready at all times to serve the "good wishes" of his customers, who he will tell you are of the very first families, and very distinguished! He holds distinguished peoples in high esteem; and several distinguished persons have no very bad opinion of him, but a much better one of his very interesting daughter, whose acquaintance (though not a lady, in the Southern acceptation of the term) they would not object to making—provided!

His little shop is lumbered with boxes and barrels, all containing relics of a by-gone age—such as broken swords, pistols of curious make, revolutionary hand-saws, planes, cuirasses, broken spurs, blunderbusses, bowie, scalping, and hunting-knives; all of which he declares our great men have a use for. Hung on a little post, and over a pair of rather suspicious-looking buckskin breeches, is a rusty helmet, which he sincerely believes was worn by a knight of the days of William the Conqueror. A little counter to the left staggers under a pile of musty old books and mustier papers, all containing valuable matter relating to the old Continentals, who, as he has it, were all Carolinians. (Dispute this, and he will go right into a passion.) Resting like good-natured policemen against this weary old counter are two sympathetic old coffins, several second-hand crutches, and a quantity of much-neglected wooden legs. These Mr. McArthur says are in great demand with our first families. No one, except Mr. Soloman Snivel, knows better what the chivalry stand in need of to prop up its declining dignity. His dirty little shelves, too, are stuffed with those cheap uniforms the State so grudgingly voted its unwilling volunteers during the Revolution.[1] Tucked in here and there, at sixes and sevens, are the scarlet and blue of several suits of cast-off theatrical wardrobe he got of Abbott, and now loans for a small trifle to Madame Flamingo and the St. Cecilia Society—the first, when she gives her very seductive *balmasques*; the second, when distinguished foreigners with titles honor its costume balls. As for Revolutionary cocked hats, epaulettes, plumes, and holsters, he has enough to supply and send off, feeling as proud as peacocks, every General and Colonel in the State— and their name, as you ought to know, reader, is legion.

The stranger might, indeed, be deceived into the belief that Absalom McArthur's curiosity shop was capable of furnishing accoutrements for that noble little army, (standing army we call it!) on which the State prides itself not a little, and spends no end of money. For ourselves, (if the reader but permit us,) we have long admired this little Spartan force, saying all the good things of it our prosy brain could invent, and in the kindest manner recommending its uniform good character as a model for our very respectable society to fashion after. Indeed, we have, in the very best nature of a modern historian, endeavored to enlighten the barbarian world outside of South Carolina as to the terrible consequences which might accrue to the Union did this noble little army assume any other than a standing character. Now that General Jackson is out of the way, and our plebeian friends over the Savannah, whom we hold in high esteem, (the Georgians,) kindly consent to let us go our own road out of the Union, nothing can be more grateful than to find our wise politicians sincerely believing that when this standing army, of which other States know so little, shall have become allied with those mighty men of Beaufort, dire consequences to this young but very respectable Federal compact will be the result. Having discharged the duties of a historian, for the benefit of those benighted beings unfortunate enough to live out of our small but highly-civilized State, we must return to McArthur.

He is a little old-maidish about his age, which for the last twenty years has not got a day more than fifty-four. Being as sensitive of his veracity as the State is of its dignity, we would not, either by implication or otherwise, lay an impeachment at his door, but rather charge the discrepancy to that sin (a treacherous memory) the legal gentry find so convenient for their purposes when they knock down their own positions. McArthur stood five feet eight exactly, when young, but age has made him lean of person, and somewhat bent. His face is long and corrugated; his expression of countenance singularly serious. A nose, neither aquiline nor Grecian, but large enough, and long enough, and red enough at the end, to make both; a sharp and curiously-projecting chin, that threatens a meeting, at no very distant day, with his nasal organ; two small, watchful blue eyes deep-set under narrow arches, fringed with long gray lashes; a deeply-furrowed, but straight and contracted forehead, and a shaggy red wig, poised upon the crown of his head, and, reader, if you except the constant working of a heavy, drooping lower lip, and the diagonal sight with which his eyes are favored, you have his most prominent features. Fashion he holds in utter contempt, nor has he the very best opinion in the world of our fashionable tailors, who are grown so rich that they hold mortgages on the very best plantations in the State, and offer themselves candidates for the Governorship. Indeed, Mr. McArthur says, one of these knights of the goose, not long since, had the pertinacity to imagine himself a great General. And to show his tenacious adherence to the examples set by the State, he dresses exactly as his grandfather's great-grandfather used to, in a blue coat, with small brass buttons, a narrow crimpy collar, and tails long enough and sharp enough for a clipper-ship's run. The periods when he provided himself with new suits are so far apart that they formed special episodes in his history; nevertheless there is always an air of neatness about him, and he will spend much time arranging a dingy ruffled shirt, a pair of gray trowsers, a black velvet waistcoat, cut in the Elizabethan style, and a high, square shirt collar, into which his head has the appearance of being jammed. This collar he ties with a much-valued red and yellow Spittlefields, the ends of which flow over his ruffle. Although the old man would not bring much at the man-shambles, we set a great deal of store by him, and would not exchange him for anything in the world but a regiment or two of heroic secessionists. Indeed we are fully aware that nothing like him exists beyond the highly perfumed atmosphere of our State. And to many other curious accomplishments the old man adds that of telling fortunes. The negroes seriously believe he has a private arrangement with the devil, of whom he gets his wisdom, and the secret of propitiating the gods.

Two days have passed since the *emeute* at the house of the old hostess. McArthur has promised the young missionary a place for Tom Swiggs, when he gets out of prison (but no one but his mother seems to have a right to let him out), and the tall figure of Mister Snivel is seen entering the little curiosity shop. "I say!—my old hero, has she been here yet?" inquires Mr. Snivel, the accommodation man. "Nay, good friend," returns the old man, rising from his sofa, and returning the salutation, "she has not yet darkened the door." The old man draws the steel-bowed spectacles from his face, and watches with a patriarchal air any change that comes over the accommodation man's countenance. "Now, good friend, if I did but know the plot," pursues the old man.

"The plot you are not to know! I gave you her history yesterday—that is, as far as I know it. You must make up the rest. You know how to tell fortunes, old boy. I need not instruct you. Mind you flatter her beauty, though—extend on the kindness of the Judge, and be sure you get it in that it was me who betrayed her at the St. Cecelia. All right old boy, eh?" and shaking McArthur by the hand warmly, he takes his departure, bowing himself into the street. The old man says he will be all ready when she comes.

Scarcely has the accommodation man passed out of sight when a sallow-faced stripling makes his appearance, and with that characteristic effrontery for borrowing and never returning, of the property-man of a country theatre, "desires" to know if Mr. McArthur will lend him a skull.

"A skull!" ejaculates the old man, his bony fingers wandering to his melancholy lip—"a skull!" and he fusses studiously round the little cell-like place, looking distrustfully at the property-man, and then turning an anxious eye towards his piles of rubbish, as if fearing some plot is on foot to remove them to the infernal regions.

"You see," interrupts Mr. Property, "we play Hamlet to-night—expect a crammed house—and our star, being scrupulous of his reputation, as all small stars are, won't go on for the scene of the grave-digger, without two skulls—he swears he won't! He raised the very roof of the theatre this morning, because his name wasn't in bigger type on the bill. And if we don't give him two skulls and plenty of bones to-night, he swears—and such swearing as it is!—he'll forfeit the manager, have the house closed, and come out with a card to the public in the morning. We are in a fix, you see! The janitor only has one, and he lent us that as if he didn't want to."

Mr. McArthur says he sees, and with an air of regained wisdom stops suddenly, and takes from a shelf a dingy old board, on which is a dingier paper, bearing curious inscriptions, no one but the old man himself would have supposed to be a schedule of stock in trade. Such it is, nevertheless. He rubs his spectacles, places them methodically upon his face, wipes and wipes the old board with his elbow. "It's here if it's anywhere!" says the old man, with a sigh. "It comes into my head that among the rest of my valuables I've Yorick's skull."

"The very skull we want!" interrupts Property. And the old man quickens the working of his lower jaw, and continues to rub at the board until he has brought out the written mystery. "My ancestors were great people," he mumbles to himself, "great people!" He runs the crusty forefinger of his right hand up and down the board, adding, "and my customers are all of the first families, which is some consolation in one's poverty. Ah! I have it here!" he exclaims, with childlike exultation, frisking his fingers over the board. "One Yorick's skull—a time-worn, tenantless, and valuable relic, in which graveyard worms have banqueted more than once. Yes, young man, presented to my ancestors by the elder Stuarts, and on that account worth seven skulls, or more." "One Yorick's skull," is written on the paper, upon which the old man presses firmly his finger. Then turning to an old box standing in the little fireplace behind the counter, saying, "it's in here—as my name's Absalom McArthur, it is," he opens the lid, and draws forth several old military coats (they have seen revolutionary days! he says, exultingly), numerous scales of brass, such as are worn on British soldiers' hats, a ponderous chapeau and epaulets, worn, he insists, by Lord Nelson at the renowned battle of Trafalgar. He has not opened, he adds, this box for more than twelve long years. Next he drags forth a military cloak of great weight and dimensions. "Ah!" he exclaims, with nervous joy, "here's the identical cloak worn by Lord Cornwallis—how my ancestors used to prize it." And as he unrolls its great folds there falls upon the floor, to his great surprise, an old buff-colored silk dress, tied firmly with a narrow, green ribbon. "Maria! Maria! Maria!" shouts the old man, as if suddenly seized with a spasm. And his little gray eyes flash with excitement, as he says—"if here hasn't come to light at last, poor Mag Munday's dress. God forgive the poor wretch, she's dead and gone, no doubt." In response to the name of "Maria" there protrudes from a little door that opens into a passage leading to a back-room, the delicate figure of a female, with a face of great paleness, overcast by a thoughtful expression. She has a finely-developed head, intelligent blue eyes, light auburn hair, and features more interesting than regular. Indeed, there is more to admire in the peculiar modesty of her demeanor than in the regularity of her features, as we shall show. "My daughter!" says the old man, as she nervously advances, her pale hand extended. "Poor woman! how she would mourn about this old dress; and say it contained something that might give her a chance in the world," she rather whispers than speaks, disclosing two rows of small white teeth. She takes from the old man's hand the package, and disappears. The anxiety she evinces over the charge discloses the fact that there is something of deep interest connected with it.

Mr. McArthur was about to relate how he came by this seemingly worthless old package, when the property-man, becoming somewhat restless, and not holding in over high respect the old man's rubbish, as he called it in his thoughts, commences drawing forth, piece after piece of the old relics. The old man will not allow this. "There, young man!" he says, touching him on the elbow, and resuming his labor. At length he draws forth the dust-tenanted skull, coated on the outer surface with greasy mould. "There!" he says, with an unrestrained exclamation of joy, holding up the wasting bone, "this was in its time poor Yorick's skull. It was such a skull, when Yorick lived! Beneath this filthy remnant of past greatness (I always think of greatness when I turn to the past), this empty tenement, once the domain of wisdom, this poor bone, what thoughts did not come out?" And the old man shakes his head, mutters inarticulately, and weeps with the simplicity of a child.

"The Star'll have skulls and bones enough to make up for his want of talent now—I reckon," interposes the property-man. "But!—I say, mister, this skull couldn't a bin old Yorick's, you know—"

"Yorick's!—why not?" interrupts the old man.

"Because Yorick—Yorick was the King's jester, you see—no nigger; and no one would think of importing anything but a nigger's skull into Charleston—"

"Young man!—if this skull had consciousness; if this had a tongue it would rebuke thee;" the old man retorts hastily, "for my ancestors knew Yorick, and Yorick kept up an intimate acquaintance with the ancestors of the very first families in this State, who were not shoemakers and milliners, as hath been maliciously charged, but good and pious Huguenots." To the end that he may convince the unbelieving Thespian of the truth of his assertion, he commences to rub away the black coating with the sleeve of his coat, and there, to his infinite delight, is written, across the crown, in letters of red that stand out as bold as the State's chivalry—"Alas! poor Yorick."

Tears of sympathy trickle down the old man's cheeks, his eyes sparkle with excitement, and with womanly accents he mutters: "the days of poetry and chivalry are gone. It is but a space of time since this good man's wit made Kings and Princes laugh with joy."

This skull, and a coral pin, which he said was presented to his ancestors by Lord Cornwallis, who they captured, now became his hobby; and he referred to it in all his conversation, and made them as much his idol as our politicians do secession. In this instance, he dare not entrust his newly-discovered jewel to the vulgar hands of Mr. Property, but pledged his honor—a ware the State deals largely in notwithstanding it has become exceedingly cheap—it would be forthcoming at the requisite time.

CHAPTER XII
IN WHICH ARE MATTERS THE READER MAY HAVE ANTICIPATED

Mr. Soloman Snivel has effected a reconciliation between old Judge Sleepyhorn and the beautiful Anna Bonard, and he has flattered the weak-minded George Mullholland into a belief that the old Judge, as he styles him, is his very best friend. So matters go on swimmingly at the house of Madame Flamingo. Indeed Mr. Soloman can make himself extremely useful in any affair requiring the exercise of nice diplomatic skill—no matter whether it be of love or law. He gets people into debt, and out of debt; into bankruptcy and out of bankruptcy; into jail and out of jail; into society and out of society. He has officiated in almost every capacity but that of a sexton. If you want money, Mr. Soloman can always arrange the little matter for you. If you have old negroes you want to get off your hands at a low figure, he has a customer. If you want to mortgage your negro property, a thing not uncommon with our very first families, Mr. Soloman is your man. Are you worth a fee, and want legal advice, he will give it exactly to your liking. Indeed, he will lie you into the most hopeless suit, and with equal pertinacity lie you out of the very best. Every judge is his friend and most intimate acquaintance. He is always rollicking, frisking, and insinuating himself into something, affects to be the most liberal sort of a companion, never refuses to drink when invited, but never invites any one unless he has a motive beyond friendship. Mr. Keepum, the wealthy lottery broker, who lives over the way, in Broad street, in the house with the mysterious signs, is his money-man. This Keepum, the man with the sharp visage and guilty countenance, has an excellent standing in society, having got it as the reward of killing two men. Neither of these deeds of heroism, however, were the result of a duel. Between these worthies there exists relations mutually profitable, if not the most honorable. And notwithstanding Mr. Soloman is forever sounding Mr. Keepum's generosity, the said Keepum has a singular faculty for holding with a firm grasp all he gets, the extent of his charities being a small mite now and then to Mr. Hadger, the very pious agent for the New York Presbyterian Tract Society. Mr. Hadger, who by trading in things called negroes, and such like wares, has become a man of great means, twice every year badgers the community in behalf of this society, and chuckles over what he gets of Keepum, as if a knave's money was a sure panacea for the cure of souls saved through the medium of those highly respectable tracts the society publishes to suit the tastes of the god slavery. Mr. Keepum, too, has a very high opinion of this excellent society, as he calls it, and never fails to boast of his contributions.

It is night. The serene and bright sky is hung with brighter stars. Our little fashionable world has got itself arrayed in its best satin—and is in a flutter. Carriages, with servants in snobby coats, beset the doors of the theatre. A flashing of silks, satins, brocades, tulle and jewelry, distinguished the throng pressing eagerly into the lobbies, and seeking with more confusion than grace seats in the dress circle. The orchestra has played an overture, and the house presents a lively picture of bright-colored robes. Mr. Snivel's handsome figure is seen looming out of a private box in the left-hand proceniums, behind the curtain of which, and on the opposite side, a mysterious hand every now and then frisks, makes a small but prudent opening, and disappears. Again it appears, with delicate and chastely-jeweled fingers. Cautiously the red curtain moves aside apace, and the dark languishing eyes of a female, scanning over the dress-circle, are revealed. She recognizes the venerable figure of Judge Sleepyhorn, who has made a companion of George Mullholland, and sits at his side in the parquette. Timidly she closes the curtain.

In the right-hand procenium box sits, resplendent of jewels and laces, and surrounded by her many admirers, the beautiful and very fashionable Madame Montford, a woman of singularly regular features, and more than ordinary charms. Opinion is somewhat divided on the early history of Madame Montford. Some have it one thing, some another. Society is sure to slander a woman of transcendent beauty and intellect. There is nothing in the world more natural, especially when those charms attract fashionable admirers. It is equally true, too, that if you would wipe out any little taint that may hang about the skirts of your character you must seek the panacea in a distant State, where, with the application of a little diplomacy you may become the much sought for wonder of a new atmosphere and new friends, as is the case with Madame Montford, who rebukes her New York neighbors of the Fifth Avenue (she has a princely mansion there), with the fact that in Charleston she is, whenever she visits it, the all-absorbing topic with fashionable society. For four successive winters Madame Montford has honored the elite of Charleston with her presence. The advent of her coming, too, has been duly heralded in the morning papers—to the infinite delight of the St. Cecilia Society, which never fails to distinguish her arrival with a ball. And this ball is sure to be preceded with no end of delicately-perfumed cards, and other missives, as full of compliments as it is capable of cramming them. There is, notwithstanding all these ovations in honor of her coming, a mystery hanging over her periodical visits, for the sharp-eyed persist that they have seen her disguised, and in suspicious places, making singular inquiries about a woman of the name of Mag Munday. And these suspicions have given rise to whisperings, and these whisperings have crept into the ears of several very old and highly-respectable "first families," which said families have suddenly dropped her acquaintance. But what is more noticeable in the features of Madame Montford, is the striking similarity between them and Anna Bonard's. Her most fervent admirers have noticed it; while strangers have not failed to discover it, and to comment upon it. And the girl who sits in the box with Mr. Snivel, so cautiously fortifying herself with the curtain, is none other than Anna. Mr. Snivel has brought her here as an atonement for past injuries.

Just as the curtain is about to rise, Mr. McArthur, true to his word, may be seen toddling to the stage door, his treasure carefully tied up in a handkerchief. He will deliver it to no one but the manager, and in spite of his other duties that functionary is compelled to receive it in person. This done, the old man, to the merriment of certain wags who delight to speculate on his childlike credulity, takes a seat in the parquette, wipes clean his venerable spectacles, and placing them methodically over his eyes, forms a unique picture in the foreground of the audience. McArthur, with the aid of his glasses, can recognize objects at a distance; and as the Hamlet of the night is decidedly Teutonic in his appearance and pronunciation, he has no great relish for the Star, nor a hand of applause to bestow on his genius. Hamlet, he is sure, never articulated with a coarse brogue. So turning from the stage, he amuses himself with minutely scanning the faces of the audience, and resolving in his mind that something will turn up in the grave-digger's scene, of which he is an enthusiastic admirer. It is, indeed, he thinks to himself, very doubtful, whether in this wide world the much-abused William Shakspeare hath a more ardent admirer of this curious but faithful illustration of his genius. Suddenly his attention seems riveted on the private box, in which sits the stately figure of Madame Montford, flanked in a half-circle by her perfumed and white-gloved admirers. "What!" exclaims the old man, in surprise, rubbing and replacing his glasses, "if I'm not deceived! Well—I can't be. If there isn't the very woman, a little altered, who has several times looked into my little place of an evening. Her questions were so curious that I couldn't make out what she really wanted (she never bought anything); but she always ended with inquiring about poor Mag Munday. People think because I have all sorts of things, that I must know about all sorts of things. I never could tell her much that satisfied her, for Mag, report had it, was carried off by the yellow fever, and nobody ever thought of her afterwards. And because I couldn't tell this woman any more, she would go away with tears in her eyes." Mr. McArthur whispers to a friend on his right, and touches him on the arm, "Pooh! pooh!" returns the man, with measured indifference, "that's the reigning belle of the season—Madame Montford, the buxom widow, who has been just turned forty for some years."

The play proceeds, and soon the old man's attention is drawn from the Widow Montford by the near approach to the scene of the grave-digger. And as that delineator enters the grave, and commences his tune, the old man's anxiety increases.

A twitching and shrugging of the shoulders, discovers Mr. McArthur's feelings. The grave-digger, to the great delight of the Star, bespreads the stage with a multiplicity of bones. Then he follows them with a skull, the appearance of which causes Mr. McArthur to exclaim, "Ah! that's my poor Yorick." He rises from his seat, and abstractedly stares at the Star, then at the audience. The audience gives out a spontaneous burst of applause, which the Teutonic Hamlet is inclined to regard as an indignity offered to superior talent. A short pause and his face brightens with a smile, the grave-digger shoulders his pick, and with the thumb of his right hand to his nasal organ, throws himself into a comical attitude. The audience roar with delight; the Star, ignorant of the cause of what he esteems a continued insult, waves his plumes to the audience, and with an air of contempt walks off the stage.

CHAPTER XIII
MRS. SWIGGS COMES TO THE RESCUE OF THE HOUSE OF THE FOREIGN MISSIONS

"An excellent society—excellent, I assure you, Madame—"

"Truly, Mr. Hadger," interrupted Mrs. Swiggs, "your labors on behalf of this Tract Society will be rewarded in heaven—"

"Dear-a-me," Mr. Hadger returns, ere Mrs. Swiggs can finish her sentence, "don't mention such a thing. I assure you it is a labor of love."

"Their tracts are so carefully got up. If my poor old negro property could only read—(Mrs. Swiggs pauses.) I was going to say—if it wasn't for the law (again she pauses), we couldn't prejudice our cause by letting our negroes read them—"

"Excuse the interruption," Mr. Hadger says, "but it wouldn't, do, notwithstanding (no one can be more liberal than myself on the subject of enlightening our negro property!) the Tract Society exhibits such an unexceptionable regard to the requirements of our cherished institution."

This conversation passes between Mrs. Swiggs and Mr. Hadger, who, as he says with great urbanity of manner, just dropped in to announce joyous tidings. He has a letter from Sister Abijah Slocum, which came to hand this morning, enclosing one delicately enveloped for Sister Swiggs. "The Lord is our guide," says Mrs. Swiggs, hastily reaching out her hand and receiving the letter. "Heaven will reward her for the interest she takes in the heathen world."

"Truly, if she hath not now, she will have there a monument of gold," Mr. Hadger piously pursues, adding a sigh.

"There! there!—my neuralgy; it's all down my left side. I'm not long for this world, you see!" Mrs. Swiggs breaks out suddenly, then twitches her head and oscillates her chin. And as if some electric current had changed the train of her thoughts, she testily seizes hold of her Milton, and says: "I have got my Tom up again—yes I have, Mr. Hadger."

Mr. Hadger discovers the sudden flight her thoughts have taken: "I am sure," he interposes, "that so long as Sister Slocum remains a member of the Tract Society we may continue our patronage."

Mrs. Swiggs is pleased to remind Mr. Hadger, that although her means have been exceedingly narrowed down, she has not, for the last ten years, failed to give her mite, which she divides between the house of the "Foreign Missions," and the "Tract Society."

A nice, smooth-faced man, somewhat clerically dressed, straight and portly of person, and most unexceptionable in his morals, is Mr. Hadger. A smile of Christian resignation and brotherly love happily ornaments his countenance; and then, there is something venerable about his nicely-combed gray whiskers, his white cravat, his snowy hair, his mild brown eyes, and his pleasing voice. One is almost constrained to receive him as the ideal of virtue absolved in sackcloth and ashes. As an evidence of our generosity, we regard him an excellent Christian, whose life hath been purified with an immense traffic in human——(perhaps some good friend will crack our skull for saying it).

In truth (though we never could find a solution in the Bible for it), as the traffic in human property increased Mr. Hadger's riches, so also did it in a corresponding ratio increase his piety. There is, indeed, a singular connection existing between piety and slavery; but to analyze it properly requires the mind of a philosopher, so strange is the blending.

Brother Hadger takes a sup of ice-water, and commences reading Sister Slocum's letter, which runs thus:

"New York, May —, 1850.

"Dear Brother Hadger:

"Justice and Mercy is the motto of the cause we have lent our hands and hearts to promote. Only yesterday we had a gathering of kind spirits at the Mission House in Centre street, where, thank God, all was peace and love. We had, too, an anxious gathering at the 'Tract Society's rooms.' There it was not so much peace and love as could have been desired. Brother Bight seemed earnest, but said many unwise things; and Brother Scratch let out some very unwise indiscretions which you will find in the reports I send. There was some excitement, and something said about what we got from the South not being of God's chosen earnings. And there was something more let off by our indiscreet Brothers against the getting up of the tracts. But we had a majority, and voted down our indiscreet Brothers, inasmuch as it was shown to be necessary not to offend our good friends in the South. Not to give offence to a Brother is good in the sight of the Lord, and this

Brother Primrose argued in a most Christian speech of four long hours or more, and which had the effect of convincing every one how necessary it was to free the *tracts* of everything offensive to your cherished institution. And though we did not, Brother Hadger, break up in the continuance of that love we were wont to when you were among us, we sustained the principle that seemeth most acceptable to you—we gained the victory over our disaffected Brothers. And I am desired on behalf of the Society, to thank you for the handsome remittance, hoping you will make it known, through peace and love, to those who kindly contributed toward it. The Board of 'Foreign Missions,' as you will see by the report, also passed a vote of thanks for your favor. How grateful to think what one will do to enlighten the heathen world, and how many will receive a tract through the medium of the other.

"We are now in want of a few thousand dollars, to get the Rev. Singleton Spyke, a most excellent person, off to Antioch. Aid us with a mite, Brother Hadger, for his mission is one of God's own. The enclosed letter is an appeal to Sister Swiggs, whose yearly mites have gone far, very far, to aid us in the good but mighty work now to be done. Sister Swiggs will have her reward in heaven for these her good gifts. How thankful should she be to Him who provides all things, and thus enableth her to bestow liberally.

"And now, Brother, I must say adieu! May you continue to live in the spirit of Christian love. And may you never feel the want of these mites bestowed in the cause of the poor heathen.

"Sister Abijah Slocum."

"May the good be comforted!" ejaculates Mrs. Swiggs, as Mr. Hadger concludes. She has listened with absorbed attention to every word, at times bowing, and adding a word of approval. Mr. Hadger hopes something may be done in this good cause, and having interchanged sundry compliments, takes his departure, old Rebecca opening the door.

"Glad he's gone!" the old lady says to herself. "I am so anxious to hear the good tidings Sister Slocum's letter conveys." She wipes and wipes her venerable spectacles, adjusts them piquantly over her small, wicked eyes, gives her elaborate cap-border a twitch forward, frets her finger nervously over the letter, and gets herself into a general state of confritteration. "There!" she says, entirely forgetting her Milton, which has fallen on the floor, to the great satisfaction of the worthy old cat, who makes manifest his regard for it by coiling himself down beside it, "God bless her. It makes my heart leap with joy when I see her writing," she pursues, as old Rebecca stands contemplating her, with serious and sullen countenance. Having prilled and fussed over the letter, she commences reading in a half whisper:

"No. —,4th Avenue, New York,

May —, 1850.

"Much Beloved Sister:

"I am, as you know, always overwhelmed with business; and having hoped the Lord in his goodness yet spares you to us, and gives you health and bounty wherewith to do good, must be pardoned for my brevity. The Lord prospers our missions among the heathen, and the Tract Society continues to make its labors known throughout the country. It, as you will see by the tracts I send herewith, still continues that scrupulous regard to the character of your domestic institution which has hitherto characterized it. Nothing is permitted to creep into them that in any way relates to your domestics, or that can give pain to the delicate sensibilities of your very excellent and generous people. We would do good to all without giving pain to any one. Oh! Sister, you know what a wicked world this is, and how it becomes us to labor for the good of others. But what is this world compared with the darkness of the heathen world, and those poor wretches ('Sure enough!' says Mrs. Swiggs) who eat one another, never have heard of a God, and prefer rather to worship idols of wood and stone. When I contemplate this dreadful darkness, which I do night and day, day and night, I invoke the Spirit to give me renewed strength to go forward in the good work of bringing from darkness ('Just as I feel,' thinks Mrs. Swiggs) unto light those poor benighted wretches of the heathen world. How often I have wished you could be here with us, to add life and spirit to our cause— to aid us in beating down Satan, and when we have got him down not to let him up. The heathen world never will be what it should be until Satan is bankrupt, deprived of his arts, and chained to the post of humiliation— never! ('I wish I had him where my Tom is!' Mrs. Swiggs mutters to herself.) Do come on here, Sister. We will give you an excellent reception, and make you so happy while you sojourn among us. And now, Sister, having never appealed to you in vain, we again extend our hand, hoping you will favor the several very excellent projects we now have on hand. First, we have a project—a very excellent one, on hand, for evangelizing the world; second, in consideration of what has been done in the reign of the Seven Churches— Pergamos Thyatira, Magnesia, Cassaba, Demish, and Baindir, where all is darkness, we have conceived a mission to Antioch; and third, we have been earnestly engaged in, and have spent a few thousand dollars over a project of the 'Tract Society,' which is the getting up of no less than one or two million of their excellent tracts, for the Dahomy field of missionary labor—

such as the Egba mission, the Yoruba mission, and the Ijebu missions. Oh! Sister, what a field of labor is here open to us. And what a source of joy and thankfulness it should be to us that we have the means to labor in those fields of darkness. We have selected brother Singleton Spyke, a young man of great promise, for this all-important mission to Antioch. He has been for the last four years growing in grace and wisdom. No expense has been spared in everything necessary to his perfection, not even in the selection of a partner suited to his prospects and future happiness. We now want a few thousand dollars to make up the sum requisite to his mission, and pay the expenses of getting him off. Come to our assistance, dear Sister—do come! Share with us your mite in this great work of enlightening the heathen, and know that your deeds are recorded in heaven. ('Verily!' says the old lady.) And now, hoping the Giver of all good will continue to favor you with His blessing, and preserve you in that strength of intellect with which you have so often assisted us in beating down Satan, and hoping either to have the pleasure of seeing you, or hearing from you soon, I will say adieu! subscribing myself a servant in the cause of the heathen, and your sincere Sister,

"Mrs. Abijah Slocum.

"P.S.—Remember, dear Sister, that the amount of money expended in idol-worship—in erecting monster temples and keeping them in repair, would provide comfortable homes and missions for hundreds of our very excellent young men and women, who are now ready to buckle on the armor and enter the fight against Satan.

"A.S."

"Dear-a-me," she sighs, laying the letter upon the table, kicking the cat as she resumes her rocking, and with her right hand restoring her Milton to its accustomed place on the table. "Rebecca," she says, "will get a pillow and place it nicely at my back." Rebecca, the old slave, brings the pillow. "There, there! now, not too high, nor too low, Rebecca!" her thin, sharp voice echoes, as she works her shoulders, and permits her long fingers to wander over her cap-border. "When 'um got just so missus like, say—da he is!" mumbles the old negress in reply. "Well, well—a little that side, now—" The negress moves the pillow a little to the left. "That's too much, Rebecca—a slight touch the other way. You are so stupid, I will have to sell you, and get Jewel to take care of me. I would have done it before but for the noise of her crutch—I would, Rebecca! You never think of me—you only think of how much hominy you can eat." The old negress makes a motion to move the pillow a little to the right, when Mrs. Swiggs settles her head and shoulders into it, saying, "there!"

"Glad'um suit—fo'h true!" retorts the negress, her heavy lips and sullen face giving out the very incarnation of hatred.

"Now don't make a noise when you go out." Rebecca in reply says she is "gwine down to da kitchen to see Isaac," and toddles out of the room, gently closing the door after her.

Resignedly Mrs. Swiggs closes her eyes, moderates her rocking, and commences evolving and revolving the subject over in her mind. "I haven't much of this world's goods—no, I haven't; but I'm of a good family, and its name for hospitality must be kept up. Don't see that I can keep it up better than by helping Sister Slocum and the *Tract Society* out," she muses. But the exact way to effect this has not yet come clear to her mind. Times are rather hard, and, as we have said before, she is in straightened circumstances, having, for something more than ten years, had nothing but the earnings of eleven old negroes, five of whom are cripples, to keep up the dignity of the house of the Swiggs. "There's old Zeff," she says, "has took to drinking, and Flame, his wife, ain't a bit better; and neither one of them have been worth anything since I sold their two children—which I had to do, or let the dignity of the family suffer. I don't like to do it, but I must. I must send Zeff to the workhouse—have him nicely whipped, I only charge him eighteen dollars a month for himself, and yet he will drink, and won't pay over his wages. Yes!—he shall have it. The extent of the law, well laid on, will learn him a lesson. There's old Cato pays me twenty dollars a month, and Cato's seventy-four—four years older than Zeff. In truth, my negro property is all getting careless about paying wages. Old Trot runs away whenever he can get a chance; Brutus has forever got something the matter with him; and Cicero has come to be a real skulk. He don't care for the cowhide; the more I get him flogged the worse he gets. Curious creature! And his old woman, since she broke her leg, and goes with a crutch, thinks she can do just as she pleases. There is plenty of work in her—plenty; she has no disposition to let it come out, though! And she has kept up a grumbling ever since I sold her girls. Well, I didn't want to keep them all the time at the whipping-post; so I sold them to save their characters." Thus Mrs. Swiggs muses until she drops into a profound sleep, in which she remains, dreaming that she has sold old Mumma Molly, Cicero's wife, and with the proceeds finds herself in New York, hob-nobbing it with Sister Slocum, and making one extensive donation to the Tract Society, and another to the fund for getting Brother Singleton Spyke off to Antioch. Her arrival in Gotham, she dreams, is a great event. The Tract Society (she is its guest) is smothering her with its attentions. Indeed, a whole column and a half of the very conservative and highly respectable old *Observer* is taken up with an elaborate and well-written history of her many virtues.

The venerable old lady dreams herself into dusky evening, and wakes to find old Rebecca summoning her to tea. She is exceedingly sorry the old slave disturbed her. However, having great faith in dreams, and the one she has just enjoyed bringing the way to aid Sister Slocum in carrying out her projects of love so clear to her mind, she is resolved to lose no time in carrying out its principles. Selling old Molly won't be much; old Molly is not worth much to her; and the price of old Molly (she'll bring something!) will do so much to enlighten the heathen, and aid the Tract Society in giving out its excellent works. "And I have for years longed to see Sister Slocum, face to face, before I die," she says. And with an affixed determination to carry out this pious resolve, Mrs. Swiggs sips her tea, and retires to her dingy little chamber for the night.

A bright and cheerful sun ushers in the following morning. The soft rays steal in at the snuffy door, at the dilapidated windows, through the faded curtains, and into the "best parlor," where, at an early hour, sits the antique old lady, rummaging over some musty old papers piled on the centre-table. The pale light plays over and gives to her features a spectre-like hue; while the grotesque pieces of furniture by which she is surrounded lend their aid in making complete the picture of a wizard's abode. The paper she wants is nowhere to be found. "I must exercise a little judgment in this affair," she mutters, folding a bit of paper, and seizing her pen. Having written—

"To the Master of the Work-house:

"I am sorry I have to trouble you so often with old Cicero. He will not pay wages all I can do. Give him at least thirty—well laid on. I go to New York in a few days, and what is due you from me for punishments will be paid any time you send your bill.

"Sarah Pringle Hughes Swiggs."

"Well! he deserves what he gets," she shakes her head and ejaculates. Having summoned Rebecca, Master Cicero, a hard-featured old negro, is ordered up, and comes tottering into the room, half-bent with age, his hair silvered, and his face covered with a mossy-white beard—the picture of a patriarch carved in ebony. "Good mornin', Missus," he speaks in a feeble and husky voice, standing hesitatingly before his august owner. "You are— well, I might as well say it—you're a miserable old wretch!" Cicero makes a nervous motion with his left hand, as the fingers of his right wander over the bald crown of his head, and his eyes give out a forlorn look. She has no pity for the poor old man—none. "You are, Cicero—you needn't pretend you ain't," she pursues; and springing to her feet with an incredible nimbleness, she advances to the window, tucks up the old curtain, and says, "There; let the light reflect on your face. Badness looks out of it, Cicero! you never was a good nigger—"

"Per'aps not, Missus; but den I'se old."

"Old! you ain't so old but you can pay wages," the testy old woman interrupts, tossing her head. "You're a capital hand at cunning excuses. This will get you done for, at the workhouse." She hands him a delicately enveloped and carefully superscribed *billet*, and commands him to proceed forthwith to the workhouse. A tear courses slowly down his time-wrinkled face, he hesitates, would speak one word in his own defence. But the word of his owner is absolute, and in obedience to the wave of her hand he totters to the door, and disappears. His tears are only those of a slave. How useless fall the tears of him who has no voice, no power to assert his manhood! And yet, in that shrunken bosom—in that figure, bent and shattered of age, there burns a passion for liberty and hatred of the oppressor more terrible than the hand that has made him the wretch he is. That tear! how forcibly it tells the tale of his sorrowing soul; how eloquently it foretells the downfall of that injustice holding him in its fierce chains!

Cicero has been nicely got out of the way. Molly, his wife, is summoned into the presence of her mistress, to receive her awful doom. "To be frank with you, Molly, and I am always outspoken, you know, I am going to sell you. We have been long enough together, and necessity at this moment forces me to this conclusion," says our venerable lady, addressing herself to the old slave, who stands before her, leaning on her crutch, for she is one of the cripples. "You will get a pious owner, I trust; and God will be merciful to you."

The old slave of seventy years replies only with an expression of hate in her countenance, and a drooping of her heavy lip. "Now," Mrs. Swiggs pursues, "take this letter, go straight to Mr. Forcheu with it, and he will sell you. He is very kind in selling old people—very!" Molly inquires if Cicero may go. Mrs. Swiggs replies that nobody will buy two old people together.

The slave of seventy years, knowing her entreaties will be in vain, approaches her mistress with the fervency of a child, and grasping warmly her hand, stammers out: "Da—da—dah Lord bless um, Missus. Tan't many days fo'h we meet in t'oder world—good-bye."

"God bless you—good-bye, Molly. Remember what I have told you so many times—long suffering and forbearance make the true Christian. Be a Christian—seek to serve your Master faithfully; such the Scripture teacheth. Now tie your handkerchief nicely on your head, and get your clean apron on, and mind to look good-natured when Mr. Forcheu sells you." This admonition, methodically addressed to the old slave, and Mrs. Swiggs waves her hand, resumes her Milton, and settles herself back into her chair. Reader! if you have a heart in the right place it will be needless for us to dwell upon the feelings of that old slave, as she drags her infirm body to the shambles of the extremely kind vender of people.

CHAPTER XIV
MR. McARTHUR MAKES A DISCOVERY

On his return from the theatre, Mr. McArthur finds his daughter, Maria, waiting him in great anxiety. "Father, father!" she says, as he enters his little back parlor, "this is what that poor woman, Mag Munday, used to take on so about; here it is." She advances, her countenance wearing an air of great solicitude, holds the old dress in her left hand, and a stained letter in her right. "It fell from a pocket in the bosom," she pursues. The old man, with an expression of surprise, takes the letter and prepares to read it. He pauses. "Did it come from the dress I discovered in the old chest?" he inquires, adjusting his spectacles. Maria says it did. She has no doubt it might have relieved her suffering, if it had been found before she died. "But, father, was there not to you something strange, something mysterious about the manner she pursued her search for this old dress? You remember how she used to insist that it contained something that might be a fortune to her in her distress, and how there was a history connected with it that would not reflect much credit on a lady in high life!"

The old man interrupts by saying he well remembers it; remembers how he thought she was a maniac to set so much value on the old dress, and make so many sighs when it could not be found. "It always occurred to me there was something more than the dress that made her take on so," the old man concludes, returning the letter to Maria, with a request that she will read it. Maria resumes her seat, the old man draws a chair to the table, and with his face supported in his left hand listens attentively as she reads:

"Washington Square, New York,

May 14, 18—

"I am glad to hear from Mr. Sildon that the child does well. Poor little thing, it gives me so many unhappy thoughts when I think of it; but I know you are a good woman, Mrs. Munday, and will watch her with the care of a mother. She was left at our door one night, and as people are always too ready to give currency to scandal, my brother and I thought that it would not be prudent to adopt it at once, more especially as I have been ill for the last few months, and have any quantity of enemies. I am going to close my house, now that my deceased husband's estate is settled, and spend a few years in Europe. Mr. Thomas Sildon is well provided with funds for the care of the child during my absence, and will pay you a hundred dollars every quarter. Let no one see this letter, not even your husband. And when I return I will give you an extra remuneration, and adopt the child as my own. Mr. Sildon will tell you where to find me when I return."

Your friend,

"C.A.M."

"There, father," says Maria, "there is something more than we know about, connected with this letter. One thing always discovers another — don't you think it may have something to do with that lady who has two or three times come in here, and always appeared so nervous when she inquired about Mag Munday? and you recollect how she would not be content until we had told her a thousand different things concerning her. She wanted, she said, a clue to her; but she never could get a clue to her. There is something more than we know of connected with this letter," and she lays the old damp stained and crumpled letter on the table, as the old servant enters bearing on a small tray their humble supper.

"Now, sit up, my daughter," says the old man, helping her to a sandwich while she pours out his dish of tea, "our enjoyment need be none the less because our fare is humble. As for satisfying this lady about Mag Munday, why, I have given that up. I told her all I knew, and that is, that when she first came to Charleston — one never knows what these New Yorkers are — she was a dashing sort of woman, had no end of admirers, and lived in fine style. Then it got out that she wasn't the wife of the man who came with her, but that she was the wife of a poor man of the name of Munday, and had quit her husband; as wives will when they take a notion in their heads. And as is always the way with these sort of people, she kept gradually getting down in the world, and as she kept getting more and more down so she took more and more to drink, and drink brought on grief, and grief soon wasted her into the grave. I took pity on her, for she seemed not a bad woman at heart, and always said she was forced by necessity into the house of Madame Flamingo — a house that hurries many a poor creature to her ruin. And she seemed possessed of a sense of honor not common to these people; and when Madame Flamingo turned her into the street, — as she does every one she has succeeded in making a wretch of, — and she could find no one to take her in, and had nowhere to lay her poor head, as she used to say, I used to lend her little amounts, which she always managed somehow to repay. As to there being anything valuable in the dress, I never gave it a thought; and when she would say if she could have restored to her the dress, and manage to get money enough to get to New York, I thought it was only the result of her sadness."

"You may remember, father," interrupts Maria, "she twice spoke of a child left in her charge; and that the child was got away from her. If she could only trace that poor child, she would say, or find out what had become of it, she could forget her own sufferings and die easy. But the thought of what had become of that child forever haunted her; she knew that unless she atoned in some way the devil would surely get her." The old man says, setting down his cup, it all comes fresh to his mind. Mr. Soloman (he has not a doubt) could let some light upon the subject; and, as he seems acquainted with the lady that takes so much interest in what became of the woman Munday, he may relieve her search. "I am sure she is dead, nevertheless; I say this, knowing that having no home she got upon the Neck, and then associated with the negroes; and the last I heard of her was that the fever carried her off. This must have been true, or else she had been back here pleading for the bundles we could not find." Thus saying, Mr. McArthur finishes his humble supper, kisses and fondles his daughter, whom he dotingly loves, and retires for the night.

CHAPTER XV
WHAT MADAME FLAMINGO WANTS TO BE

Tom Swiggs has enjoyed, to the evident satisfaction of his mother, a seven months' residence in the old prison. The very first families continue to pay their respects to the good old lady, and she in return daily honors them with mementoes of her remembrance. These little civilities, exchanging between the stately old lady and our first families, indicate the approach of the fashionable season. Indeed, we may as well tell you the fashionable season is commencing in right good earnest. Our elite are at home, speculations are rife as to what the "Jockey Club" will do, we are recounting our adventures at northern watering-places, chuckling over our heroism in putting down those who were unwise enough to speak disrespectful of our cherished institutions, and making very light of what we would do to the whole north. You may know, too, that our fashionable season is commenced by what is taking place at the house of Madame Flamingo on the one side, and the St. Cecilia on the other. We recognize these establishments as institutions. That they form the great fortifications of fashionable society, flanking it at either extreme, no one here doubts.

We are extremely sensitive of two things—fashion, and our right to sell negroes. Without the former we should be at sea; without the latter, our existence would indeed be humble. The St. Cecilia Society inaugurates the fashionable season, the erudite Editor of the Courier will tell you, with an entertainment given to the elite of its members and a few very distinguished foreigners. Madame Flamingo opens her forts, at the same time, with a grand supper, which she styles a very select entertainment, and to which she invites none but "those of the highest standing in society." If you would like to see what sort of a supper she sets to inaugurate the fashionable season, take our arm for a few minutes.

Having just arrived from New York, where she has been luxuriating and selecting her wares for the coming season, (New York is the fountain ejecting its vice over this Union,) Madame looks hale, hearty, and exceedingly cheerful. Nor has she spared any expense to make herself up with becoming youthfulness—as the common people have it. She has got her a lace cap of the latest fashion, with great broad striped blue and red strings; and her dress is of orange-colored brocade, trimmed with tulle, and looped with white blossoms. Down the stomacher it is set with jewels. Her figure seems more embonpoint than when we last saw her; and as she leans on the arm of old Judge Sleepyhorn, forms a striking contrast to the slender figure of that singular specimen of judicial infirmity. Two great doors are opened, and Madame leads the way into what she calls her upper and private parlor, a hall of some fifty feet by thirty, in the centre of which a sumptuously decorated table is set out. Indeed there is a chasteness and richness about the furniture and works of art that decorate this apartment, singularly at variance with the bright-colored furniture of the room we have described in a former chapter. "Ladies and gentlemen!" ejaculates the old hostess, "imagine this a palace, in which you are all welcome. As the legal gentry say (she casts a glance at the old Judge), when you have satisfactorily imagined that, imagine me a princess, and address me—"

"High ho!" interrupts Mr. Soloman.

"I confess," continues the old woman, her little, light-brown curls dangling across her brow, and her face crimsoning, "I would like to be a princess."

"You can," rejoins the former speaker, his fingers wandering to his chin.

"Well! I have my beadle—beadles, I take, are inseparable from royal blood—and my servants in liveries. After all (she tosses her head) what can there be in beadles and liveries? Why! the commonest and vulgarest people of New York have taken to liveries. If you chance to take an elegant drive up the 'Fifth Avenue,' and meet a dashing equipage—say with horses terribly caparisoned, a purloined crest on the carriage-door, a sallow-faced footman covered up in a green coat, all over big brass buttons, stuck up behind, and a whiskey-faced coachman half-asleep in a great hammercloth, be sure it belongs to some snob who has not a sentence of good English in his head. Yes! perhaps a soap-chandler, an oil-dealer, or a candy-maker. Brainless people always creep into plush—always! People of taste and learning, like me, only are entitled to liveries and crests." This Madame says, inviting her guests to take seats at her banquet-table, at the head of which she stands, the Judge on her right, Mr. Soloman on her left. Her china is of the most elaborate description, embossed and gilt; her plate is of pure silver, and massive; she has vases and candelabras of the same metal; and her cutlery is of the most costly description. No house in the country can boast a more exact taste in their selection. At each plate a silver holder stands, bearing a bouquet of delicately-arranged flowers. A trellis of choice flowers, interspersed here and there with gorgeous bouquets in porcelain vases, range along the centre of the table; which presents the appearance of a bed of fresh flowers variegated with delicious fruits. Her guests are to her choicer than her fruits; her fruits are choicer than her female wares. No entertainment of this kind would be complete without Judge Sleepyhorn and Mr. Soloman. They countenance vice in its most insidious form—they foster crime; without crime their trade would be damaged. The one cultivates, that the other may reap the harvest and maintain his office.

"I see," says Mr. Soloman, in reply to the old hostess, "not the slightest objection to your being a princess—not the slightest! And, to be frank about the matter, I know of no one who would better ornament the position."

"Your compliments are too liberally bestowed, Mr. Soloman."

"Not at all! 'Pon my honor, now, there is a chance for you to bring that thing about in a very short time. There is Grouski, the Polish exile, a prince of pure blood. Grouski is poor, wants to get back to Europe. He wants a wife, too. Grouski is a high old fellow—a most celebrated man, fought like a hero for the freedom of his country; and though an exile here, would be received with all the honors due to a prince in either Italy, France or England.

"A very respectable gentleman, no doubt; but a prince of pure blood, Mr. Soloman, is rather a scarce article these days."

"Not a bit of it—why there is lots of exiled Princes all over this country. They are modest men, you know, like me; and having got it into their heads that we don't like royal blood, rather keep the fact of their birth to themselves. As for Grouski! why his history is as familiar to every American who takes any interest in these things, as is the history of poor Kossuth. I only say this, Madame Flamingo, to prove to you that Grouski is none of your mock articles. And what is more, I have several times heard him speak most enthusiastically of you."

"Of me!" interrupts the old hostess, blushing. "I respect Grouski, and the more so for his being a poor prince in exile." Madame orders her servants, who are screwed into bright liveries, to bring on some sparkling Moselle. This done, and the glasses filled with the sparkling beverage, Mr. Soloman rises to propose a toast; although, as he says, it is somewhat out of place, two rounds having only succeeded the soup: "I propose the health of our generous host, to whom we owe so much for the superb manner in which she has catered for our amusement. Here's that we may speedily have the pleasure of paying our respects to her as the Princess Grouski." Madame Flamingo bows, the toast is drunk with cheers, and she begins to think there is something in it after all.

"Make as light of it as you please, ladies and gentlemen—many stranger things have come to pass. As for the exile, Grouski, I always esteemed him a very excellent gentleman."

"Exactly!" interposes the Judge, tipping his glass, and preparing his appetite for the course of game—broiled partridges, rice-birds, and grouse—which is being served by the waiters. "No one more worthy," he pursues, wiping his sleepy face with his napkin, "of being a princess. Education, wealth, and taste, you have; and with Grouski, there is nothing to prevent the happy consummation—nothing! I beg to assure you," Madame Flamingo makes a most courteous bow, and with an air of great dignity condescends to say she hopes gentlemen of the highest standing in Charleston have for ten years or more had the strongest proofs of her ability to administer the offices of a lady of station. "But you know," she pursues, hoping ladies and gentlemen will be kind enough to keep their glasses full, "people are become so pious now-a-days that they are foolish enough to attach a stigma to our business."

"Pooh, pooh!" interrupts the accommodation man, having raised his glass in compliment to a painted harlot. "Once in Europe, and under the shadow of the wife of Prince Grouski, the past would be wiped out; your money would win admirers, while your being a princess would make fashionable society your tool. The very atmosphere of princesses is full of taint; but it is sunk in the rank, and rather increases courtiers. In France your untainted princess would prognosticate the second coming of—, well, I will not profane."

"Do not, I beg of you," says Madame, blushing. "I am scrupulously opposed to profanity." And then there breaks upon the ear music that seems floating from an enchanted chamber, so soft and dulcet does it mingle with the coarse laughing and coarser wit of the banqueters. At this feast of flowers may be seen the man high in office, the grave merchant, the man entrusted with the most important affairs of the commonwealth—the sage and the charlatan. Sallow-faced and painted women, more undressed than dressed, sit beside them, hale companions. Respectable society regards the Judge a fine old gentleman; respectable society embraces Mr. Soloman, notwithstanding he carries on a business, as we shall show, that brings misery upon hundreds. Twice has he received a large vote as candidate for the General Assembly.

A little removed from the old Judge (excellent man) sits Anna Bonard, like a jewel among stones less brilliant, George Mullholland on her left. Her countenance wears an expression of gentleness, sweet and touching. Her silky black hair rolls in wavy folds down her voluptuous shoulders, a fresh carnatic flush suffuses her cheeks, her great black eyes, so beautifully arched with heavy lashes, flash incessantly, and to her bewitching charms is added a pensive smile that now lights up her features, then subsides into melancholy.

"What think you of my statuary?" inquired the old hostess, "and my antiques? Have I not taste enough for a princess?" How soft the carpet, how rich its colors! Those marble mantel-pieces, sculptured in female figures, how massive! How elegantly they set off each end of the hall, as we shall call this room; and how sturdily they bear up statuettes, delicately executed in alabaster and Parian, of Byron, Goethe, Napoleon, and Charlemagne—two on each. And there, standing between two Gothic windows on the front of the hall, is an antique side-table, of curious design. The windows are draped with curtains of rich purple satin, with embroidered cornice skirts and heavy tassels. On this antique table, and between the undulating curtains, is a marble statue of a female in a reclining posture, her right hand supporting her head, her dishevelled hair flowing down her shoulder. The features are soft, calm, and almost grand. It is simplicity sleeping, Madame Flamingo says. On the opposite side of the hall are pedestals of black walnut, with mouldings in gilt, on which stand busts of Washington and Lafayette, as if they were unwilling spectators of the revelry. A venerable recline, that may have had a place in the propylæa, or served to decorate the halls of Versailles in the days of Napoleon, has here a place beneath the portrait of Jefferson. This humble tribute the old hostess says she pays to democracy. And at each end of the hall are double alcoves, over the arches of which are great spread eagles, holding in their beaks the points of massive maroon-colored drapery that falls over the sides, forming brilliant depressions. In these alcoves are groups of figures and statuettes, and parts of statuettes, legless and armless, and all presenting a rude and mutilated condition. What some of them represented it would have puzzled the ancient Greeks to decypher. Madame, nevertheless, assures her guests she got them from among the relics of Italian and Grecian antiquity. You may do justice to her taste on living statuary; but her rude and decrepit wares, like those owned and so much valued by our New York patrons of the arts, you may set down as belonging to a less antique age of art. And there are chairs inlaid with mosaic and pearl, and upholstered with the richest and brightest satin damask,—revealing, however, that uncouthness of taste so characteristic of your Fifth Avenue aristocrat.

Now cast your eye upward to the ceiling. It is frescoed with themes of a barbaric age. The finely-outlined figure of a female adorns the centre. Her loins are enveloped in what seems a mist; and in her right hand, looking as if it were raised from the groundwork, she holds gracefully the bulb of a massive chandelier, from the jets of which a refulgent light is reflected upon the flowery banquet table. Madame smilingly says it is the Goddess of Love, an exact copy of the one in the temple of Jupiter Olympus. Another just opposite, less voluptuous in its outlines, she adds, is intended for a copy of the fabled goddess, supposed by the ancients to have thrown off her wings to illustrate the uncertainty of fortune.

Course follows course, of viands the most delicious, and sumptuously served. The wine cup now flows freely, the walls reëcho the coarse jokes and coarser laughs of the banqueters, and leaden eyelids, languid faces, and reeling brains, mark the closing scene. Such is the gorgeous vice we worship, such the revelries we sanction, such the insidious debaucheries we shield with the mantle of our laws—laws made for the accommodation of the rich, for the punishment only of the poor. And a thousand poor in our midst suffer for bread while justice sleeps.

Midnight is upon the banqueters, the music strikes up a last march, the staggering company retire to the stifled air of resplendent chambers. The old hostess contemplates herself as a princess, and seriously believes an alliance with Grouski would not be the strangest thing in the world. There is, however, one among the banqueters who seems to have something deeper at heart than the transitory offerings on the table—one whose countenance at times assumes a thoughtfulness singularly at variance with those around her. It is Anna Bonard.

Only to-day did George Mullholland reveal to her the almost hopeless condition of poor Tom Swiggs, still confined in the prison, with criminals for associates, and starving. She had met Tom when fortune was less ruthless; he had twice befriended her while in New York. Moved by that sympathy for the suffering which is ever the purest offspring of woman's heart, no matter how low her condition, she resolved not to rest until she had devised the means of his release. Her influence over the subtle-minded old Judge she well knew, nor was she ignorant of the relations existing between him and the accommodation man.

On the conclusion of the feast she invites them to her chamber. They are not slow to accept the invitation. "Be seated, gentlemen, be seated," she says, preserving a calmness of manner not congenial to the feelings of either of her guests. She places chairs for them at the round table, upon the marble top of which an inlaid portfolio lies open.

"Rather conventional," stammers Mr. Snivel, touching the Judge significantly on the arm, as they take seats. Mr. Snivel is fond of good wine, and good wine has so mellowed his constitution that he is obliged to seek support for his head in his hands.

"I'd like a little light on this 'ere plot. Peers thar's somethin' a foot," responds the Judge.

Anna interposes by saying they shall know quick enough. Placing a pen and inkstand on the table, she takes her seat opposite them, and commences watching their declining consciousness. "Thar," ejaculates the old Judge, his moody face becoming dark and sullen, "let us have the wish."

"You owe me an atonement, and you can discharge it by gratifying my desire."

"Women," interposes the old Judge, dreamily, "always have wishes to gratify. W-o-l, if its teu sign a warrant, hang a nigger, tar and feather an abolitionist, ride the British Consul out a town, or send a dozen vagrants to the whipping-post—I'm thar. Anything my hand's in at!" incoherently mumbles this judicial dignitary.

Mr. Snivel having reminded the Judge that ten o'clock to-morrow morning is the time appointed for meeting Splitwood, the "nigger broker," who furnishes capital with which they start a new paper for the new party, drops away into a refreshing sleep, his head on the marble.

"Grant me, as a favor, an order for the release of poor Tom Swiggs. You cannot deny me this, Judge," says Anna, with an arch smile, and pausing for a reply.

"Wol, as to that," responds this high functionary, "if I'd power, 'twouldn't be long afore I'd dew it, though his mother'd turn the town upside down; but I hain't no power in the premises. I make it a rule, on and off the bench, never to refuse the request of a pretty woman. Chivalry, you know."

"For your compliment, Judge, I thank you. The granting my request, however, would be more grateful to my feelings."

"It speaks well of your heart, my dear girl; but, you see, I'm only a Judge. Mr. Snivel, here, probably committed him ('Snivel! here, wake up!' he says, shaking him violently), he commits everybody. Being a Justice of the Peace, you see, and justices of the peace being everything here, I may prevail on him to grant your request!" pursues the Judge, brightening up at the earnest manner in which Anna makes her appeal. "Snivel! Snivel!— Justice Snivel, come, wake up. Thar is a call for your sarvices." The Judge continues to shake the higher functionary violently. Mr. Snivel with a modest snore rouses from his nap, says he is always ready to do a bit of a good turn. "If you are, then," interposes the fair girl, "let it be made known now. Grant me an order of release for Tom Swiggs. Remember what will be the consequence of a refusal!"

"Tom Swiggs! Tom Swiggs!—why I've made a deal of fees of that fellow. But, viewing it in either a judicial or philosophical light, he's quite as well where he is. They don't give them much to eat in jail I admit, but it is a great place for straightening the morals of a rum-head like Tom. And he has got down so low that all the justices in the city couldn't make him fit for respectable society." Mr. Snivel yawns and stretches his arms athwart.

"But you can grant me the order independent of what respectable society will do."

Mr. Snivel replies, bowing, a pretty woman is more than a match for the whole judiciary. He will make a good amount of fees out of Tom yet; and what his testy old mother declines to pay, he will charge to the State, as the law gives him a right to do.

"Then I am to understand!" quickly retorts Anna, rising from her chair, with an expression of contempt on her countenance, and a satirical curl on her lip, "you have no true regard for me then; your friendship is that of the knave, who has nothing to give after his ends are served. I will leave you!" The Judge takes her gently by the arm; indignantly she pushes him from her, as her great black eyes flash with passion, and she seeks for the door. Mr. Snivel has placed himself against it, begs she will be calm. "Why," he says, "get into a passion at that which was but a joke." The Judge touches him on the arm significantly, and whispers in his ear, "grant her the order— grant it, for peace sake, Justice Snivel."

"Now, if you will tell me why you take so deep an interest in getting them fellows out of prison, I will grant the order of release," Mr. Snivel says, and with an air of great gallantry leads her back to her chair.

"None but friendship for one who served me when he had it in his power."

"I see! I see!" interrupts our gallant justice; "the renewal of an old acquaintance; you are to play the part of Don Quixote,—he, the mistress. It's well enough there should be a change in the knights, and that the stripling who goes about in the garb of the clergy, and has been puzzling his wits how to get Tom out of prison for the last six months—"

"Your trades never agree;" parenthesises Anna.

"Should yield the lance to you."

"Who better able to wield it in this chivalrous atmosphere? It only pains my own feelings to confess myself an abandoned woman; but I have a consolation in knowing how powerful an abandoned woman may be in Charleston."

An admonition from the old Judge, and Mr. Snivel draws his chair to the table, upon which he places his left elbow, rests his head on his hand. "This fellow will get out; his mother—I have pledged my honor to keep him fast locked up—will find it out, and there'll be a fuss among our first families," he whispers. Anna pledges him her honor, a thing she never betrays, that the secret of Tom's release shall be a matter of strict confidence. And having shook hands over it, Mr. Snivel seizes the pen and writes an order of release, commanding the jailer to set at liberty one Tom Swiggs, committed as a vagrant upon a justice's warrant, &c., &c., &c. "There," says Justice Snivel, "the thing is done—now for a kiss;" and the fair girl permits him to kiss her brow. "Me too; the bench and the bar!" rejoins the Judge, following the example of his junior. And with an air of triumph the victorious girl bears away what at this moment she values a prize.

CHAPTER XVI
IN WHICH TOM SWIGGS GAINS HIS LIBERTY, AND WHAT BEFALLS HIM

Anna gives George Mullholland the letter of release, and on the succeeding morning he is seen entering at the iron gate of the wall that encloses the old prison. "Bread! give me bread," greets his ear as soon as he enters the sombre old pile. He walks through the debtors' floor, startles as he hears the stifled cry for bread, and contemplates with pained feelings the wasting forms and sickly faces that everywhere meet his eye. The same piercing cry grates upon his senses as he sallies along the damp, narrow aisle of the second floor, lined on both sides with small, filthy cells, in which are incarcerated men whose crime is that of having committed "assault and battery," and British seamen innocent of all crime except that of having a colored skin. If anything less than a gentleman commit assault and battery, we punish him with imprisonment; we have no law to punish gentlemen who commit such offences.

Along the felon's aisle—in the malarious cells where "poor" murderers and burglars are chained to die of the poisonous atmosphere, the same cry tells its mournful tale. Look into the dark vista of this little passage, and you will see the gleaming of flabby arms and shrunken hands. Glance into the apertures out of which they protrude so appealingly, you will hear the dull clank of chains, see the glare of vacant eyes, and shudder at the pale, cadaverous faces of beings tortured with starvation. A low, hoarse whisper, asks you for bread; a listless countenance quickens at your footfall. Oh! could you but feel the emotion that has touched that shrunken form which so despondingly waits the coming of a messenger of mercy. That system of cruelty to prisoners which so disgraced England during the last century, and which for her name she would were erased from her history, we preserve here in all its hideousness. The Governor knows nothing, and cares nothing about the prison; the Attorney-General never darkens its doors; the public scarce give a thought for those within its walls—and to one man, Mr. Hardscrabble, is the fate of these wretched beings entrusted. And so prone has become the appetite of man to speculate on the misfortunes of his fellow-man, that this good man, as we shall call him, tortures thus the miserable beings entrusted to his keeping, and makes it a means of getting rich. Pardon, reader, this digression.

George, elated with the idea of setting Tom at liberty, found the young theologian at the prison, and revealed to him the fact that he had got the much-desired order. To the latter this seemed strange—not that such a person as George could have succeeded in what he had tried in vain to effect, but that there was a mystery about it. It is but justice to say that the young theologian had for six months used every exertion in his power, without avail, to procure an order of release. He had appealed to the Attorney-General, who declared himself powerless, but referred him to the Governor. The Governor could take no action in the premises, and referred him to the Judge of the Sessions. The Judge of the Sessions doubted his capacity to interfere, and advised a petition to the Clerk of the Court. The Clerk of the Court, who invariably took it upon himself to correct the judge's dictum, decided that the judge could not interfere, the case being a committal by a Justice of the Peace, and not having been before the sessions. And against these high functionaries—the Governor, Attorney-General, Judge of the Sessions, and Clerk of the Court, was Mr. Soloman and Mrs. Swiggs all-powerful. There was, however, another power superior to all, and that we have described in the previous chapter.

Accompanied by the brusque old jailer, George and the young theologian make their way to the cell in which Tom is confined.

"Hallo! Tom," exclaims George, as he enters the cell, "boarding at the expense of the State yet, eh?" Tom lay stretched on a blanket in one corner of the cell, his faithful old friend, the sailor, watching over him with the solicitude of a brother. "I don't know how he'd got on if it hadn't bin for the old sailor, yonder," says the jailer, pointing to Spunyarn, who is crouched down at the great black fireplace, blowing the coals under a small pan. "He took to Tom when he first came in, and hasn't left him for a day. He'll steal to supply Tom's hunger, and fight if a prisoner attempts to impose upon his charge. He has rigged him out, you see, with his pea-coat and overalls," continues the man, folding his arms.

"I am sorry, Tom—"

"Yes," says Tom, interrupting the young theologian, "I know you are. You don't find me to have kept my word; and because I haven't you don't find me improved much. I can't get out; and if I can't get out, what's the use of my trying to improve? I don't say this because I don't want to improve. I have no one living who ought to care for me, but my mother. And she has shown what she cares for me."

"Everything is well. (The young theologian takes Tom by the hand.) We have got your release. You are a free man, now."

"My release!" exclaims the poor outcast, starting to his feet, "my release?"

"Yes," kindly interposes the jailer, "you may go, Tom. Stone walls, bolts and chains have no further use for you." The announcement brings tears to his eyes; he cannot find words to give utterance to his emotions. He drops the young theologian's hand, grasps warmly that of George Mullholland, and says, the tears falling fast down his cheeks, "now I will be a new man."

"God bless Tom," rejoins the old sailor, who has left the fireplace and joined in the excitement of the moment. "I alwas sed there war better weather ahead, Tom." He pats him encouragingly on the shoulder, and turns to the bystanders, continuing with a childlike frankness: "he's alwas complained with himself about breaking his word and honor with you, sir—"

The young theologian says the temptation was more than he could withstand.

"Yes sir!—that was it. He, poor fellow, wasn't to blame. One brought him in a drop, and challenged him; then another brought him in a drop, and challenged him; and the vote-cribber would get generous now and then, and bring him a drop, saying how he would like to crib him if he was only out, on the general election coming on, and make him take a drop of what he called election whiskey. And you know, sir, it's hard for a body to stand up against all these things, specially when a body's bin disappointed in love. It's bin a hard up and down with him. To-day he would make a bit of good weather, and to-morrow he'd be all up in a hurricane." And the old sailor takes a fresh quid of tobacco, wipes Tom's face, gets the brush and fusses over him, and tells him to cheer up, now that he has got his clearance.

"Tom would know if his mother ordered it."

"No! she must not know that you are at large," rejoins George.

"Not that I am at large?"

"I have," interposes the young theologian, "provided a place for you. We have a home for you, a snug little place at the house of old McArthur—"

"Old McArthur," interpolates Tom, smiling, "I'm not a curiosity."

George Mullholland says he may make love to Maria, that she will once more be a sister. Touched by the kindly act on his behalf, Tom replies saying she was always kind to him, watched over him when no one else would, and sought with tender counsels to effect his reform, to make him forget his troubles.

"Thank you!—my heart thanks you more forcibly than my tongue can. I feel a man. I won't touch drink again: no I won't. You won't find me breaking my honor this time. A sick at heart man, like me, has no power to buffet disappointment. I was a wretch, and like a wretch without a mother's sympathy, found relief only in drinks—"

"And such drinks!" interposes the old sailor, shrugging his shoulders. "Good weather, and a cheer up, now and then, from a friend, would have saved him."

Now there appears in the doorway, the stalworth figure of the vote-cribber, who, with sullen face, advances mechanically toward Tom, pauses and regards him with an air of suspicion. "You are not what you ought to be, Tom," he says, doggedly, and turns to the young Missionary. "Parson," he continues, "this 'ere pupil of yourn's a hard un. He isn't fit for respectable society. Like a sponge, he soaks up all the whiskey in jail." The young man turns upon him a look more of pity than scorn, while the jailer shakes his head admonishingly. The vote-cribber continues insensible to the admonition. He, be it known, is a character of no small importance in the political world. Having a sort of sympathy for the old jail he views his transient residences therein rather necessary than otherwise. As a leading character is necessary to every grade of society, so also does he plume himself the aristocrat of the prison. Persons committed for any other than offences against the election laws, he holds in utter contempt. Indeed, he says with a good deal of truth, that as fighting is become the all necessary qualification of our Senators and Representatives to Congress, he thinks of offering himself for the next vacancy. The only rival he fears is "handsome Charley."[2] The accommodations are not what they might be, but, being exempt from rent and other items necessary to a prominent politician, he accepts them as a matter of economy.

The vote-cribber is sure of being set free on the approach of an election. We may as well confess it before the world—he is an indispensable adjunct to the creating, of Legislators, Mayors, Congressmen, and Governors. Whiskey is not more necessary to the reputation of our mob-politicians than are the physical powers of Milman Mingle to the success of the party he honors with his services. Nor do his friends scruple at consulting him on matters of great importance to the State while in his prison sanctuary.

"I'm out to-morrow, parson," he resumes; the massive fingers of his right hand wandering into his crispy, red beard, and again over his scarred face. "Mayor's election comes off two weeks from Friday—couldn't do without me—can knock down any quantity of men—you throw a plumper, I take it?" The young Missionary answers in the negative by shaking his head, while the kind old sailor continues to fuss over and prepare Tom for his departure. "Tom is about to leave us," says the old sailor, by way of diverting the vote-cribber's attention. That dignitary, so much esteemed by our fine old statesmen, turns to Tom, and inquires if he has a vote.

Tom has a vote, but declares he will not give it to the vote-cribber's party. The politician says "p'raps," and draws from his bosom a small flask. "Whiskey, Tom," he says,—"no use offering it to parsons, eh? (he casts an insinuating look at the parson.) First-chop election whiskey—a sup and we're friends until I get you safe under the lock of my crib. Our Senators to Congress patronize this largely." The forlorn freeman, with a look of contempt for the man who thus upbraids him, dashes the drug upon the floor, to the evident chagrin of the politician, who, to conceal his feelings, turns to George Mulholland, and mechanically inquires if *he* has a vote. Being answered in the negative, he picks up his flask and walks away, saying: "what rubbish!"

Accompanied by his friends and the old sailor, Tom sallies forth into the atmosphere of sweet freedom. As the old jailer swings back the outer gate, Spunyarn grasps his friend and companion in sorrow warmly by the hand, his bronzed face brightens with an air of satisfaction, and like pure water gushing from the rude rock his eyes fill with tears. How honest, how touching, how pure the friendly lisp—good bye! "Keep up a strong heart, Tom,—never mind me. I don't know by what right I'm kept here, and starved; but I expect to get out one of these days; and when I do you may reckon on me as your friend. Keep the craft in good trim till then; don't let the devil get master. Come and see us now and then, and above all, never give up the ship during a storm." Tom's emotions are too deeply touched. He has no reply to make, but presses in silence the hand of the old sailor, takes his departure, and turns to wave him an adieu.

CHAPTER XVII
IN WHICH THERE IS AN
INTERESTING MEETING

Our very chivalric dealers in human merchandise, like philosophers and philanthropists, are composed merely of flesh and blood, while their theories are alike influenced by circumstances. Those of the first, we (the South) are, at times, too apt to regard as sublimated and refined, while we hold the practices of the latter such as divest human nature of everything congenial. Nevertheless we can assure our readers that there does not exist a class of men who so much pride themselves on their chivalry as some of our opulent slave-dealers. Did we want proof to sustain what we have said we could not do better than refer to Mr. Forsheu, that very excellent gentleman. Mrs. Swiggs held him in high esteem, and so far regarded his character for piety and chivalry unblemished, that she consigned to him her old slave of seventy years—old Molly. Molly must be sold, the New York Tract Society must have a mite, and Sister Abijah Slocum's very laudable enterprise of getting Brother Singleton Spyke off to Antioch must be encouraged. And Mr. Forsheu is very kind to the old people he sells. It would, indeed, be difficult for the distant reader to conceive a more striking instance of a man, grown rich in a commerce that blunts all the finer qualities of our nature, preserving a gentleness, excelled only by his real goodness of heart.

When the old slave, leaning on her crutch, stood before Mr. Forsheu, her face the very picture of age and starvation, his heart recoiled at the thought of selling her in her present condition. He read the letter she bore, contemplated her with an air of pity, and turning to Mr. Benbow, his methodical book-keeper of twenty years, who had added and subtracted through a wilderness of bodies and souls, ordered him to send the shrunken old woman into the pen, on feed. Mr. Forsheu prided himself on the quality of people sold at his shambles, and would not for the world hazard his reputation on old Molly, till she was got in better condition. Molly rather liked this, inasmuch as she had been fed on corn and prayers exclusively, and more prayers than corn, which is become the fashion with our much-reduced first families. For nearly four months she enjoyed, much to the discomfiture of her august owner, the comforts of Mr. Forsheu's pen. Daily did the anxious old lady study her Milton, and dispatch a slave to inquire if her piece of aged property had found a purchaser. The polite vender preserved, with uncommon philosophy, his temper. He enjoined patience. The condition and age of the property were, he said, much in the way of sale. Then Mrs. Swiggs began questioning his ability as a merchant. Aspersions of this kind, the polite vender of people could not bear with. He was a man of enormous wealth, the result of his skill in the sale of people. He was the president of an insurance company, a bank director, a commissioner of the orphan asylum, and a steward of the jockey club. To his great relief, for he began to have serious misgivings about his outlay on old Molly, there came along one day an excellent customer. This was no less a person than Madame Flamingo. What was singular of this very distinguished lady was, that she always had a use for old slaves no one else ever thought of. Her yard was full of aged and tottering humanity. One cleaned knives, another fetched ice from the ice-house, a third blacked boots, a fourth split wood, a fifth carried groceries, and a sixth did the marketing. She had a decayed negro for the smallest service; and, to her credit be it said, they were as contented and well fed a body of tottering age as could be found in old Carolina.

Her knife-cleaning machine having taken it into his head to die one day, she would purchase another. Mr Forsheu, with that urbanity we so well understand how to appreciate, informed the distinguished lady that he had an article exactly suited to her wants. Forthwith, Molly was summoned into her presence. Madame Flamingo, moved almost to tears at the old slave's appearance, purchased her out of pure sympathy, as we call it, and to the great relief of Mr. Forsheu, lost no time in paying one hundred and forty dollars down in gold for her. In deference to Mr. Hadger, the House of The Foreign Missions, and the very excellent Tract Society, of New York, we will not here extend on how the money was got. The transaction was purely commercial: why should humanity interpose? We hold it strictly legal that institutions created for the purpose of enlightening the heathen have no right to ask by what means the money constituting their donations is got.

The comforts of Mr. Forsheu's pen,—the hominy, grits, and rest, made the old slave quite as reluctant about leaving him as she had before been in parting with Lady Swiggs. Albeit, she shook his hand with equal earnestness, and lisped "God bless Massa," with a tenderness and simplicity so touching, that had not Madame Flamingo been an excellent diplomat, reconciling the matter by assuring her that she would get enough to eat, and clothes to wear, no few tears would have been shed. Madame, in addition to this incentive, intimated that she might attend a prayer meeting now and then—perhaps see Cicero. However, Molly could easily have forgotten

Cicero, inasmuch as she had enjoyed the rare felicity of thirteen husbands, all of whom Lady Swiggs had sold when it suited her own convenience.

Having made her purchase, Madame very elegantly bid the gallant merchant good morning, hoping he would not forget her address, and call round when it suited his convenience. Mr. Forsheu, his hat doffed, escorted her to her carriage, into the amber-colored lining of which she gracefully settled her majestic self, as a slightly-browned gentleman in livery closed the bright door, took her order with servile bows, and having motioned to the coachman, the carriage rolled away, and was soon out of sight. Monsieur Gronski, it may be well to add here, was discovered curled up in one corner; he smiled, and extended his hand very graciously to Madame as she entered the carriage.

Like a pilgrim in search of some promised land, Molly adjusted her crutch, and over the sandy road trudged, with truculent face, to her new home, humming to herself "dah-is-a-time-a-comin, den da Lor' he be good!!"

On the following morning, Lady Swiggs received her account current, Mr. Forsheu being exceedingly prompt in business. There was one hundred and twenty-nine days' feed, commissions, advertising, and sundry smaller charges, which reduced the net balance to one hundred and three dollars. Mrs. Swiggs, with an infatuation kindred to that which finds the State blind to its own poverty, stubbornly refused to believe her slaves had declined in value. Hence she received the vender's account with surprise and dissatisfaction. However, the sale being binding, she gradually accommodated her mind to the result, and began evolving the question of how to make the amount meet the emergency. She must visit the great city of New York; she must see Sister Slocum face to face; Brother Spyke's mission must have fifty dollars; how much could she give the Tract Society? Here was a dilemma—one which might have excited the sympathy of the House of the "Foreign Missions." The dignity of the family, too, was at stake. Many sleepless nights did this difficult matter cause the august old lady. She thought of selling another cripple! Oh! that would not do. Mr. Keepum had a lien on them; Mr. Keepum was a man of iron-heart. Suddenly it flashed upon her mind that she had already been guilty of a legal wrong in selling old Molly. Mr. Soloman had doubtless described her with legal minuteness in the bond of security for the two hundred dollars. Her decrepit form; her corrugated face; her heavy lip; her crutch, and her piety—everything, in a word, but her starvation, had been set down. Well! Mr. Soloman might, she thought, overlook in the multiplicity of business so small a discrepancy. She, too, had a large circle of distinguished friends. If the worst came to the worst she would appeal to them. There, too, was Sir Sunderland Swiggs' portrait, very valuable for its age; she might sell the family arms, such things being in great demand with the chivalry; her antique furniture, too, was highly prized by our first families. Thus Lady Swiggs contemplated these mighty relics of past greatness. Our celtic Butlers and Brookses never recurred to the blood of their querulous ancestors with more awe than did this memorable lady to her decayed relics. Mr. Israel Moses, she cherished a hope, would give a large sum for the portrait; the family arms he would value at a high figure; the old furniture he would esteem a prize. But to Mr. Moses and common sense, neither the blood of the Butlers, nor Lady Swiggs' rubbish, were safe to loan money upon. The Hebrew gentleman was not so easily beguiled.

The time came when it was necessary to appeal to Mr. Hadger. That gentleman held the dignity of the Swiggs family in high esteem, but shook his head when he found the respectability of the house the only security offered in exchange for a loan. Ah! a thought flashed to her relief, the family watch and chain would beguile the Hebrew gentleman. With these cherished mementoes of the high old family, (she would under no other circumstance have parted with for uncounted gold,) she in time seduced Mr. Israel Moses to make a small advance. Duty, stern and demanding, called her to New York. Forced to reduce her generosity, she, not without a sigh, made up her mind to give only thirty dollars to each of the institutions she had made so many sacrifices to serve. And thus, with a reduced platform, as our politicians have it, she set about preparing for the grand journey. Regards the most distinguished were sent to all the first families; the St. Cecilia had notice of her intended absence; no end of tea parties were given in honor of the event. Apparently happy with herself, with every one but poor Tom, our august lady left in the Steamer one day. With a little of that vanity the State deals so largely in, Mrs. Swiggs thought every passenger on board wondering and staring at her.

While then she voyages and dreams of the grand reception waiting her in New York,—of Sister Slocum's smiles, of the good of the heathen world, and of those nice evening gatherings she will enjoy with the pious, let us, gentle reader, look in at the house of Absalom McArthur.

To-day Tom Swiggs feels himself free, and it is high noon. Downcast of countenance he wends his way along the fashionable side of King-street. The young theologian is at his side. George Mullholland has gone to the house of Madame Flamingo. He will announce the glad news to Anna. The old antiquarian dusts his little counter with a stubby broom, places various curiosities in the windows, and about the doors, stands contemplating them with an air of satisfaction, then proceeds to drive a swarm of flies that hover upon the ceiling, into a curiously-arranged trap that he has set.

"What!—my young friend, Tom Swiggs!" exclaims the old man, toddling toward Tom, and grasping firmly his hand, as he enters the door. "You are welcome to my little place, which shall be a home." Tom hangs down his head, receives the old man's greeting with shyness. "Your poor father and me, Tom, used to sit here many a time. (The old man points to an old sofa.) We were friends. He thought much of me, and I had a high opinion of him; and so we used to sit for hours, and talk over the deeds of the old continentals. Your mother and him didn't get along over-well together; she had more dignity than he could well digest: but that is neither here nor there."

"I hope, in time," interrupts Tom, "to repay your kindness. I am willing to ply myself to work, though it degrades one in the eyes of our society."

"As to that," returns the old man, "why, don't mention it. Maria, you know, will be a friend to you. Come away now and see her." And taking Tom by the hand, (the theologian has withdrawn,) he becomes enthusiastic, leads him through the dark, narrow passage into the back parlor, where he is met by Maria, and cordially welcomed. "Why, Tom, what a change has come over you," she ejaculates, holding his hand, and viewing him with the solicitude of a sister, who hastens to embrace a brother returned after a long absence. Letting fall his begrimed hand, she draws up the old-fashioned rocking chair, and bids him be seated. He shakes his head moodily, says he is not so bad as he seems, and hopes yet to make himself worthy of her kindness. He has been the associate of criminals; he has suffered punishment; he feels himself loathed by society; he cannot divest himself of the odium clinging to his garments. Fain would he go to some distant clime, and there seek a refuge from the odium of felons.

"Let no such thoughts enter your mind, Tom," says the affectionate girl; "divest yourself at once of feelings that can only do you injury. You have engaged my thoughts during your troubles. Twice I begged your mother to honor me with an interview. We were humble people; she condescended at last. But she turned a deaf ear to me when I appealed to her for your release, merely inquiring if—like that other jade—I had become enamored of—" Maria pauses, blushing.

"I would like to see my mother," interposes Tom.

"Had I belonged to our grand society, the case had been different," resumes Maria.

"Truly, Maria," stammers Tom, "had I supposed there was one in the world who cared for me, I had been a better man."

"As to that, why we were brought up together, Tom. We knew each other as children, and what else but respect could I have for you? One never knows how much others think of them, for the—" Maria blushes, checks herself, and watches the changes playing over Tom's countenance. She was about to say the tongue of love was too often silent.

It must be acknowledged that Maria had, for years, cherished a passion for Tom. He, however, like many others of his class, was too stupid to discover it. The girl, too, had been overawed by the dignity of his mother. Thus, with feelings of pain did she watch the downward course of one in whose welfare she took a deep interest.

"Very often those for whom we cherish the fondest affections, are coldest in their demeanor towards us," pursues Maria.

"Can she have thought of me so much as to love me?" Tom questions within himself; and Maria put an end to the conversation by ringing the bell, commanding the old servant to hasten dinner. A plate must be placed at the table for Tom.

The antiquarian, having, as he says, left the young people to themselves, stands at his counter furbishing up sundry old engravings, horse-pistols, pieces of coat-of-mail, and two large scimitars, all of which he has piled together in a heap, and beside which lay several chapeaus said to have belonged to distinguished Britishers. Mr. Soloman suddenly makes his appearance in the little shop, much to Mr. McArthur's surprise. "Say— old man! centurion!" he exclaims, in a maudlin laugh, "Keepum's in the straps—is, I do declare; Gadsden and he bought a lot of niggers—a monster drove of 'em, on shares. He wants that trifle of borrowed money—must have it. Can have it back in a few days."

"Bless me," interrupts the old man, confusedly, "but off my little things it will be hard to raise it. Times is hard, our people go, like geese, to the North. They get rid of all their money there, and their fancy—you know that, Mr. Snivel—is abroad, while they have, for home, only a love to keep up slavery."

"I thought it would come to that," says Mr. Snivel, facetiously. The antiquarian seems bewildered, commences offering excuses that rather involve himself deeper, and finally concludes by pleading for a delay. Scarce any one would have thought a person of Mr. McArthur's position, indebted to Mr. Keepum; but so it was. It is very difficult to tell whose negroes are not mortgaged to Mr. Keepum, how many mortgages of plantation he has foreclosed, how many high old families he has reduced to abject poverty, or how many poor but respectable families he has disgraced. He has a reputation for loaning money to parents, that he may rob their daughters of that jewel the world refuses to give them back. And yet our best society honor him, fawn over him, and bow to him. We so worship the god of slavery, that our minds are become debased, and yet we seem unconscious of it. Mr. Keepum did not lend money to the old antiquarian without a purpose. That purpose, that justice which accommodates itself to the popular voice, will aid him in gaining.

Mr. Snivel affects a tone of moderation, whispers in the old man's ear, and says: "Mind you tell the fortune of this girl, Bonard, as I have directed. Study what I have told you. If she be not the child of Madame Montford, then no faith can be put in likenesses. I have got in my possession what goes far to strengthen the suspicions now rife concerning the fashionable New Yorker."

"There surely is a mystery about this woman, Mr. Snivel, as you say. She has so many times looked in here to inquire about Mag Munday, a woman in a curious line of life who came here, got down in the world, as they all do, and used now and then to get the loan of a trifle from me to keep her from starvation." (Mr. Snivel says, in parentheses, he knows all about her.)

"Ha! ha! my old boy," says Mr. Snivel, frisking his fingers through his light Saxon beard, "I have had this case in hand for some time. It is strictly a private matter, nevertheless. They are a bad lot—them New Yorkers, who come here to avoid their little delicate affairs. I may yet make a good thing out of this, though. As for that fellow, Mullholland, I intend getting him the whipping post. He is come to be the associate of gentlemen; men high in office shower upon him their favors. It is all to propitiate the friendship of Bonard—I know it." Mr. Snivel concludes hurriedly, and departs into the street, as our scene changes.

CHAPTER XVIII
ANNA BONARD SEEKS AN INTERVIEW WITH THE ANTIQUARY

It is night. King street seems in a melancholy mood, the blue arch of heaven is bespangled with twinkling stars, the moon has mounted her high throne, and her beams, like messengers of love, dance joyously over the calm waters of the bay, so serenely skirted with dark woodland. The dull tramp of the guardman's horse now breaks the stillness; then the measured tread of the heavily-armed patrol, with which the city swarms at night, echoes and re-echoes along the narrow streets. A theatre reeking with the fumes of whiskey and tobacco; a sombre-looking guard-house, bristling with armed men, who usher forth to guard the fears of tyranny, or drag in some wretched slave; a dilapidated "Court House," at the corner, at which lazy-looking men lounge; a castellated "Work House," so grand without, and so full of bleeding hearts within; a "Poor House" on crutches, and in which infirm age and poverty die of treatment that makes the heart sicken — these are all the public buildings we can boast. Like ominous mounds, they seem sleeping in the calm and serene night. Ah! we had almost forgotten the sympathetic old hospital, with its verandas; the crabbed looking "City Hall," with its port holes; and the "Citadel," in which, when our youths have learned to fight duels, we learn them how to fight their way out of the Union. Duelling is our high art; getting out of the Union is our low. And, too, we have, and make no small boast that we have, two or three buildings called "Halls." In these our own supper-eating men riot, our soldiers drill (soldiering is our presiding genius), and our mob-politicians waste their spleen against the North. Unlike Boston, towering all bright and vigorous in the atmosphere of freedom, we have no galleries of statuary; no conservatories of paintings; no massive edifices of marble, dedicated to art and science; no princely school-houses, radiating their light of learning over a peace and justice-loving community; no majestic exchange, of granite and polished marble, so emblematic of a thrifty commerce;—we have no regal "State House" on the lofty hill, no glittering colleges everywhere striking the eye. The god of slavery—the god we worship, has no use for such temples; public libraries are his prison; his civilization is like a dull dead march; he is the enemy of his own heart, vitiating and making drear whatever he touches. He wages war on art, science, civilization! he trembles at the sight of temples reared for the enlightening of the masses. Tyranny is his law, a cotton-bag his judgment-seat. But we pride ourselves that we are a respectable people—what more would you have us?

The night is chilly without, in the fireplace of the antiquary's back parlor there burns a scanty wood fire. Tom has eaten his supper and retired to a little closet-like room overhead, where, in bed, he muses over what fell from Maria's lips, in their interview. Did she really cherish a passion for him? had her solicitude in years past something more than friendship in it? what did she mean? He was not one of those whose place in a woman's heart could never be supplied. How would an alliance with Maria affect his mother's dignity? All these things Tom evolves over and over in his mind. In point of position, a mechanic's daughter was not far removed from the slave; a mechanic's daughter was viewed only as a good object of seduction for some nice young gentleman. Antiquarians might get a few bows of planter's sons, the legal gentry, and cotton brokers (these make up our aristocracy), but practically no one would think of admitting them into decent society. They, of right, belong to that vulgar herd that live by labor at which the slave can be employed. To be anything in the eyes of good society, you must only live upon the earnings of slaves.

"Why," says Tom, "should I consult the dignity of a mother who discards me? The love of this lone daughter of the antiquary, this girl who strives to know my wants, and to promote my welfare, rises superior to all. I will away with such thoughts! I will be a man!" Maria, with eager eye and thoughtful countenance, sits at the little antique centre-table, reading Longfellow's Evangeline, by the pale light of a candle. A lurid glare is shed over the cavern-like place. The reflection plays curiously upon the corrugated features of the old man, who, his favorite cat at his side, reclines on a stubby little sofa, drawn well up to the fire. The poet would not select Maria as his ideal of female loveliness; and yet there is a touching modesty in her demeanor, a sweet smile ever playing over her countenance, an artlessness in her conversation that more than makes up for the want of those charms novel writers are pleased to call transcendent. "Father!" she says, pausing, "some one knocks at the outer door." The old man starts and listens, then hastens to open it. There stands before him the figure of a strange female, veiled. "I am glad to find you, old man. Be not suspicious of my coming at this hour, for my mission is a strange one." The old man's crooked eyes flash, his deep curling lip quivers, his hand vibrates the candle he holds before him. "If on a mission to do nobody harm," he responds, "then you are welcome." "You will pardon me; I have seen you before. You have wished me well," she whispers in a musical voice. Gracefully she raises her veil over her Spanish hood, and advances cautiously, as the old man closes the door behind her. Then she uncovers her head, nervously. The white, jewelled fingers of her right hand, so delicate and tapering, wander over and smooth her silky black hair, that falls in waves over her Ion-like brow. How exquisite those features just revealed; how full of soul those flashing black eyes; her dress, how chaste! "They call me Anna Bonard," she speaks, timorously, "you may know me?—"

"Oh, I know you well," interrupts the old man, "your beauty has made you known. What more would you have?"

"Something that will make me happy. Old man, I am unhappy. Tell me, if you have the power, who I am. Am I an orphan, as has been told me; or have I parents yet living, affluent, and high in society? Do they seek me and cannot find me? Oh! let the fates speak, old man, for this world has given me nothing but pain and shame. Am I—" she pauses, her eyes wander to the floor, her cheeks crimson, she seizes the old man by the hand, and her bosom heaves as if a fierce passion had just been kindled within it.

The old man preserves his equanimity, says he has a fortune to tell her. Fortunes are best told at midnight. The stars, too, let out their secrets more willingly when the night-king rules. He bids her follow him, and totters back to the little parlor. With a wise air, he bids her be seated on the sofa, saying he never mistakes maidens when they call at this hour.

Maria, who rose from the table at the entrance of the stranger, bows, shuts her book mechanically, and retires. Can there be another face so lovely? she questions within herself, as she pauses to contemplate the stranger ere she disappears. The antiquary draws a chair and seats himself beside Anna. "Thy life and destiny," he says, fretting his bony fingers over the crown of his wig. "Blessed is the will of providence that permits us to know the secrets of destiny. Give me your hand, fair lady." Like a philosopher in deep study, he wipes and adjusts his spectacles, then takes her right hand and commences reading its lines. "Your history is an uncommon one—"

"Yes," interrupts the girl, "mine has been a chequered life."

"You have seen sorrow enough, but will see more. You come of good parents; but, ah!—there is a mystery shrouding your birth." ("And that mystery," interposes the girl, "I want to have explained.") "There will come a woman to reclaim you—a woman in high life; but she will come too late—" (The girl pales and trembles.) "Yes," pursues the old man, looking more studiously at her hand, "she will come too late. You will have admirers, and even suitors; but they will only betray you, and in the end you will die of trouble. Ah! there is a line that had escaped me. You may avert this dark destiny—yes, you may escape the end that fate has ordained for you. In neglect you came up, the companion of a man you think true to you. But he is not true to you. Watch him, follow him—you will yet find him out. Ha! ha! ha! these men are not to be trusted, my dear. There is but one man who really loves you. He is an old man, a man of station. He is your only true friend. I here see it marked." He crosses her hand, and says there can be no mistaking it. "With that man, fair girl, you may escape the dark destiny. But, above all things, do not treat him coldly. And here I see by the sign that Anna Bonard is not your name. The name was given you by a wizard."

"You are right, old man," speaks Anna, raising thoughtfully her great black eyes, as the antiquary pauses and watches each change of her countenance; "that name was given me by Hag Zogbaum, when I was a child in her den, in New York, and when no one cared for me. What my right name was has now slipped my memory. I was indeed a wretched child, and know little of myself."

"Was it Munday?" inquires the old man. Scarce has he lisped the name before she catches it up and repeats it, incoherently, "Munday! Munday! Munday!" her eyes flash with anxiety. "Ah, I remember now. I was called Anna Munday by Mother Bridges. I lived with her before I got to the den of Hag Zogbaum. And Mother Bridges sold apples at a stand at the corner of a street, on West street. It seems like a dream to me now. I do not want to recall those dark days or my childhood. Have you not some revelation to make respecting my parents?" The old man says the signs will not aid him further. "On my arm," she pursues, baring her white, polished arm, "there is a mark. I know not who imprinted it there. See, old man." The old man sees high up on her right arm two hearts and a broken anchor, impressed with India ink blue and red. "Yes," repeats the antiquary, viewing it studiously, "but it gives out no history. If you could remember who put it there." Of that she has no recollection. The old man cannot relieve her anxiety, and arranging her hood she bids him good night, forces a piece of gold into his hand, and seeks her home, disappointed.

The antiquary's predictions were founded on what Mr. Soloman Snivel had told him, and that gentleman got what he knew of Anna's history from George Mullholland. To this, however, he added what suggestions his suspicions gave rise to. The similarity of likeness between Anna and Madame Montford was striking; Madame Montford's mysterious searches and inquiries for the woman Munday had something of deep import in them. Mag Munday's strange disappearance from Charleston, and her previous importuning for the old dress left in pawn with McArthur, were not to be overlooked. These things taken together, and Mr. Snivel saw a case there could be no mistaking. That case became stronger when his fashionable friend engaged his services to trace out what had become of the woman Mag Munday, and to further ascertain what the girl Anna Bonard knew of her own history.

CHAPTER XIX
A SECRET INTERVIEW

While the scene we have related in the foregoing chapter was being enacted, there might be seen pacing the great colonnade of the Charleston hotel, the tall figure of a man wrapped in a massive talma. Heedless of the throng of drinkers gathered in the spacious bar-room, making the very air echo with their revelry, he pauses every few moments, watches intently up and then down Meeting street, now apparently contemplating the twinkling stars, then turning as if disappointed, and resuming his sallies. "He will not come to night," he mutters, as he pauses at the "Ladies' door," then turns and rings the bell. The well-dressed and highly-perfumed servant who guards the door, admits him with a scrutinizing eye. "Beg pardon," he says, with a mechanical bow. He recognizes the stranger, bows, and motions his hands. "Twice," continues the servant, "she has sent a messenger to inquire of your coming." The figure in the talma answers with a bow, slips something into the hand of the servant, passes softly up the great stairs, and is soon lost to sight. In another minute he enters, without knocking, a spacious parlor, decorated and furnished most sumptuously. "How impatiently I have waited your coming," whispers, cautiously, a richly-dressed lady, as she rises from a velvet covered lounge, on which she had reclined, and extends her hand to welcome him.

"Madame, your most obedient," returns the man, bowing and holding her delicate hand in his. "You have something of importance,—something to relieve my mind?" she inquires, watching his lips, trembling, and in anxiety. "Nothing definite," he replies, touching her gently on the arm, as she begs him to be seated in the great arm-chair. He lays aside his talma, places his gloves on the centre-table, which is heaped with an infinite variety of delicately-enveloped missives and cards, all indicative of her position in fashionable society. "I may say, Madame, that I sympathize with you in your anxiety; but as yet I have discovered nothing to relieve it." Madame sighs, and draws her chair near him, in silence. "That she is the woman you seek I cannot doubt. While on the Neck, I penetrated the shanty of one Thompson, a poor mechanic—our white mechanics, you see, are very poor, and not much thought of—who had known her, given her a shelter, and several times saved her from starvation. Then she left the neighborhood and took to living with a poor wretch of a shoemaker."

"Poor creature," interrupts Madame Montford, for it is she whom Mr. Snivel addresses. "If she be dead—oh, dear! That will be the end. I never shall know what became of that child. And to die ignorant of its fate will—" Madame pauses, her color changes, she seems seized with some violent emotion. Mr. Snivel perceives her agitation, and begs she will remain calm. "If that child had been my own," she resumes, "the responsibility had not weighed heavier on my conscience. Wealth, position, the pleasures of society—all sink into insignificance when compared with my anxiety for the fate of that child. It is like an arrow piercing my heart, like a phantom haunting me in my dreams, like an evil spirit waking me at night to tell me I shall die an unhappy woman for having neglected one I was bound by the commands of God to protect—to save, perhaps, from a life of shame." She lets fall the satin folds of her dress, buries her face in her hands, and gives vent to her tears in loud sobs. Mr. Snivel contemplates her agitation with unmoved muscle. To him it is a true index to the sequel. "If you will pardon me, Madame," he continues, "as I was about to say of this miserable shoemaker, he took to drink, as all our white mechanics do, and then used to abuse her. We don't think anything of these people, you see, who after giving themselves up to whiskey, die in the poor house, a terrible death. This shoemaker, of whom I speak, died, and she was turned into the streets by her landlord, and that sent her to living with a 'yellow fellow,' as we call them. Soon after this she died—so report has it. We never know much, you see, about these common people. They are a sort of trash we can make nothing of, and they get terribly low now and then." Madame Montford's swelling breast heaves, her countenance wears an air of melancholy; again she nervously lays aside the cloud-like skirts of her brocade dress. "Have you not," she inquires, fretting her jewelled fingers and displaying the massive gold bracelets that clasp her wrists, "some stronger evidence of her death?" Mr. Snivel says he has none but what he gathered from the negroes and poor mechanics, who live in the by-lanes of the city. There is little dependence, however, to be placed in such reports. Madame, with an air of composure, rises from her chair, and paces twice or thrice across the room, seemingly in deep study. "Something," she speaks, stopping suddenly in one of her sallies—"something (I do not know what it is) tells me she yet lives: that this is the child we see, living an abandoned life."

"As I was going on to say, Madame," pursues Mr. Snivel, with great blandness of manner, "when our white trash get to living with our negroes they are as well as dead. One never knows what comes of them after that.

Being always ready to do a bit of a good turn, as you know, I looked in at Sam Wiley's cabin. Sam Wiley is a negro of some respectability, and generally has an eye to what becomes of these white wretches. I don't—I assure you I don't, Madame—look into these places except on professional business. Sam, after making inquiry among his neighbors—our colored population view these people with no very good opinion, when they get down in the world—said he thought she had found her way through the gates of the poor man's graveyard."

"Poor man's graveyard!" repeats Madame Montford, again resuming her chair.

"Exactly! We have to distinguish between people of position and those white mechanics who come here from the North, get down in the world, and then die. We can't sell this sort of people, you see. No keeping their morals straight without you can. However, this is not to the point. (Mr. Solomon Snivel keeps his eyes intently fixed upon the lady.)

"I sought out the old Sexton, a stupid old cove enough. He had neither names on his record nor graves that answered the purpose. In a legal sense, Madame, this would not be valid testimony, for this old cove being only too glad to get rid of our poor, and the fees into his pocket, is not very particular about names. If it were one of our 'first families,' the old fellow would be so obsequious about having the name down square—"

Mr. Snivel frets his fingers through his beard, and bows with an easy grace.

"Our first families!" repeats Madame Montford.

"Yes, indeed! He is extremely correct over their funerals. They are of a fashionable sort, you see. Well, while I was musing over the decaying dead, and the distinction between poor dead and rich dead, there came along one Graves, a sort of wayward, half simpleton, who goes about among churchyards, makes graves a study, knows where every one who has died for the last century is tucked away, and is worth six sextons at pointing out graves. He never knows anything about the living, for the living, he says, won't let him live; and that being the case, he only wants to keep up his acquaintance with the dead. He never has a hat to his head, nor a shoe to his foot; and where, and how he lives, no one can tell. He has been at the whipping-post a dozen times or more, but I'm not so sure that the poor wretch ever did anything to merit such punishment. Just as the crabbed old sexton was going to drive him out of the gate with a big stick, I says, more in the way of a joke than anything else: 'Graves, come here!—I want a word or two with you.' He came up, looking shy and suspicious, and saying he wasn't going to harm anybody, but there was some fresh graves he was thinking over."

"Some fresh graves!" repeats Madame Montford, nervously.

"Bless you!—a very common thing," rejoins Mr. Snivel, with a bow. "Well, this lean simpleton said they (the graves) were made while he was sick. That being the case, he was deprived—and he lamented it bitterly—of being present at the funerals, and getting the names of the deceased. He is a great favorite with the grave-digger, lends him a willing hand on all occasions, and is extremely useful when the yellow fever rages. But to the sexton he is a perfect pest, for if a grave be made during his absence he will importune until he get the name of the departed. 'Graves,' says I, 'where do they bury these unfortunate women who die off so, here in Charleston?' 'Bless you, my friend,' says Graves, accompanying his words with an idiotic laugh, 'why, there's three stacks of them, yonder. They ship them from New York in lots, poor things; they dies here in droves, poor things; and we buries them yonder in piles, poor things. They go—yes, sir, I have thought a deal of this thing—fast through life; but they dies, and nobody cares for them—you see how they are buried.' I inquired if he knew all their names. He said of course he did. If he didn't, nobody else would. In order to try him, I desired he would show me the grave of Mag Munday. He shook his head smiled, muttered the name incoherently, and said he thought it sounded like a dead name. 'I'll get my thinking right,' he pursued, and brightening up all at once, his vacant eyes flashed, then he touched me cunningly on the arm, and with a wink and nod of the head there was no mistaking, led the way to a great mound located in an obscure part of the graveyard—"

"A great mound! I thought it would come to that," sighs Madame Montford, impatiently.

"We bury these wretched creatures in an obscure place. Indeed, Madame, I hold it unnecessary to have anything to distinguish them when once they are dead. Well, this poor forlorn simpleton then sat down on a grave, and bid me sit beside him. I did as he bid me, and soon he went into a deep study, muttering the name of Mag Munday the while, until I thought he never would stop. So wild and wandering did the poor fellow seem, that I began to think it a pity we had not a place, an insane hospital, or some sort of benevolent institution, where such poor creatures could be placed and cared for. It would be much better than sending them to the whipping-post—"

"I am indeed of your opinion—of your way of thinking most certainly," interpolates Madame Montford, a shadow of melancholy darkening her countenance.

"At length, he went at it, and repeated over an infinite quantity of names. It was wonderful to see how he could keep them all in his head. 'Well, now,' says he, turning to me with an inoffensive laugh, 'she ben't dead. You may bet on that. There now!' he spoke, as if suddenly becoming conscious of a recently-made discovery. 'Why, she runned wild about here, as I does, for a time; was abused and knocked about by everybody. Oh, she had a hard time enough, God knows that.' 'But that is not disclosing to me what became of her,' says I; 'come, be serious, Graves.' (We call him this, you see, Madame, for the reason that he is always among graveyards.) Then he went into a singing mood, sang two plaintive songs, and had sung a third and fourth, if I had not stopped him. 'Well,' he says, 'that woman ain't dead, for I've called up in my mind the whole graveyard of names, and her's is not among them. Why not, good gentleman, (he seized me by the arm as he said this,) inquire of Milman Mingle, the vote-cribber? He is a great politician, never thinks of poor Graves, and wouldn't look into a graveyard for the world. The vote-cribber used to live with her, and several times he threatened to hang her, and would a hanged her—yes, he would, sir—if it hadn't a been for the neighbors. I don't take much interest in the living, you know. But I pitied her, poor thing, for she was to be pitied, and there was nobody but me to do it. Just inquire of the vote-cribber.' I knew the simpleton never told an untruth, being in no way connected with our political parties."

"Never told an untruth, being in no way connected with our political parties!" repeats Madame Montford, who has become more calm.

"I gave him a few shillings, he followed me to the gate, and left me muttering, 'Go, inquire of the vote-cribber.'"

"And have you found this man?" inquires the anxious lady.

"I forthwith set about it," replies Mr. Snivel, "but as yet, am unsuccessful. Nine months during the year his residence is the jail—"

"The jail!"

"Yes, Madame, the jail. His profession, although essential to the elevation of our politicians and statesmen, is nevertheless unlawful. And he being obliged to practice it in opposition to the law, quietly submits to the penalty, which is a residence in the old prison for a short time. It's a nominal thing, you see, and he has become so habituated to it that I am inclined to the belief that he prefers it. I proceeded to the prison and found he had been released. One of our elections comes off in a few days. The approach of such an event is sure to find him at large. I sought him in all the drinking saloons, in the gambling dens, in the haunts of prostitution—in all the low places where our great politicians most do assemble and debauch themselves. He was not to be found. Being of the opposite party, I despatched a spy to the haunt of the committee of the party to which he belongs, and for which he cribs. I have paced the colonnade for more than an hour, waiting the coming of this spy. He did not return, and knowing your anxiety in the matter I returned to you. To-morrow I will seek him out; to-morrow I will get from him what he knows of this woman you seek.

"And now, Madame, here is something I would have you examine." (Mr. Snivel methodically says he got it of McArthur, the antiquary.) "She made a great ado about a dress that contained this letter. I have no doubt it will tell a tale." Mr. Snivel draws from his breast-pocket the letter found concealed in the old dress, and passes it to Madame Montford, who receives it with a nervous hand. Her eyes become fixed upon it, she glances over its defaced page with an air of bewilderment, her face crimsons, then suddenly pales, her lips quiver—her every nerve seems unbending to the shock. "Heavens! has it come to this?" she mutters, confusedly. Her strength fails her; the familiar letter falls from her fingers.—For a few moments she seems struggling to suppress her emotions, but her reeling brain yields, her features become like marble, she shrieks and swoons ere Mr. Snivel has time to clasp her in his arms.

CHAPTER XX
LADY SWIGGS ENCOUNTERS DIFFICULTIES
ON HER ARRIVAL IN NEW YORK

A pleasant passage of sixty hours, a good shaking up at the hands of that old tyrant, sea-sickness, and Lady Swiggs finds the steamer on which she took passage gliding majestically up New York Bay. There she sits, in all her dignity, an embodiment of our decayed chivalry, a fair representative of our first families. She has taken up her position on the upper deck, in front of the wheel house. As one after another the objects of beauty that make grand the environs of that noble Bay, open to her astonished eyes, she contrasts them favorably or unfavorably with some familiar object in Charleston harbor. There is indeed a similarity in the conformation. And though ours, she says, may not be so extensive, nor so grand in its outlines, nor so calm and soft in its perspective, there is a more aristocratic air about it. Smaller bodies are always more select and respectable. The captain, to whom she has put an hundred and one questions which he answers in monosyllables, is not, she thinks, so much of a gentleman as he might have been had he been educated in Charleston. He makes no distinction in favor of people of rank.

Lady Swiggs wears that same faded silk dress; her black crape bonnet, with two saucy red artificial flowers tucked in at the side, sits so jauntily; that dash of brown hair is smoothed so exactly over her yellow, shrivelled forehead; her lower jaw oscillates with increased motion; and her sharp, gray eyes, as before, peer anxiously through her great-eyed spectacles. And, generous reader, that you may not mistake her, she has brought her inseparable Milton, which she holds firmly grasped in her right hand. "You have had a tedious time of it, Madam," says a corpulent lady, who is extensively dressed and jewelled, and accosts her with a familiar air. Lady Swiggs says not so tedious as it might have been, and gives her head two or three very fashionable twitches.

"Your name, if you please?"

"The Princess Grouski. My husband, the Prince Grouski," replies the corpulent lady, turning and introducing a fair-haired gentleman, tall and straight of person, somewhat military in his movements, and extremely fond of fingering his long, Saxon moustache. Lady Swiggs, on the announcement of a princess, rises suddenly to her feet, and commences an unlimited number of courtesies. She is, indeed, most happy to meet, and have the honor of being fellow-voyager with their Royal Highnesses—will remember it as being one of the happiest events of her life,—and begs to assure them of her high esteem. The corpulent lady gives her a delicate card, on which is described the crown of Poland, and beneath, in exact letters, "The Prince and Princess Grouski." The Prince affects not to understand English, which Lady Swiggs regrets exceedingly, inasmuch as it deprives her of an interesting conversation with a person of royal blood. The card she places carefully between the leaves of her Milton, having first contemplated it with an air of exultation. Again begging to thank the Prince and Princess for this mark of their distinguished consideration, Lady Swiggs inquires if they ever met or heard of Sir Sunderland Swiggs. The rotund lady, for herself and the prince, replies in the negative. "He was," she pursues, with a sigh of disappointment, "he was very distinguished, in his day. Yes, and I am his lineal descendant. Your highnesses visited Charleston, of course?"

"O dear," replies the rotund lady, somewhat laconically, "the happiest days of my life were spent among the chivalry of South Carolina. Indeed, Madam, I have received the attention and honors of the very first families in that State."

This exclamation sets the venerable lady to thinking how it could be possible that their highnesses received the attentions of the first families and she not know it. No great persons ever visited the United States without honoring Charleston with their presence, it was true; but how in the world did it happen that she was kept in ignorance of such an event as that of the Prince and Princess paying it a visit. She began to doubt the friendship of her distinguished acquaintances, and the St. Cecilia Society. She hopes that should they condescend to pay the United States a second visit, they will remember her address. This the rotund lady, who is no less a person than the distinguished Madame Flamingo, begs to assure her she will.

Let not this happy union between Grouski and the old hostess, surprise you, gentle reader. It was brought about by Mr. Snivel, the accommodation man, who, as you have before seen, is always ready to do a bit of a good turn. Being a skilful diplomatist in such matters, he organized the convention, superintended the wooing, and for a lusty share of the spoils, secured to him by Grouski, brought matters to an issue "highly acceptable" to all parties. A sale of her palace of licentiousness, works of art, costly furniture, and female wares, together with the good will of all concerned, (her friends of the "bench and bar" not excepted,) was made for the nice little sum of sixty-seven thousand dollars, to Madame Grace Ashley, whose inauguration was one of the most gorgeous *fêtes* the history of Charleston can boast. The new occupant was a novice. She had not sufficient funds to pay ready money for the purchase, hence Mr. Doorwood, a chivalric and very excellent gentleman, according to report, supplies the necessary, taking a mortgage on the institution; which proves to be quite as good property as the Bank, of which he is president. It is not, however, just that sort of business upon which an already seared conscience can repose in quiet, hence he applies that antidote too frequently used by knaves—he never lets a Sunday pass without piously attending church.

The money thus got, through this long life of iniquity, was by Madame Flamingo handed over to the Prince, in exchange for his heart and the title she had been deluded to believe him capable of conferring. Her reverence for Princes and exiled heroes, (who are generally exiled humbugs,) was not one jot less than that so pitiably exhibited by our self-dubbed fashionable society all over this Union. It may be well to add, that this distinguished couple, all smiling and loving, are on their way to Europe, where they are sure of receiving the attentions of any quantity of "crowned heads." Mr. Snivel, in order not to let the affair lack that *eclat* which is the crowning point in matters of high life, got smuggled into the columns of the highly respectable and very authentic old "Courier," a line or two, in which the fashionable world was thrown into a flutter by the announcement that Prince Grouski and his wealthy bride left yesterday, *en route* for Europe. This bit of gossip the "New York Herald" caught up and duly itemised, for the benefit of its upper-ten readers, who, as may be easily imagined, were all on tip-toe to know the address of visitors so distinguished, and leave cards.

Mrs. Swiggs has (we must return to her mission) scarcely set foot on shore, when, thanks to a little-headed corporation, she is fairly set upon by a dozen or more villanous hack-drivers, each dangling his whip in her face, to the no small danger of her bonnet and spectacles. They jostle her, utter vile imprecations, dispute for the right of carrying her, each in his turn offering to do it a shilling less. Lady Swiggs is indeed an important individual in the hands of the hack-drivers, and by them, in a fair way of being torn to pieces. She wonders they do not recognize her as a distinguished person, from the chivalric State of South Carolina. The captain is engaged with his ship, passengers are hurrying ashore, too anxious to escape the confinement of the cabin; every one seems in haste to leave her, no one offers to protect her from the clutches of those who threaten to tear her into precious pieces. She sighs for Sister Slocum, for Mr. Hadger, for any one kind enough to raise a friendly voice in her behalf. Now one has got her black box, another her corpulent carpet-bag—a third exults in a victory over her band-box. Fain would she give up her mission in disgust, return to the more aristocratic atmosphere of Charleston, and leave the heathen to his fate. All this might have been avoided had Sister Slocum sent her carriage. She will stick by her black-box, nevertheless. So into the carriage with it she gets, much discomfited. The driver says he would drive to the Mayor's office "and 'ave them ar two coves what's got the corpulent carpet-bag and the band-box, seed after, if it wern't that His Honor never knows anything he ought to know, and is sure to do nothing. They'll turn up, Mam, I don't doubt," says the man, "but it's next to los'in' on 'em, to go to the Mayor's office. Our whole corporation, Mam, don't do nothin' but eats oysters, drinks whiskey, and makes presidents;—them's what they do, Marm." Lady Swiggs says what a pity so great a city was not blessed with a bigger-headed corporation.

"That it is, Marm," returns the methodical hack-driver, "he an't got a very big head, our corporation." And Lady Swiggs, deprived of her carpet-bag and band-box, and considerably out of patience, is rolled away to the mansion of Sister Slocum, on Fourth Avenue. Instead of falling immediately into the arms and affections of that worthy and very enterprising lady, the door is opened by a slatternly maid of all work—her greasy dress, and hard, ruddy face and hands—her short, flabby figure, and her coarse, uncombed hair, giving out strong evidence of being overtaxed with labor. "Is it Mrs. Slocum hersel' ye'd be seein'?" inquires the maid, wiping her soapy hands with her apron, and looking querulously in the face of the old lady, who, with the air of a Scotch metaphysician, says she is come to spend a week in friendly communion with her, to talk over the cause of the poor, benighted heathen. "Troth an' I'm not as sure ye'll do that same, onyhow; sure she'd not spend a week at home in the blessed year; and the divil another help in the house but mysel' and himsel', Mr. Slocum. A decent man is that same Slocum, too," pursues the maid, with a laconic indifference to the wants of the guest. A dusty hat-stand ornaments one side of the hall, a patched and somewhat deformed sofa the other. The walls wear a dingy air; the fumes of soapsuds and stewed onions offend the senses. Mrs. Swiggs hesitates in the doorway. Shall I advance, or retreat to more congenial quarters? she asks herself. The wily hack-driver (he agreed for four and charged her twelve shillings) leaves her black box on the step and drives away. She may be thankful he did not charge her twenty. They make no allowance for distinguished people; Lady Swiggs learns this fact, to her great annoyance. To the much-confused maid of all work she commences relating the loss of her luggage. With one hand swinging the door and the other tucked under her dowdy apron, she says, "Troth, Mam, and ye ought to be thankful, for the like of that's done every day."

Mrs. Swiggs would like a room for the night at least, but is told, in a somewhat confused style, that not a room in the house is in order. That a person having the whole heathen world on her shoulders should not have her house in order somewhat surprises the indomitable lady. In answer to a question as to what time Mr. Slocum will be home, the maid of all work says: "Och! God love the poor man, there's no tellin'. Sure there's not much left of the poor man. An' the divil a one more inoffensive than poor Slocum. It's himsel' works all day in the Shurance office beyant. He comes home dragged out, does a dale of writing for Mrs. Slocum hersel', and goes to bed sayin' nothin' to nobody." Lady Swiggs says: "God bless me He no doubt labors in a good cause—an excellent cause—he will have his reward hereafter."

It must here be confessed that Sister Slocum, having on hand a newly-married couple, nicely suited to the duties of a mission to some foreign land, has conceived the very laudable project of sending them to Aleppo, and is now spending a few weeks among the Dutch of Albany, who are expected to contribute the necessary funds. A few thousand dollars expended, a few years' residence in the East, a few reports as to what might have been done if something had not interposed to prevent it, and there is not a doubt that this happy couple will return home crowned with the laurels of having very nearly Christianized one Turk and two Tartars.

The maid of all work suddenly remembers that Mrs. Slocum left word that if a distinguished lady arrived from South Carolina she could be comfortably accommodated at Sister Scudder's, on Fourth Street. Not a little disappointed, the venerable old lady calls a passing carriage, gets herself and black box into it, and orders the driver to forthwith proceed to the house of Sister Scudder. Here she is—and she sheds tears that she is—cooped up in a cold, closet-like room, on the third story, where, with the ends of her red shawl, she may blow and warm her fingers. Sister Scudder is a crispy little body, in spectacles. Her features are extremely sharp, and her countenance continually wears a wise expression. As for her knowledge of scripture, it is truly wonderful, and a decided improvement when contrasted with the meagre set-out of her table. Tea time having arrived, Lady Swiggs is invited down to a cup by a pert Irish servant, who accosts her with an independence she by no means approves. Entering the room with an air of stateliness she deems necessary to the position she desires to maintain, Sister Scudder takes her by the hand and introduces her to a bevy of nicely-conditioned, and sleek-looking gentlemen, whose exactly-combed mutton chop whiskers, smoothly-oiled hair, perfectly-tied white cravats, cloth so modest and fashionable, and mild, studious countenances, discover their profession. Sister Scudder, motioning Lady Swiggs aside, whispers in her ear: "They are all very excellent young men. They will improve on acquaintance. They are come up for the clergy." They, in turn, receive the distinguished stranger in a manner that is rather abrupt than cold, and ere she has dispensed her stately courtesy, say; "how do you do marm," and turn to resume with one another their conversation on the wicked world. It is somewhat curious to see how much more interested these gentry become in the wicked world when it is afar off.

Tea very weak, butter very strong, toast very thin, and religious conversation extremely thick, make up the repast. There is no want of appetite. Indeed one might, under different circumstances, have imagined Sister Scudder's clerical boarders contesting a race for an extra slice of her very thin toast. Not the least prominent among Sister Scudder's boarders is Brother Singleton Spyke, whom Mrs. Swiggs recognizes by the many compliments he lavishes upon Sister Slocum, whose absence is a source of great regret with him. She is always elbow deep in some laudable pursuit. Her presence sheds a radiant light over everything around; everybody mourns her when absent. Nevertheless, there is some satisfaction in knowing that her absence is caused by her anxiety to promote some mission of good: Brother Spyke thus muses. Seeing that there is come among them a distinguished stranger, he gives out that to-morrow evening there will be a gathering of the brethren at the "House of the Foreign Missions," when the very important subject of funds necessary to his mission to Antioch, will be discussed. Brother Spyke, having levelled this battery at the susceptibility of Mrs. Swiggs, is delighted to find some fourteen voices chiming in—all complimenting his peculiar fitness for, and the worthy object of the mission. Mrs. Swiggs sets her cup in her saucer, and in a becoming manner, to the great joy of all present, commences an eulogium on Mr. Spyke. Sister Slocum, in her letters, held him before her in strong colors; spoke in such high praise of his talent, and gave so many guarantees as to what he would do if he only got among the heathen, that her sympathies were enlisted— she resolved to lose no time in getting to New York, and, when there, put her shoulder right manfully to the wheel. This declaration finds her, as if by some mysterious transport, an object of no end of praise. Sister Scudder adjusts her spectacles, and, in mildest accents, says, "The Lord will indeed reward such disinterestedness." Brother Mansfield says motives so pure will ensure a passport to heaven, he is sure. Brother Sharp, an exceedingly lean and tall youth, with a narrow head and sharp nose (Mr. Sharp's father declared he made him a preacher because he could make him nothing else), pronounces, with great emphasis, that such self-sacrifice should be written in letters of gold. A unanimous sounding of her praises convinces Mrs. Swiggs that she is indeed a person of great importance. There is, however, a certain roughness of manner about her new friends, which does not harmonize with her notions of aristocracy. She questions within herself whether they represent the "first families" of New York. If the "first families" could only get their heads together, the heathen world would be sure to knock under. No doubt, it can be effected in time by common people. If Sister Slocum, too, would evangelize the world—if she would give the light of heaven to the benighted, she must employ willing hearts and strong hands. Satan, she says, may be chained, subdued, and made to abjure his wickedness. These cheering contemplations more than atone for the cold reception she met at the house of Sister Slocum. Her only regret now is that she did not sell old Cicero. The money so got would have enabled her to bestow a more substantial token of her soul's sincerity.

Tea over, thanks returned, a prayer offered up, and Brother Spyke, having taken a seat on the sofa beside Mrs. Swiggs, opens his batteries in a spiritual conversation, which he now and then spices with a few items of his own history. At the age of fifteen he found himself in love with a beautiful young lady, who, unfortunately, had made up her mind to accept only the hand of a clergyman: hence, she rejected his. This so disturbed his thoughts, that he resolved on studying theology. In this he was aided by the singular discovery, that he had a talent, and a "call to preach." He would forget his amour, he thought, become a member of the clergy, and go preach to the heathen. He spent his days in reading, his nights in the study of divine truths. Then he got on the kind side of a committee of very excellent ladies, who, having duly considered his qualities, pronounced him exactly suited to the study of theology. Ladies were generally good judges of such matters, and Brother Spyke felt he could not do better than act up to their opinions. To all these things Mrs. Swiggs listens with delight.

Spyke, too, is in every way a well made-up man, being extremely tall and lean of figure, with nice Saxon hair and whiskers, mild but thoughtful blue eyes, an anxious expression of countenance, a thin, squeaking voice, and features sufficiently delicate and regular for his calling. His dress, too, is always exactly clerical. If he be cold and pedantic in his manner, the fault must be set down to the errors of the profession, rather than to any natural inclination of his own. But what is singular of Brother Spyke is, that, notwithstanding his passion for delving the heathen world, and dragging into Christian light and love the benighted wretches there found, he has never in his life given a thought for that heathen world at his own door—a heathen world sinking in the blackest pool of misery and death, in the very heart of an opulent city, over which it hurls its seething pestilence, and scoffs at the commands of high heaven. No, he never thought of that Babylon of vice and crime—that heathen world pleading with open jaws at his own door. He had no thought for how much money might be saved, and how much more good done, did he but turn his eyes; go into this dark world (the Points) pleading at his feet, nerve himself to action, and lend a strong hand to help drag off the film of its degradation. In addition to this, Brother Spyke was sharp enough to discover the fact that a country parson does not enjoy the most enviable situation. A country parson must put up with the smallest salary; he must preach the very best of sermons; he must flatter and flirt with all the marriageable ladies of his church; he must consult the tastes, but offend none of the old ladies; he must submit to have the sermon he strained his brain to make perfect, torn to pieces by a dozen wise old women, who claim the right of carrying the church on their shoulders; he must have dictated to him what sort of dame he may take for wife;—in a word, he must bear meekly a deal of pestering and starvation, or be in bad odor with the senior members of the sewing circle. Duly appreciating all these difficulties, Brother Spyke chose a mission to Antioch, where the field of his labors would be wide, and the gates not open to restraints. And though he could not define the exact character of his mission to Antioch, he so worked upon the sympathies of the credulous old lady, as to well-nigh create in her mind a resolve to give the amount she had struggled to get and set apart for the benefit of those two institutions ("the Tract Society," and "The Home of the Foreign Missions"), all to the getting himself off to Antioch.

CHAPTER XXI
MR. SNIVEL PURSUES HIS SEARCH FOR THE VOTE-CRIBBER

While Mrs. Swiggs is being entertained by Sister Scudder and her clerical friends in New York, Mr. Snivel is making good his demand on her property in Charleston. As the agent of Keepum, he has attached her old slaves, and what few pieces of furniture he could find; they will in a few days be sold for the satisfaction of her debts. Mrs. Swiggs, it must be said, never had any very nice appreciation of debt-paying, holding it much more legitimate that her creditors accept her dignity in satisfaction of any demand they chanced to have against her. As for her little old house, the last abode of the last of the great Swiggs family,—that, like numerous other houses of our "very first families," is mortgaged for more than it is worth, to Mr. Staple the grocer. We must, however, turn to Mr. Snivel.

Mr. Snivel is seen, on the night after the secret interview at the Charleston Hotel, in a happy mood, passing down King street. A little, ill-featured man, with a small, but florid face, a keen, lecherous eye, leans on his arm. They are in earnest conversation.

"I think the mystery is nearly cleared up, Keepum" says Snivel.

"There seems no getting a clue to the early history of this Madame Montford, 'tis true. Even those who introduced her to Charleston society know nothing of her beyond a certain period. All anterior to that is wrapped in suspicion," returns Keepum, fingering his massive gold chain and seals, that pend from his vest, then releasing his hold of Mr. Snivel's arm, and commencing to button closely his blue dress coat, which is profusely decorated with large gilt buttons. "She's the mother of the dashing harlot, or I'm no prophet, nevertheless," he concludes, shaking his head significantly.

"You may almost swear it—a bad conscience is a horrid bore; d—n me, if I can't see through the thing. (Mr. Snivel laughs.) Better put our female friends on their guard, eh?"

"They had better drop her as quietly as possible," rejoins Mr. Keepum, drawing his white glove from off his right hand, and extending his cigar case.

Mr. Snivel having helped himself to a cigar, says: "D—n me, if she didn't faint in my arms last night. I made a discovery that brought something of deep interest back to her mind, and gave her timbers such a shock! I watched, and read the whole story in her emotions. One accustomed to the sharps of the legal profession can do this sort of thing. She is afraid of approaching this beautiful creature, Anna Bonard, seeing the life she lives, and the suspicions it might create in fashionable society, did she pursue such a course to the end of finding out whether she be really the lost child of the relative she refers to so often. Her object is to find one Mag Munday, who used to knock about here, and with whom the child was left. But enough of this for the present." Thus saying, they enter the house of the old antiquary, and finding no one but Maria at home, Mr. Snivel takes the liberty of throwing his arms about her waist. This done, he attempts to drag her across the room and upon the sofa. "Neither your father nor you ever had a better friend," he says, as the girl struggles from his grasp, shrinks at his feet, and, with a look of disdain, upbraids him for his attempt to take advantage of a lone female.

"High, ho!" interposes Keepum, "what airs these sort of people put on, eh? Don't amount to much, no how; they soon get over them, you know. A blasted deal of assumption, as you say. Ha, ha, ha! I rather like this sort of modesty. 'Tisn't every one can put it cleverly." Mr. Snivel winks to Keepum, who makes an ineffectual attempt to extinguish the light, which Maria seizes in her hand, and summoning her courage, stands before them in a defiant attitude, an expression of hate and scorn on her countenance. "Ah, fiend! you take this liberty—you seek to destroy me because I am poor—because you think me humble—an easy object to prey upon. I am neither a stranger to the world nor your cowardly designs; and so long as I have life you shall not gloat over the destruction of my virtue. Approach me at your peril—knaves! You have compromised my father; you have got him in your grasp, that you may the more easily destroy me. But you will be disappointed, your perfidy will recoil on yourselves: though stripped of all else, I will die protecting that virtue you would not dare to offend but for my poverty." This unexpected display of resolution has the effect of making the position of the intruders somewhat uncomfortable. Mr. Keepum, whose designs Snivel would put in execution, sinks, cowardly, upon the sofa, while his compatriot (both are celebrated for their chivalry) stands off apace endeavoring to palliate the insult with facetious remarks. (This chivalry of ours is a mockery, a convenient word in the foul mouths of fouler ruffians.) Mr. Snivel makes a second attempt to overcome the unprotected girl. With every expression of hate and scorn rising to her face, she bids him defiance. Seeing himself thus firmly repulsed, he begs to assure her, on the word of a gentleman—a commodity always on hand, and exceedingly cheap with us—he was far from intending an insult. He meant it for a bit of a good turn—nothing more. "Always fractious at first—these sort of people are," pursues Keepum, relighting his cigar as he sits on the sofa, squinting his right eye. "Take bravely to gentlemen after a little display of modesty—always! Try her again, Squire." Mr. Snivel dashes the candle from her hand, and in the darkness grasps her wrists. The enraged girl shrieks, and calls aloud for assistance. Simultaneously a blow fells Mr. Snivel to the floor. The voice of Tom Swiggs is heard, crying: "Wretch! villain!—what brings you here? (Mr. Keepum, like the coward, who fears the vengeance he has merited, makes good his escape.) Will you never cease polluting the habitations of the poor? Would to God there was justice for the poor, as well as law for the rich; then I would make thee bite the dust, like a dying viper. You should no longer banquet on poor virtue. Wretch!—I would teach thee that virtue has its value with the poor as well as the rich;—that with the true gentleman it is equally sacred." Tom stands a few moments over the trembling miscreant, Maria sinks into a chair, and with her elbows resting on the table, buries her face in her hands and gives vent to her tears.

"Never did criminal so merit punishment; but I will prove thee not worth my hand. Go, wretch, go! and know that he who proves himself worthy of entering the habitations of the humble is more to be prized than kings and princes." Tom relights the candle in time to see Mr. Snivel rushing into the street.

The moon sheds a pale light over the city as the two chivalric gentlemen, having rejoined and sworn to have revenge, are seen entering a little gate that opens to a dilapidated old building, fronted by a neglected garden, situate on the north side of Queen street, and in days gone by called "Rogues' Retreat." "Rogues' Retreat" has scared vines creeping over its black, clap-boarded front, which viewed from the street appears in a squatting mood, while its broken door, closed shutters—the neglected branches of grape vines that depend upon decayed trellise and arbors, invest it with a forlorn air: indeed, one might without prejudicing his faculties imagine it a fit receptacle for our deceased politicians and our whiskey-drinking congressmen—the last resting-place of our departed chivalry. Nevertheless, generous reader, we will show you that "Rogues' Retreat" serves a very different purpose. Our mob-politicians, who make their lungs and fists supply the want of brains, use it as their favorite haunt, and may be seen on the eve of an election passing in and out of a door in the rear. Hogsheads of bad whiskey have been drunk in "Rogues' Retreat;" it reeks with the fumes of uncounted cigars; it has been the scene of untold villanies. Follow us; we will forego politeness, and peep in through a little, suspicious-looking window, in the rear of the building. This window looks into a cavern-like room, some sixteen feet by thirty, the ceiling of which is low, and blotched here and there with lamp-smoke and water-stains, the plastering hanging in festoons from the walls, and lighted by the faint blaze of a small globular lamp, depending from the centre, and shedding a lurid glare over fourteen grotesque faces, formed round a broad deal-table. Here, at one side of the table sits Judge Sleepyhorn, Milman Mingle, the vote-cribber, on his right; there, on the other, sits Mr. Snivel and Mr. Keepum. More conspicuous than anything else, stands, in the centre of the table, bottles and decanters of whiskey, of which each man is armed with a stout glass. "I am as well aware of the law as my friend who has just taken his seat can be. But we all know that the law can be made subordinate; and it must be made subordinate to party ends. We must not (understand me, I do not say this in my judicial capacity) be too scrupulous when momentous issues are upon us. The man who has not nerve enough to make citizens by the dozen—to stuff double-drawered ballot-boxes, is not equal to the times we live in;—this is a great moral fact." This is said by the Judge, who, having risen with an easy air, sits down and resumes his glass and cigar.

"Them's my sentiments—exactly," interposes the vote-cribber, his burly, scarred face, and crispy red hair and beard, forming a striking picture in the pale light. "I have given up the trade of making Presidents, what I used to foller when, you see, I lived in North Caroliner; but, I tell you on the faith of my experience, that to carry the day we must let the law slide, and crib with a free chain: there's no gettin' over this."

"It is due," interrupts the Judge, again rising to his feet and bowing to the cribber, "to this worthy man, whose patriotism has been tried so often within prison-walls, that we give weight to his advice. He bears the brunt of the battle like a hero—he is a hero!" (The vote-cribber acknowledges the compliment by filling his glass and drinking to the Judge.)

"Of this worthy gentleman I have, as a member of the learned profession, an exalted opinion. His services are as necessary to our success as steam to the speed of a locomotive. I am in favor of leaving the law entirely out of the question. What society sanctions as a means to party ends, the law in most cases fails to reach," rejoins a tall, sandy-complexioned man, of the name of Booper, very distinguished among lawyers and ladies. Never was truth spoken with stronger testimony at hand. Mr. Keepum could boast of killing two poor men; Mr. Snivel could testify to the fallacy of the law by gaining him an honorable acquittal. There were numerous indictments against Mr. Keepum for his dealings in lottery tickets, but they found their way into the Attorney-General's pocket, and it was whispered he meant to keep them there. It was indeed pretty well known he could not get them out in consequence of the gold Keepum poured in. Not a week passes but men kill each other in the open streets. We call these little affairs, "rencontres;" the fact is, we are become so accustomed to them that we rather like them, and regard them as evidences of our advanced civilization. We are infested with slave-hunters, and slave-killers, who daily disgrace us with their barbarities; yet the law is weak when the victor is strong. So we continue to live in the harmless belief that we are the most chivalrous people in the world.

"Mr. Booper!" ejaculates Mr. Snivel, knocking the ashes from his cigar and rising to his feet, "you have paid no more than a merited compliment to the masterly completeness of this excellent man's cribbing. (He points to the cribber, and bows.) Now, permit me to say here, I have at my disposal a set of fellows, (he smiles,) who can fight their way into Congress, duplicate any system of sharps, and stand in fear of nothing. Oh! gentlemen, (Mr. Snivel becomes enthusiastic.) I was—as I have said, I believe—enjoying a bottle of champagne with my friend Keepum here, when we overheard two Dutchmen—the Dutch always go with the wrong party—discoursing about a villanous caucus held to-night in King street. There is villany up with these Dutch! But, you see, we—that is, I mean I—made some forty or more citizens last year. We have the patent process; we can make as many this year."

Mr. Sharp, an exceedingly clever politician, who has meekly born any number of cudgellings at the polls, and hopes ere long to get the appointment of Minister to Paris, interrupts by begging that Mr. Soloman will fill his glass, and resume his seat. Mr. Snivel having taking his seat, Mr. Sharp proceeds: "I tell you all what it is, says I, the other day to a friend— these ponderous Dutch ain't to be depended on. Then, says I, you must separate the Irish into three classes, and to each class you must hold out a different inducement, says I. There's the Rev. Father Flaherty, says I, and he is a trump card at electioneering. He can form a breach between his people and the Dutch, and, says I, by the means of this breach we will gain the whole tribe of Emeralds over to our party. I confess I hate these vagabonds right soundly; but necessity demands that we butter and sugar the mover until we carry our ends. You must not look at the means, says I, when the ends are momentous."

"The staunch Irish," pursues the Judge, rising as Mr. Sharp sits down, "are noble fellows, and with us. To the middle class—the grocers and shopkeepers—we must, however, hold out flattering inducements; such as the reduction of taxes, the repeal of our oppressive license laws, taking the power out of the hands of our aristocracy—they are very tender here—and giving equal rights to emigrants. These points we must put as Paul did his sermons—with force and ingenuity. As for the low Irish, all we have to do is to crib them, feed and pickle them in whiskey for a week. To gain an Irishman's generosity, you cannot use a better instrument than meat, drink, and blarney. I often contemplate these fellows when I am passing sentence upon them for crime."

"True! I have the same dislike to them personally; but politically, the matter assumes quite a different form of attraction. The laboring Irish—the dull-headed—are what we have to do with. We must work them over, and over, and over, until we get them just right. Then we must turn them all into legal voting citizens—"

"That depends on how long they have been in the country," interrupts a brisk little man, rising quickly to his feet, and assuming a legal air.

"Mr. Sprig! you are entirely behind the age. It matters not how long these gentlemen from Ireland have been in the country. They take to politics like rats to good cheese. A few months' residence, and a little working over, you know, and they become trump voters. The Dutch are a different sort of animal; the fellows are thinkers," resumes the Judge.

Mr. Snivel, who has been sipping his whiskey, and listening very attentively to the Judge, rises to what he calls the most important order. He has got the paper all ready, and proposes the gentlemen he thinks best qualified for the naturalization committee. This done, Mr. Snivel draws from his pocket a copy of the forged papers, which are examined, and approved by every one present. This instrument is surmounted with the eagle and arms of the United States, and reads thus:

"*STATE OF NEW YORK.*

"In the Court of Common Pleas for the city and county of New York:

"I—— do declare on oath, that it is *bonâ fide* my intention to become a citizen of the United States, and to renounce forever all allegiance and fidelity to any foreign prince, potentate, State or sovereignty whatever, and particularly to the Queen of the United Kingdom of Great Britain and Ireland, of whom I am a subject."

Signed this—— day of—— 184-.

James Connor, Clerk.

"Clerk's office, Court of Common Pleas for the city and county of New York."

"I hereby certify that the foregoing is a true copy of an original declaration of intention remaining on record in my office, &c., &c., &c."

"There! it required skill and practice to imitate like that" Mr. Snivel exultingly exclaims. "We require to make thirty-seven citizens, and have prepared the exact number of papers. If the cribbers do their duty, the day is ours." Thus is revealed one of the scenes common to "Rogues' Retreat." We shrink at the multiplicity of crime in our midst; we too seldom trace the source from whence it flows. If we did but turn our eyes in the right direction we would find the very men we have elected our guardians, protecting the vicious, whose power they covet—sacrificing their high trust to a low political ambition. You cannot serve a political end by committing a wrong without inflicting a moral degradation on some one. Political intrigue begets laxity of habits; it dispels that integrity without which the unfixed mind becomes vicious; it acts as a festering sore in the body politic.

Having concluded their arrangements for the Mayor's election, the party drinks itself into a noisy mood, each outshouting the other for the right to speak, each refilling and emptying his glass, each asserting with vile imprecations, his dignity as a gentleman. Midnight finds the reeling party adjourning in the midst of confusion.

Mr. Snivel winks the vote-cribber into a corner, and commences interrogating him concerning Mag Munday. The implacable face of the vote-cribber reddens, he contorts his brows, frets his jagged beard with the fingers of his left hand, runs his right over the crown of his head, and stammers: "I know'd her, lived with her—she used to run sort of wild, and was twice flogged. She got crazed at last!" He shrugs his stalworth shoulders and pauses. "Being a politician, you see, a body can't divest their minds of State affairs sufficiently to keep up on women matters," he pursues: "She got into the poor-house, that I knows—"

"She is dead then?" interposes Mr. Snivel.

"As like as not. The poor relatives of our 'first families' rot and die there without much being said about it. Just look in at that institution—it's a terrible place to kill folks off!—and if she be not there then come to me. Don't let the keepers put you off. Pass through the outer gate, into and through the main building, then turn sharp to the left, and advance some twenty feet up a filthy passage, then enter a passage on the right, (have a light with you,) that leads to a dozen or fourteen steps, wet and slippery. Then you must descend into a sort of grotto, or sickly vault, which you will cross and find yourself in a spacious passage, crawling with beetles and lizards. Don't be frightened, sir; keep on till you hear moanings and clankings of chains. Then you will come upon a row of horrid cells, only suited for dog kennels.

In these cells our crazy folks are chained and left to die. Give Glentworthy a few shillings for liquor, sir, and he, having these poor devils in charge, will put you through. It's a terrible place, sir, but our authorities never look into it, and few of our people know of its existence."

Mr. Snivel thanks the vote-cribber, who pledges his honor he would accompany him, but for the reason that he opens crib to-morrow, and has in his eye a dozen voters he intends to look up. He has also a few recently-arrived sons of the Emerald Isle he purposes turning into citizens.

CHAPTER XXII
MRS. SWIGGS FALLS UPON A MODERN HEATHEN WORLD

Purged of all the ill-humors of her mind, Mrs. Swiggs finds herself, on the morning following the excellent little gathering at Sister Scudder's, restored to the happiest of tempers. The flattery administered by Brother Spyke, and so charmingly sprinkled with his pious designs on the heathen world, has had the desired effect. This sort of drug has, indeed, a wonderful efficacy in setting disordered constitutions to rights. It would not become us to question the innocence, or the right to indulge in such correctives; it is enough that our venerable friend finds herself in a happy vein, and is resolved to spend the day for the benefit of that heathen world, the darkness of which Brother Spyke pictured in colors so terrible.

Breakfast is scarcely over when Sister Slocum, in great agitation, comes bustling into the parlor, offers the most acceptable apologies for her absence, and pours forth such a vast profusion of solicitude for Mrs. Swiggs' welfare, that that lady is scarce able to withstand the kindness. She recounts the numerous duties that absorb her attention, the missions she has on hand, the means she uses to keep up an interest in them, the amount of funds necessary to their maintenance. A large portion of these funds she raises with her own energy. She will drag up the heathen world; she will drag down Satan. Furnishing Mrs. Swiggs with the address of the House of the Foreign Missions, in Centre street, she excuses herself. How superlatively happy she would be to accompany Mrs. Swiggs. A report to present to the committee on finance, she regrets, will prevent this. However, she will join her precisely at twelve o'clock, at the House. She must receive the congratulations of the Board. She must have a reception that will show how much the North respects her co-laborers of the South. And with this, Sister Slocum takes leave of her guest, assuring her that all she has to do is to get into the cars in the Bowery. They will set her down at the door.

Ten o'clock finds our indomitable lady, having preferred the less expensive mode of walking, entering a strange world. Sauntering along the Bowery she turns down Bayard street. Bayard street she finds lined with filthy looking houses, swarming with sickly, ragged, and besotted poor; the street is knee-deep with corrupting mire; carts are tilted here and there at intervals; the very air seems hurling its pestilence into your blood. Ghastly-eyed and squalid children, like ants in quest of food, creep and swarm over the pavement, begging for bread or uttering profane oaths at one another. Mothers who never heard the Word of God, nor can be expected to teach it to their children, protrude their vicious faces from out reeking gin shops, and with bare breasts and uncombed hair, sweep wildly along the muddy pavement, disappear into some cavern-like cellar, and seek on some filthy straw a resting place for their wasting bodies. A whiskey-drinking Corporation might feast its peculative eyes upon hogs wallowing in mud; and cellars where swarming beggars, for six cents a night, cover with rags their hideous heads—where vice and crime are fostered, and into which your sensitive policeman prefers not to go, are giving out their seething miasma. The very neighborhood seems vegetating in mire. In the streets, in the cellars, in the filthy lanes, in the dwellings of the honest poor, as well as the vicious, muck and mire is the predominating order. The besotted remnants of depraved men, covered with rags and bedaubed with mire, sit, half sleeping in disease and hunger on decayed door-stoops. Men with bruised faces, men with bleared eyes, men in whose every feature crime and dissipation is stamped, now drag their waning bodies from out filthy alleys, as if to gasp some breath of air, then drag themselves back, as if to die in a desolate hiding-place. Engines of pestilence and death the corporation might see and remove, if it would, are left here to fester—to serve a church-yard as gluttonous as its own belly. The corporation keeps its eyes in its belly, its little sense in its big boots, and its dull action in the whiskey-jug. Like Mrs. Swiggs, it cannot afford to do anything for this heathen world in the heart of home. No, sir! The corporation has the most delicate sense of its duties. It is well paid to nurture the nucleus of a pestilence that may some day break out and sweep over the city like an avenging enemy. It thanks kind Providence, eating oysters and making Presidents the while, for averting the dire scourge it encourages with its apathy. Like our humane and very fashionable preachers, it contents itself with looking into the Points from Broadway. What more would you ask of it?

Mrs. Swiggs is seized with fear and trembling. Surely she is in a world of darkness. Can it be that so graphically described by Brother Syngleton Spyke? she questions within herself. It might, indeed, put Antioch to shame: but the benighted denizens with which it swarms speak her own tongue. "It is a deal worse in Orange street,[3] Marm—a deal, I assure you!" speaks a low, muttering voice. Lady Swiggs is startled. She only paused a moment to view this sea of vice and wretchedness she finds herself surrounded with.

Turning quickly round she sees before her a man, or what there is left of a man. His tattered garments, his lean, shrunken figure, his glassy eyes, and pale, haggard face, cause her to shrink back in fright. He bows, touches his shattered hat, and says, "Be not afraid good Madam. May I ask if you have not mistaken your way?" Mrs. Swiggs looks querulously through her spectacles and says, "Do tell me where I am?" "In the Points, good Madam. You seem confused, and I don't wonder. It's a dreadful place. I know it, madam, to my sorrow." There is a certain politeness in the manner of this man—an absence of rudeness she is surprised to find in one so dejected. The red, distended nose, the wild expression of his countenance, his jagged hair, hanging in tufts over his ragged coat collar, give him a repulsiveness not easily described. In answer to an inquiry he says, "They call me, Madam, and I'm contented with the name,—they call me Tom Toddleworth, the Chronicle. I am well down—not in years, but sorrow. Being sick of the world I came here, have lived, or rather drifted about, in this sea of hopeless misery, homeless and at times foodless, for ten years or more. Oh! I have seen better days, Madam. You are a stranger here. May God always keep you a stranger to the sufferings of those who dwell with us. I never expect to be anything again, owe nothing to the world, and never go into Broadway."

"Never go into Broadway," repeats Mrs. Swiggs, her fingers wandering to her spectacles. Turning into Orange street, Mr. Toddleworth tenders his services in piloting Mrs. Swiggs into Centre street, which, as he adds, will place her beyond harm. As they advance the scene becomes darker and darker. Orange street seems that centre from which radiates the avenues of every vice known to a great city. One might fancy the world's outcasts hurled by some mysterious hand into this pool of crime and misery, and left to feast their wanton appetites and die. "And you have no home, my man?" says Mrs. Swiggs, mechanically. "As to that, Madam," returns the man, with a bow, "I can't exactly say I have no home. I kind of preside over and am looked up to by these people. One says, 'come spend a night with me, Mr. Toddleworth,' another says, 'come spend a night with me, Mr. Tom Toddleworth.' I am a sort of respectable man with them, have a place to lay down free, in any of their houses. They all esteem me, and say, come spend a night with me, Mr. Toddleworth. It's very kind of them. And whenever they get a drop of gin I'm sure of a taste. Surmising what I was once, they look up to me, you see. This gives me heart." And as he says this he smiles, and draws about him the ragged remnants of his coat, as if touched by shame. Arrived at the corner of Orange street, Mr. Toddleworth pauses and begs his charge to survey the prospect. Look whither she will nothing but a scene of desolation—a Babylon of hideous, wasting forms, mucky streets, and reeking dens, meet her eye. The Jews have arranged themselves on one side of Orange street, to speculate on the wasted harlotry of the other. "Look you, Madam!" says Mr. Toddleworth, leaning on his stick and pointing towards Chatham street. "A desert, truly," replies the august old lady, nervously twitching her head. She sees to the right ("it is wantonness warring upon misery," says Mr. Toddleworth) a long line of irregular, wooden buildings, black and besmeared with mud. Little houses with decrepit doorsteps; little houses with decayed platforms in front; little dens that seem crammed with rubbish; little houses with black-eyed, curly-haired, and crooked-nosed children looking shyly about the doors; little houses with lusty and lecherous-eyed Jewesses sitting saucily in the open door; little houses with open doors, broken windows, and shattered shutters, where the devil's elixir is being served to ragged and besotted denizens; little houses into which women with blotched faces slip suspiciously, deposit their almost worthless rags, and pass out to seek the gin-shop; little houses with eagle-faced men peering curiously out at broken windows, or beckoning some wayfarer to enter and buy from their door; little houses piled inside with the cast-off garments of the poor and dissolute, and hung outside with smashed bonnets, old gowns, tattered shawls; flaunting—red, blue, and yellow, in the wind, emblematic of those poor wretches, on the opposite side, who have pledged here their last offerings, and blazed down into that stage of human degradation, which finds the next step the grave— all range along, forming a picturesque but sad panorama. Mr. Moses, the man of the eagle face, who keeps the record of death, as the neighbors call it, sits opulently in his door, and smokes his cigar; while his sharp-eyed daughters estimate exactly how much it is safe to advance on the last rag some lean wretch would pledge. He will tell you just how long that brawny harlot, passing on the opposite side, will last, and what the few rags on her back will be worth when she is "shoved into Potters' Field." At the sign of the "Three Martyrs" Mr. Levy is seen, in his fashionable coat, and a massive chain falling over his tight waistcoat, registering the names of his grotesque customers, ticketing their little packages, and advancing each a shilling or two, which they will soon spend at the opposite druggery. Thus bravely wages the war. London has nothing so besotted, Paris nothing so vicious, Naples nothing so dark and despairing, as this heathen world we pass by so heedlessly. Beside it even the purlieus of Rome sink into insignificance. Now run your eye along the East side of Orange street. A sidewalk sinking in mire; a long line of one-story wooden shanties, ready to cave-in with decay; dismal looking groceries, in which the god, gin, is sending his victims by hundreds to the greedy graveyard; suspicious looking dens with dingy fronts, open doors, and windows stuffed with filthy rags—in which crimes are nightly perpetrated, and where broken-hearted victims of seduction and neglect, seeking here a last refuge, are held in a slavery delicacy forbids our describing; dens where negro dancers nightly revel, and make the very air re-echo their profaning voices; filthy lanes leading to haunts up alleys and in narrow passages, where thieves and burglars hide their vicious heads; mysterious looking steps leading to cavern-like cellars, where swarm and lay prostrate wretched beings made drunk by the "devil's elixir"—all these beset the East side of Orange street. Wasted nature, blanched and despairing, ferments here into one terrible pool. Women in gaudy-colored dresses, their bared breasts and brawny arms contrasting curiously with their wicked faces, hang lasciviously over "half-doors," taunt the dreamy policeman on his round, and beckon the unwary stranger into their dens. Piles of filth one might imagine had been thrown up by the devil or the street commissioner, and in which you might bury a dozen fat aldermen without missing one; little shops where unwholesome food is sold; corner shops where idlers of every color, and sharpers of all grades, sit dreaming out the day over their gin—are here to be found. Young Ireland would, indeed, seem to have made this the citadel from which to vomit his vice over the city.

"They're perfectly wild, Madam—these children are," says Mr. Toddleworth, in reply to a question Mrs. Swiggs put respecting the immense number of ragged and profaning urchins that swarm the streets. "They never heard of the Bible, nor God, nor that sort of thing. How could they hear of it? No one ever comes in here—that is, they come in now and then, and throw a bit of a tract in here and there, and are glad to get out with a whole coat. The tracts are all Greek to the dwellers here. Besides that, you see, something must be done for the belly, before you can patch up the head. I say this with a fruitful experience. A good, kind little man, who seems earnest in the welfare of these wild little children that you see running about here—not the half of them know their parents—looks in now and then, acts as if he wasn't afraid of us, (that is a good deal, Madam) and the boys are beginning to take to him. But, with nothing but his kind heart and earnest resolution, he'll find a rugged mountain to move. If he move it, he will deserve a monument of fairest marble erected to his memory, and letters of gold to emblazon his deeds thereon. He seems to understand the key to some of their affections. It's no use mending the sails without making safe the hull."

At this moment Mrs. Swiggs' attention is attracted by a crowd of ragged urchins and grotesque-looking men, gathered about a heap of filth at that corner of Orange street that opens into the Points.

"They are disinterring his Honor, the Mayor," says Mr. Toddleworth. "Do this sort of thing every day, Madam; they mean no harm, you see."

Mrs. Swiggs, curious to witness the process of disinterring so distinguished a person, forgets entirely her appointment at the House of the Foreign Missions, crowds her way into the filthy throng, and watches with intense anxiety a vacant-looking idiot, who has seen some sixteen summers, lean and half clad, and who has dug with his staff a hole deep in the mud, which he is busy piling up at the edges.

"Deeper, deeper!" cries out a dozen voices, of as many mischievous urchins, who are gathered round in a ring, making him the victim of their sport. Having cast his glassy eyes upward, and scanned vacantly his audience, he sets to work again, and continues throwing out dead cats by the dozen, all of which he exults over, and pauses now and then for the approbation of the bystanders, who declare they bear no resemblance to his Honor, or any one of the Board of Aldermen. One chubby urchin, with a bundle of *Tribunes* under his arm, looks mischievously into the pit, and says, "His 'Onor 'ill want the *Tribune*." Another, of a more taciturn disposition, shrugs his shoulders, gives his cap a pull over his eyes, and says, spicing his declaration with an oath, "He'll buy two *Heralds!* —he will." The taciturn urchin draws them from his bundle with an air of independence, flaunts them in the face of his rival, and exults over their merits. A splashing of mud, followed by a deafening shout, announces that the persevering idiot has come upon the object he seeks. One proclaims to his motley neighbors that the whole corporation is come to light; another swears it is only his Honor and a dead Alderman. A third, more astute than the rest, says it is only the head and body of the Corporation—a dead pig and a decaying pumpkin! Shout after shout goes up as the idiot, exultingly, drags out the prostrate pig, following it with the pumpkin. Mr. Toddleworth beckons Lady Swiggs away. The wicked-faced harlots are gathering about her in scores. One has just been seen fingering her dress, and hurrying away, disappearing suspiciously into an Alley.

"You see, Madam," says Mr. Toddleworth, as they gain the vicinity of Cow Bay, "it is currently reported, and believed by the dwellers here, that our Corporation ate itself out of the world not long since; and seeing how much they suffer by the loss of such—to have a dead Corporation in a great city, is an evil, I assure you—an institution, they adopt this method of finding it. It affords them no little amusement. These swarming urchins will have the filthy things laid out in state, holding with due ceremony an inquest over them, and mischievously proposing to the first policeman who chances along, that he officiate as coroner. Lady Swiggs has not a doubt that light might be valuably reflected over this heathen world. Like many other very excellent ladies, however, she has no candles for a heathen world outside of Antioch."

Mr. Toddleworth escorts her safely into Centre street, and directs her to the House of the Foreign Missions.

"Thank you! thank you!—may God never let you want a shilling," he says, bowing and touching his hat as Mrs. Swiggs puts four shillings into his left hand.

"One shilling, Madam," he pursues, with a smile, "will get me a new collar. A clean collar now and then, it must be said, gives a body a look of respectability."

Mr. Toddleworth has a passion for new collars, regards them as a means of sustaining his respectability. Indeed, he considers himself in full dress with one mounted, no matter how ragged the rest of his wardrobe. And when he walks out of a morning, thus conditioned, his friends greet him with: "Hi! ho! Mister Toddleworth is uppish this morning." He has bid his charge good morning, and hurries back to his wonted haunts. There is a mysterious and melancholy interest in this man's history, which many have attempted but failed to fathom. He was once heard to say his name was not Toddleworth—that he had sunk his right name in his sorrows. He was sentimental at times, always used good language, and spoke like one who had seen better days and enjoyed a superior education. He wanted, he would say, when in one of his melancholy moods, to forget the world, and have the world forget him. Thus he shut himself up in the Points, and only once or twice had he been seen in the Bowery, and never in Broadway during his sojourn among the denizens who swarm that vortex of death. How he managed to obtain funds, for he was never without a shilling, was equally involved in mystery. He had no very bad habits, seemed inoffensive to all he approached, spoke familiarly on past events, and national affairs, and discovered a general knowledge of the history of the world. And while he was always ready to share his shilling with his more destitute associates, he ever maintained a degree of politeness and civility toward those he was cast among not common to the place. He was ready to serve every one, would seek out the sick and watch over them with a kindness almost paternal, discovering a singular familiarity with the duties of a physician. He had, however, an inveterate hatred of fashionable wives; and whenever the subject was brought up, which it frequently was by the denizens of the Points, he would walk away, with a sigh. "Fashionable wives," he would mutter, his eyes filling with tears, "are never constant. Ah! they have deluged the world with sorrow, and sent me here to seek a hiding place."

CHAPTER XXIII
IN WHICH THE VERY BEST INTENTIONS ARE SEEN TO FAIL

The city clock strikes one as Mrs. Swiggs, nervous and weary, enters the House of the Foreign Missions. Into a comfortably-furnished room on the right, she is ushered by a man meekly dressed, and whose countenance wears an expression of melancholy. Maps and drawings of Palestine, Hindostan, and sundry other fields of missionary labor, hang here and there upon the walls. These are alternated with nicely-framed engravings and lithographs of Mission establishments in the East, all located in some pretty grove, and invested with a warmth and cheerfulness that cannot fail to make a few years' residence in them rather desirable than otherwise. These in turn are relieved with portraits of distinguished missionaries. Earnest-faced busts, in plaster, stand prominently about the room, periodicals and papers are piled on little shelves, and bright bookcases are filled with reports and various documents concerning the society, all bound so exactly. The good-natured man of the kind face sits in refreshing ease behind a little desk; the wise-looking lean man, in the spectacles, is just in front of him, buried in ponderous folios of reports. In the centre of the room stands a highly-polished mahogany table, at which Brother Spyke is seated, his elbow rested, and his head leaning thoughtfully in his hand. The rotund figure and energetic face of Sister Slocum is seen, whisking about conspicuously among a bevy of sleek but rather lean gentlemen, studious of countenance, and in modest cloth. For each she has something cheerful to impart; each in his turn has some compliment to bestow upon her. Several nicely-dressed, but rather meek-looking ladies, two or three accompanied by their knitting work, have arranged themselves on a settee in front of the wise man in the spectacles.

Scarcely has the representative of our chivalry entered the room when Sister Slocum, with all the ardor of a lover of seventeen, runs to her with open arms, embraces her, and kisses her with an affection truly grateful. Choking to relate her curious adventure, she is suddenly heaped with adulations, told how the time of her coming was looked to, as an event of no common occurrence—how Brothers Sharp, Spyke, and Phills, expressed apprehensions for her safety this morning, each in turn offering in the kindest manner to get a carriage and go in pursuit. The good-natured fat man gets down from his high seat, and receives her with pious congratulations; the man in the spectacles looks askant, and advances with extended hand. To use a convenient phrase, she is received with open arms; and so meek and good is the aspect, that she finds her thoughts transported to an higher, a region where only is bliss. Provided with a seat in a conspicuous place, she is told to consider herself the guest of the society. Sundry ovations, Sister Slocum gives her to understand, will be made in her honor, ere long. The fact must here be disclosed that Sister Slocum had prepared the minds of those present for the reception of an embodiment of perfect generosity.

No sooner has Lady Swiggs time to breathe freely, than she changes the wondrous kind aspect of the assembly, and sends it into a paroxysm of fright, by relating her curious adventure among the denizens of the Points. Brother Spyke nearly makes up his mind to faint; the good-natured fat man turns pale; the wise man in the spectacles is seen to tremble; the neatly-attired females, so pious-demeanored, express their horror of such a place; and Sister Slocum stands aghast. "Oh! dear, Sister Swiggs," she says, "your escape from such a vile place is truly marvellous! Thank God you are with us once more." The good-natured fat man says, "A horrible world, truly!" and sighs. Brother Spyke shrugs his shoulders, adding, "No respectable person here ever thinks of going into such a place; the people there are so corrupt." Brother Sharp says he shudders at the very thought of such a place. He has heard much said of the dark deeds nightly committed in it—of the stubborn vileness of the dwellers therein. God knows he never wants to descend into it. "Truly," Brother Phills interposes, "I walked through it once, and beheld with mine eyes such sights, such human deformity! O, God! Since then, I am content to go to my home through Broadway. I never forget to shudder when I look into the vile place from a distance, nevertheless." Brother Phills says this after the manner of a philosopher, fretting his fingers, and contorting his comely face the while. Sister Slocum, having recovered somewhat from the shock (the shock had no permanent effect on any of them), hopes Sister Swiggs did not lend an ear to their false pleadings, nor distribute charity among the vile wretches. "Such would be like scattering chaff to the winds," a dozen voices chime in. "Indeed!" Lady Swiggs ejaculates, giving her head a toss, in token of her satisfaction, "not a shilling, except to the miserable wretch who showed me the way out. And he seemed harmless enough. I never met a more melancholy object, never!" Brother Spyke raises his eyes imploringly, and says he harbors no ill-will against these vile people, but melancholy is an art with them—they make it a study. They affect it while picking one's pocket.

The body now resolves itself into working order. Brother Spyke offers up a prayer. He thanks kind Providence for the happy escape of Sister Swiggs—this generous woman whose kindness of heart has brought her here—from among the hardened wretches who inhabit that slough of despair, so terrible in all its aspects, and so disgraceful to a great and prosperous city. He thanks Him who blessed him with the light of learning—who endowed him with vigor and resolution—and told him to go forth in armor, beating down Satan, and raising up the heathen world. A mustering of spectacles follows. Sister Slocum draws from her bosom a copy of the report the wise man in the spectacles rises to read. A fashionable gold chain and gold-framed eye-glass is called to her aid; and with a massive pencil of gold, she dots and points certain items of dollars and cents her keen eye rests upon every now and then.

The wise man in the spectacles rises, having exchanged glances with Sister Slocum, and commences reading a very long, and in nowise lean report. The anxious gentlemen draw up their chairs, and turn attentive ears. For nearly an hour, he buzzes and bores the contents of this report into their ears, takes sundry sips of water, and informs those present, and the world in general, that nearly forty thousand dollars have recently been consumed for missionary labor. The school at Corsica, the missions at Canton, Ningpo, Pu-kong, Cassaba, Abheokuta, and sundry other places, the names of which could not, by any possibility, aid the reader in discovering their location—all, were doing as well as could be expected, *under the circumstances*. After many years labor, and a considerable expenditure of money, they were encouraged to go forward, inasmuch as the children of the school at Corsica were beginning to learn to read. At Casaba, Droneyo, the native scholar, had, after many years' teaching, been made conscious of the sin of idol-worship, and had given his solemn promise to relinquish it as soon as he could propitiate two favorite gods bequeathed to him by his great uncle. The furnace of "Satanic cruelty" had been broken down at Dahomey. Brother Smash had, after several years' labor, and much expense—after having broken down his health, and the health of many others—penetrated the dark regions of Arabia, and there found the very seat of Satanic power. It was firmly pegged to Paganism and Mahomedan darkness! This news the world was expected to hail with consternation. Not one word is lisped about that terrible devil holding his court of beggary and crime in the Points. He had all his furnaces in full blast there; his victims were legion! No Brother Spyke is found to venture in and drag him down. The region of the Seven Churches offers inducements more congenial. Bound about them all is shady groves, gentle breezes, and rural habitations; in the Points the very air is thick with pestilence!

A pause follows the reading. The wise man in the spectacles—his voice soft and persuasive, and his aspect meekness itself—would like to know if any one present be inclined to offer a remark. General satisfaction prevails. Brother Sharp moves, and Brother Phills seconds, that the report be accepted. The report is accepted without a dissenting voice. A second paper is handed him by Sister Slocum, whose countenance is seen to flash bright with smiles. Then there follows the proclaiming of the fact of funds, to the amount of three thousand six hundred dollars, having been subscribed, and now ready to be appropriated to getting Brother Syngleton Spyke off to Antioch. A din of satisfaction follows; every face is radiant with joy. Sister Swiggs twitches her head, begins to finger her pocket, and finally readjusts her spectacles. Having worked her countenance into a good staring condition, she sets her eyes fixedly upon Brother Spyke, who rises, saying he has a few words to offer.

The object of his mission to Antioch, so important at this moment, he would not have misunderstood. Turks, Greeks, Jews, Arabs, Armenians, and Kurds, and Yesedees—yes, brethren, Yesedees! inhabit this part of Assyria, which opens up an extensive field of missionary labor, even yet. Much had been done by the ancient Greeks for the people who roamed in these Eastern wilds—much remained for us to do; for it was yet a dark spot on the missionary map. Thousands of these poor souls were without the saving knowledge of the Gospel. He could not shrink from a duty so demanding—wringing his very heart with its pleadings! Giving the light of the Gospel to these vicious Arabs and Kurds was the end and aim of his mission. (A motion of satisfaction was here perceptible.) And while there, he would teach the Jews a just sense of their Lord's design—which was the subjugation of the heathen world. Inward light was very good, old prophecies were very grand; but Judaism was made of stubborn metal, had no missionary element in it, and could only be forced to accept light through strong and energetic movement. He had read with throbbing heart how Rome, while in her greatness, protected those Christian pilgrims who went forth into the East, to do battle with the enemy. Would not America imitate Rome, that mighty mother of Republics? A deeper responsibility rested on her at this moment. Rome, then, was semi-barbarous; America, now, was Christianized and civilized. Hence she would be held more accountable for the dissemination of light.

In those days the wandering Christian Jews undertook to instruct the polished Greeks—why could not Americans at this day inculcate the doctrines of Jesus to these educated heathen? It was a bold and daring experiment, but he was willing to try it. The Allwise worked his wonders in a mysterious way. In this irrelevant and somewhat mystical style, Brother

Spyke continues nearly an hour, sending his audience into a highly-edified state. We have said mystical, for, indeed, none but those in the secret could have divined, from Brother Spyke's logic, what was the precise nature of his mission. His speech was very like a country parson's model sermon; one text was selected, and a dozen or more (all different) preached from; while fifty things were said no one could understand.

Brother Spyke sits down—Sister Slocum rises. "Our dear and very generous guest now present," she says, addressing the good-natured fat man in the chair, as Lady Swiggs bows, "moved by the goodness that is in her, and conscious of the terrible condition of the heathen world, has come nobly to our aid. Like a true Christian she has crossed the sea, and is here. Not only is she here, but ready to give her mite toward getting Brother Spyke off to Antioch. Another donation she proposes giving the 'Tract Society,' an excellent institution, in high favor at the South. Indeed I may add, that it never has offended against its social—"

Sister Slocum hesitates. Social slavery will not sound just right, she says to her herself. She must have a term more musical, and less grating to the ear. A smile flashes across her countenance, her gold-framed eye-glasses vibrate in her fingers: "Well! I was going to say, their social arrangements," she pursues.

The assembly is suddenly thrown into a fit of excitement. Lady Swiggs is seen trembling from head to foot, her yellow complexion changing to pale white, her features contorting as with pain, and her hand clutching at her pocket. "O heavens!" she sighs, "all is gone, gone, gone: how vain and uncertain are the things here below." She drops, fainting, into the arms of Sister Slocum, who has overset the wise man in the spectacles, in her haste to catch the prostrate form. On a bench the august body is laid. Fans, water, camphor, hartshorn, and numerous other restoratives are brought into use. Persons get in each other's way, run every way but the right way, causing, as is common in such cases, very unnecessary alarm. The stately representative of the great Swiggs family lies motionless. Like the last of our chivalry, she has nothing left her but a name.

A dash or two of cold water, and the application of a little hartshorn, and that sympathy so necessary to the fainting of distinguished people— proves all-efficient. A slight heaving of the bosom is detected, the hands— they have been well chaffed—quiver and move slowly, her face resumes its color. She opens her eyes, lays her hand solicitously on Sister Slocum's arm: "It must be the will of Heaven," she lisps, motioning her head, regretfully; "it cannot now be undone—"

"Sister! sister! sister!" interrupts Sister Slocum, grasping her hand, and looking inquiringly in the face of the recovering woman, "is it an affection of the heart?—where is the pain?—what has befallen you? We are all so sorry!"

"It was there, there, there! But it is gone now." Regaining her consciousness, she lays her hand nervously upon her pocket, and pursues: "Oh! yes, sister, it was there when I entered that vile place, as you call it. What am I to do? The loss of the money does not so much trouble my mind. Oh! dear, no. It is the thought of going home deprived of the means of aiding these noble institutions."

Had Lady Swiggs inquired into the character of the purchaser of old Dolly she might now have become conscious of the fact, that whatever comes of evil seldom does good. The money she had so struggled to get together to aid her in maintaining her hypocrisy, was the result of crime. Perhaps it were better the wretch purloined it, than that the fair name of a noble institution be stained with its acceptance. Atonement is too often sought to be purchased with the gold got of infamy.

The cause of this fainting being traced to Lady Swiggs' pocket book instead of her heart, the whole scene changes. Sister Slocum becomes as one dumb, the good fat man is seized with a nervous fit, the man in the spectacles hangs his head, and runs his fingers through his crispy hair, as Brother Spyke elongates his lean body, and is seen going into a melancholy mood, the others gathering round with serious faces. Lady Swiggs commences describing with great minuteness the appearance of Mr. Tom Toddleworth. That he is the person who carried off the money, every one is certain. "He is the man!" responds a dozen voices. And as many more volunteer to go in search of Mr. Detective Fitzgerald. Brother Spyke pricks up his courage, and proceeds to initiate his missionary labors by consulting Mr. Detective Fitzgerald, with whom he starts off in pursuit of Mr. Tom Toddleworth.

CHAPTER XXIV
MR. SNIVEL ADVISES GEORGE MULLHOLLAND HOW TO MAKE STRONG LOVE

Let us leave for a time the pursuit with which we concluded the foregoing chapter, and return to Charleston. It is the still hour of midnight. There has been a ball at the fashionable house of the Flamingo, which still retains its name. In the great parlour we have before described, standing here and there upon massive tables with Egyptian marble-tops, are half-empty bottles of wine, decanters, tumblers, and viands of various descriptions. Bits of artificial flowers are strewn about the carpet, a shawl is seen thrown over one chair, a mantle over another; the light is half shut off—everything bears evidence of the gaieties of luxurious life, the sumptuous revel and the debauch. The gilded mirrors reflect but two faces, both hectic and moody of dissipation. George Mullholland and Mr. Snivel face each other, at a pier-table. Before them are several half filled bottles, from one of which Mr. Snivel fills George's glass.

"There is something in this champaign (one only gets rubbish in these houses) that compounds and elevates one's ideas," says Mr. Snivel, holding his glass in the light, and squinting his blood-shotten eyes, the lids of which he has scarce power to keep open. "Drink, George—drink! You have had your day—why let such nonsense trouble you? The whole city is in love with the girl. Her beauty makes her capricious; if the old Judge has got her, let him keep her. Indeed, I'm not so sure that she doesn't love him, and (well, I always laugh when I think of it), it is a well laid down principle among us lawyers, that no law stands good against love." Mr. Snivel's leaden eyelids close, and his head drops upon his bosom. "She never can love him—never! His wealth, and some false tale, has beguiled her. He is a hoary-headed lecher, with wealth and position to aid him in his hellish pursuits; I am poor, and an outcast! He has flattered me and showered his favors upon me, only to affect my ruin. I will have—"

"Pshaw! George," interrupts Mr. Snivel, brightening up, "be a philosopher. Chivalry, you know—chivalry! A dashing fellow like you should doff the kid to a knight of his metal: challenge him." Mr. Snivel reaches over the table and pats his opponent on the arm. "These women, George! Funny things, eh? Make any kind of love—have a sample for every sort of gallant, and can make the quantity to suit the purchaser. 'Pon my soul this is my opinion. I'm a lawyer, know pretty well how the sex lay their points. As for these unfortunate devils, as we of the profession call them (he pauses and empties his glass, saying, not bad for a house of this kind), there are so many shades of them, life is such a struggle with them; they dream of broken hopes, and they die sighing to think how good a thing is virtue. You only love this girl because she is beautiful, and beautiful women, at best, are the most capricious things in the world. D—n it, you have gone through enough of this kind of life to be accustomed to it. We think nothing of these things, in Charleston—bless you, nothing! Keep the Judge your friend—his position may give him a means to serve you. A man of the world ought at all times to have the private friendship of as many judges as he can."

"Never! poor as I am—outcast as I feel myself! I want no such friendship. Society may shun me, the community may fear me, necessity may crush me—yea! you may regard me as a villain if you will, but, were I a judge, I would scorn to use my office to serve base ends." As he says this he draws a pistol from his pocket, and throwing it defiantly upon the table, continues as his lip curls with scorn, "poor men's lives are cheap in Charleston—let us see what rich men's are worth!"

"His age, George!—you should respect that!" says Mr. Snivel, laconically.

"His age ought to be my protection."

"Ah!—you forget that the follies of our nature too often go with us to the grave."

"And am I to suffer because public opinion honors him, and gives him power to disgrace me? Can he rob me of the one I love—of the one in whose welfare my whole soul is staked, and do it with impunity?"

"D——d inconvenient, I know, George. Sympathize with you, I do. But, you see, we are governed here by the laws of chivalry. Don't let your (I am a piece of a philosopher, you see) temper get up, keep on a stiff upper lip. You may catch him napping. I respect your feelings, my dear fellow; ready to do you a bit of a good turn—you understand! Now let me tell you, my boy, he has made her his adopted, and to-morrow she moves with him to his quiet little villa near the Magnolia."

"I am a poor, forlorn wretch," interrupts George, with a sigh. "Those of whom I had a right to expect good counsel, and a helping hand, have been first to encourage me in the ways of evil—"

"Get money, Mullholland—get money. It takes money to make love strong. Say what you will, a woman's heart is sure to be sound on the gold question. Mark ye, Mullholland!—there is an easy way to get money. Do you take? (His fingers wander over his forehead, as he watches intently in George's face.) You can make names? Such things are done by men in higher walks, you know. Quite a common affair in these parts. The Judge has carried off your property; make a fair exchange—you can use his name, get money with it, and make it hold fast the woman you love. There are three things, George, you may set down as facts that will be of service to you through life, and they are these: when a man eternally rings in your ears the immoralities of the age, watch him closely; when a man makes what he has done for others a boast, set him down a knave; and when a woman dwells upon the excellent qualities of her many admirers, set her down as wanting. But, get money, and when you have got it, charm back this beautiful creature."

Such is the advice of Mr. Soloman Snivel, the paid intriguer of the venerable Judge.

CHAPTER XXV
A SLIGHT CHANGE IN THE PICTURE

The two lone revellers remain at the pier-table, moody and hectic. Mr. Snivel drops into a sound sleep, his head resting on the marble. Weak-minded, jealous, contentious—with all the attendants natural to one who leads an unsettled life, sits George Mullholland, his elbow resting on the table, and his head poised thoughtfully in his hand. "I will have revenge—sweet revenge; yes, I will have revenge to-night!" he mutters, and sets his teeth firmly.

In Anna's chamber all is hushed into stillness. The silvery moonbeams play softly through the half-closed windows, lighting up and giving an air of enchantment to the scene. Curtains hang, mist-like, from massive cornices in gilt. Satin drapery, mysteriously underlaid with lace, and floating in bewitching chasteness over a fairy-like bed, makes more voluptuous that ravishing form calmly sleeping—half revealed among the snowy sheets, and forming a picture before which fancy soars, passion unbends itself, and sentiment is led away captive. With such exquisite forms strange nature excites our love;—that love that like a little stream meanders capriciously through our feelings, refreshing life, purifying our thoughts, exciting our ambition, and modulating our actions. That love, too, like a quicksand, too often proves a destroyer to the weak-minded.

Costly chairs, of various styles carved in black walnut, stand around the chamber: lounges covered with chastely-designed tapestry are seen half concealed by the gorgeous window curtains. The foot falls upon a soft, Turkey carpet; the ceiling—in French white, and gilt mouldings—is set off with two Cupids in a circle, frescoed by a skilled hand. On a lounge, concealed in an alcove masked by curtains pending from the hands of a fairy in bronze, and nearly opposite Anna's bed, the old Judge sleeps in his judicial dignity. To-day he sentenced three rogues to the whipping-post, and two wretched negroes—one for raising his hand to a white man—to the gallows.

Calmly Anna continues to sleep, the lights in the girandoles shedding a mysterious paleness over the scene. To the eye that scans only the exterior of life, how dazzling! Like a refulgent cloud swelling golden in the evening sky, how soon it passes away into darkness and disappointment! Suddenly there appears, like a vision in the chamber, the stately figure of a female. Advancing slowly to the bed-side, for a minute she stands contemplating the sleeping beauty before her. A dark, languishing eye, an aquiline nose, beautifully-cut mouth, and a finely-oval face, is revealed by the shadow in which she stands. "How willingly," she mutters, raising the jewelled fingers of her right hand to her lips, as her eyes become liquid with emotion, and her every action betokens one whose very soul is goaded with remorse, "would I exchange all these worldly pleasures for one single day in peace of mind." She lays aside her mantle, and keeps her eyes fixed upon the object before her. A finely-rounded shoulder and exactly-developed bust is set off with a light satin bodice or corsage, cut low, opening shawl-fashion at the breast, and relieved with a stomacher of fine Brussels lace. Down the edges are rows of small, unpolished pearls, running into points. A skirt of orange-colored brocade, trimmed with tulle, and surrounded with three flounces, falls, cloud-like, from her girdle, which is set with cameos and unpolished pearls. With her left hand she raises slightly her skirts, revealing the embroidered gimps of a white taffeta underskirt, flashing in the moonlight. Small, unpolished pearls ornament the bands of her short sleeves; on her fingers are rings, set with diamonds and costly emeralds; and her wrists are clasped with bracelets of diamonds, shedding a modest lustre over her marble-like arms.

"Can this be my child? Has this crime that so like a demon haunts me— that curses me even in my dreams, driven her, perhaps against her will, to seek this life of shame?" She takes the sleeper's hand gently in her own, as the tears gush down her cheeks.

The sleeper startles, half raises herself from her pillow, parts her black, silky hair, that lays upon her gently-swelling bosom, and throws it carelessly down her shoulders, wildly setting her great black orbs on the strange figure before her. "Hush, hush!" says the speaker, "I am a friend. One who seeks you for a good purpose. Give me your confidence—do not betray me! I need not tell you by what means I gained access to you."

A glow of sadness flashes across Anna's countenance. With a look of suspicion she scans the mysterious figure from head to foot. "It is the Judge's wife!" she says within herself. "Some one has betrayed me to her; and, as is too often the case, she seeks revenge of the less guilty party." But the figure before her is in full dress, and one seeking revenge would have disguised herself. "Why, and who is it, that seeks me in this mysterious manner?"

whispers Anna, holding her delicate hand in the shadow, over her eyes. "I seek you in the hope of finding something to relieve my troubled spirit, I am a mother who has wronged her child—I have no peace of mind—my heart is lacerated—"

"Are you, then, my mother?" interrupts Anna, with a look of scorn.

"That I would answer if I could. You have occupied my thoughts day and night. I have traced your history up to a certain period. ("What I know of my own, I would fain not contemplate," interrupts Anna.) Beyond that, all is darkness. And yet there are circumstances that go far to prove you the child I seek. Last night I dreamed I saw a gate leading to a dungeon, that into the dungeon I was impelled against my will. While there I was haunted with the figure of a woman of the name of Mag Munday—a maniac, and in chains! My heart bled at the sight, for she, I thought, was the woman in whose charge I left the child I seek. I spoke—I asked her what had become of the child! She pointed with her finger, told me to go seek you here, and vanished as I awoke. I spent the day in unrest, went to the ball to-night, but found no pleasure in its gay circle. Goaded in my conscience, I left the ball-room, and with the aid of a confidant am here."

"I recognize—yes, my lady, I recognize you! You think me your abandoned child, and yet you are too much the slave of society to seek me as a mother ought to do. I am the supposed victim of your crime; you are the favored and flattered ornament of society. Our likenesses have been compared many times:—I am glad we have met. Go, woman, go! I would not, outcast as I am, deign to acknowledge the mother who could enjoy the luxuries of life and see her child a wretch."

"Woman! do not upbraid me. Spare, oh! spare my troubled heart this last pang," (she grasps convulsively at Anna's hand, then shrinks back in fright.) "Tell me! oh, tell me!" she pursues, the tears coursing down her cheeks—

Anna Bonard interrupts by saying, peremptorily, she has nothing to tell one so guilty. To be thus rebuked by an abandoned woman, notwithstanding she might be her own child, wounded her feelings deeply. It was like poison drying up her very blood. Tormented with the thought of her error, (for she evidently labored under the smart of an error in early life,) her very existence now seemed a burden to her. Gloomy and motionless she stood, as if hesitating how best to make her escape.

"Woman! I will not betray your coming here. But you cannot give me back my virtue; you cannot restore me untainted to the world—the world never forgives a fallen woman. Her own sex will be first to lacerate her heart with her shame." These words were spoken with such biting sarcasm, that the Judge, whose nap the loudness of Anna's voice had disturbed, protruded his flushed face and snowy locks from out the curtains of the alcove. "The gay Madame Montford, as I am a Christian," he exclaims in the eagerness of the moment, and the strange figure vanishes out of the door.

"A fashionable, but very mysterious sort of person," pursues the Judge, confusedly. "Ah! ha,—her case, like many others, is the want of a clear conscience. Snivel has it in hand. A great knave, but a capital lawyer, that Snivel—"

The Judge is interrupted in his remarks by the entrance of Mr. Snivel, who, with hectic face, and flushed eyes, comes rushing into the chamber. "Hollo!—old boy, there's a high bid on your head to-night. Ready to do you a bit of a good turn, you see." Mr. Snivel runs his fingers through his hair, and works his shoulders with an air of exultation. "If," he continues, "that weak-minded fellow—that Mullholland we have shown some respect to, hasn't got a pistol! He's been furbishing it up while in the parlor, and swears he will seriously damage you with it. Blasted assurance, those Northerners have. Won't fight, can't make 'em gentlemen; and if you knock 'em down they don't understand enough of chivalry to resent it. They shout to satisfy their fear and not to maintain their honor. Keep an eye out!"

The Judge, in a tone of cool indifference, says he has no fears of the renegade, and will one of these days have the pleasure of sending him to the whipping-post.

"As to that, Judge," interposes Mr. Snivel, "I have already prepared the preliminaries. I gave him the trifle you desired—to-morrow I will nail him at the Keno crib." With this the Judge and the Justice each take an affectionate leave of the frail girl, and, as it is now past one o'clock in the morning, an hour much profaned in Charleston, take their departure.

Armed with a revolver Mullholland has taken up his position in the street, where he awaits the coming of his adversaries. In doubt and anxiety, he reflects and re-reflects, recurs to the associations of his past life, and hesitates. Such reflections only bring more vividly to his mind the wrong he feels himself the victim of, and has no power to resent except with violence. His contemplations only nerve him to revenge.

A click, and the door cautiously opens, as if some votary of crime was about to issue forth in quest of booty. The hostess' head protrudes suddenly from the door, she scans first up and then down the street, then withdraws it. The Judge and Mr. Snivel, each in turn, shake the landlady by the hand, and emerge into the street. They have scarce stepped upon the sidepath when the report of a pistol resounds through the air. The ball struck a lamp-post, glanced, passed through the collar of Judge Sleepyhorn's coat, and brushed

Mr. Snivel's fashionable whiskers. Madame Ashley, successor to Madame Flamingo, shrieks and alarms the house, which is suddenly thrown into a state of confusion. Acting upon the maxim of discretion being the better part of valor, the Judge and the Justice beat a hasty retreat into the house, and secrete themselves in a closet at the further end of the back-parlor.

As if suddenly moved by some strange impulse, Madame Ashley runs from room to room, screaming at the very top of her voice, and declaring that she saw the assassin enter her house. Females rush from their rooms and into the great parlor, where they form groups of living statuary, strange and grotesque. Anxious faces—faces half painted, faces hectic of dissipation, faces waning and sallow, eyes glassy and lascivious, dishevelled hair floating over naked shoulders;—the flashing of bewitching drapery, the waving and flitting of embroidered underskirts, the tripping of pretty feet and prettier ankles, the gesticulating and swaying of half-draped bodies—such is the scene occasioned by the bench and the bar.

Madame Ashley, having inherited of Madame Flamingo the value of a scrupulous regard for the good reputation of her house, must needs call in the watch to eject the assassin, whom she swears is concealed somewhere on the premises. Mr. Sergeant Stubbs, a much respected detective, and reputed one of the very best officers of the guard, inasmuch as he never troubles his head about other people's business, and is quite content to let every one fight their own battles,—provided they give him a "nip" of whiskey when they are through, lights his lantern and goes bobbing into every room in the house. We must here inform the reader that the cause of the *emeute* was kept a profound secret between the judicial gentry. Madame Ashley, at the same time, is fully convinced the ball was intended for her, while Anna lays in a terrible fright in her chamber.

"Ho," says Mr. Stubbs, starting back suddenly as he opened the door of the closet in which the two gentlemen had concealed themselves. "I see! I see!—beg your pardon, gentlemen!" Mr. Stubbs whispers, and bows, and shuts the door quickly.

"An infernal affair this, Judge! D—n me if I wouldn't as soon be in the dock. It will all get out to-morrow," interposes Mr. Snivel, facetiously.

"Blast these improper associations!" the high functionary exclaims, fussily shrugging his shoulders, and wiping the sweat from his forehead. "I love the girl, though, I confess it!"

"Nothing more natural. A man without gallantry is like a pilgrim in the South-West Pass. You can't resist this charming creature. In truth it's a sort of longing weakness, which even the scales of justice fail to bring to a balance."

Mr. Stubbs fails to find the assassin, and enters Madame Ashley's chamber, the door of which leads into the hall. Here Mr. Stubbs's quick eye suddenly discerns a slight motion of the curtains that enclose the great, square bed, standing in one corner. "I ax your pardon, Mam, but may I look in this 'ere bed?" Mr. Stubbs points to the bed, as Madame, having thrown herself into a great rocking chair, proceeds to sway her dignity backward and forward, and give out signs of making up her mind to faint.

Mr. Stubbs draws back the curtains, when, behold! but tell it not in the by-ways, there is revealed the stalworth figure of Simon Patterson, the plantation parson. Our plantation parsons, be it known, are a singular species of depraved humanity, a sort of itinerant sermon-makers, holding forth here and there to the negroes of the rich planters, receiving a paltry pittance in return, and having in lieu of morals an excellent taste for whiskey, an article they invariably call to their aid when discoursing to the ignorant slave—telling him how content with his lot he ought to be, seeing that God intended him only for ignorance and servitude. The parson did, indeed, cut a sorry figure before the gaze of this indescribable group, as it rushed into the room and commenced heaping upon his head epithets delicacy forbids our inserting here—calling him a clerical old lecher, an assassin, and a disturber of the peace and respectability of the house. Indeed, Madame Ashley quite forgot to faint, and with a display of courage amounting almost to heroism, rushed at the poor parson, and had left him in the state he was born but for the timely precautions of Mr. Stubbs, who, finding a revolver in his possession, and wanting no better proof of his guilt, straightway took him off to the guard-house. Parson Patterson would have entered the most solemn and pious protestation of his innocence but the evidence was so strong against him, and the zeal of Mr. Sergeant Stubbs so apparent, that he held it the better policy to quietly submit to the rough fare of his new lodgings.

"I have a terror of these brawls!" says Mr. Snivel, emerging from his hiding-place, and entering the chamber, followed by the high legal functionary.

"A pretty how-do-ye-do, this is;" returns Madame Ashley, cooling her passion in the rocking-chair, "I never had much respect for parsons—"

"Parsons?" interrupts Mr. Snivel, inquiringly, "you don't mean to say it was all the doings of a parson?"

"As I'm a lady it was no one else. He was discovered behind the curtain there, a terrible pistol in his pocket—the wretch!"

Mr. Snivel exchanges a wink with the Judge, points his thumb over his left shoulder, and says, captiously: "I always had an implacable hatred of that old thief. A bad lot! these plantation parsons."

Mr. Stubbs having discovered and removed the assassin, the terrified damsels return to their chambers, and Madame Ashley proceeds to close her house, as the two legal gentlemen take their departure. Perhaps it would be well to inform the reader that a principal cause of Anna's preference for the Judge, so recently manifested, was the deep impression made on her already suspicious mind by Mr. McArthur, the antiquary, who revealed to her sincerely, as she thought, her future dark destiny.

CHAPTER XXVI
IN WHICH A HIGH FUNCTIONARY IS MADE TO PLAY A SINGULAR PART

The morning following the events detailed in the foregoing chapter, finds the august Sleepyhorn seated on his judgment-seat. The clock strikes ten as he casts his heavy eyes over the grotesque group gathered into his little, dingy court-room; and he bows to his clerk, of whom he gets his law knowledge, and with his right hand makes a sign that he is ready to admonish the erring, or pass sentence on any amount of criminals. History affords no record of a judge so unrelenting of his judgments.

A few dilapidated gentlemen of the *"learned* profession," with sharp features and anxious faces, fuss about among the crowd, reeking of whiskey and tobacco. Now they whisper suspiciously in the ears of forlorn prisoners, now they struggle to get a market for their legal nostrums. A few, more respectably clothed and less vicious of aspect, sit writing at a table inside the bar, while a dozen or more punch-faced policemen, affecting an air of superiority, drag themselves lazily through the crowd of seedy humanity, looking querulously over the railing encircling the dock, or exchanging recognitions with friends.

Some twenty "negro cases" having been disposed of without much respect to law, and being sent up for punishment (the Judge finds it more convenient to forego testimony in these cases), a daughter of the Emerald Isle, standing nearly six feet in her bare soles, and much shattered about the dress, is, against her inclination, arraigned before his Honor. "I think I have seen you before, Mrs. Donahue?" says the Judge, inquiringly.

"Arrah, good-morning, yer 'onher! Shure, it's only the sixth time these three weeks. Doesn't meself like to see yer smiling face, onyhow!" Here Mrs. Donahue commences complimenting the Judge in one breath, and laying no end of charges at the door of the very diminutive and harmless Mister Donahue in the next.

"This being the sixth time," returns his Honor, somewhat seriously, "I would advise you to compromise the matter with Donahue, and not be seen here again. The state of South Carolina cannot pay your fees so often—"

"Och, bad luck to Donahue! Troth, an' if yer onher'd put the fees down to Donahue, our acquaintance 'ouldn't be so fraquent." Mrs. Donahue says this with great unction, throwing her uncombed hair back, then daintily raising her dress apace, and inquiring of Mr. Sheriff Hardscrabble, who sits on his Honor's left, peering sharply through his spectacles, how he likes the spread of her broad, flat foot; "the charging the fees to Donahue, yer onher, 'd do it!" There was more truth in this remark than his Honor seemed to comprehend, for having heard the charge against her (Mr. Donahue having been caught in the act of taking a drop of her gin, she had well-nigh broken his head with the bottle), and having listened attentively while poor Donahue related his wrongs, and exhibited two very well blacked eyes and a broken nose, he came to the very just conclusion that it were well to save the blood of the Donahues. And to this end did he grant Mrs. Donahue board and lodging for one month in the old prison. Mrs. Donahue is led away, heaping curses on the head of Donahue, and compliments on that of his Honor.

A pale, sickly looking boy, some eleven years old, is next placed upon the stand. Mr. Sergeant Stubbs, who leans his corpulent figure against the clerk's desk, every few minutes bowing his sleepy head to some friend in the crowd, says: "A hard 'un—don't do no good about here. A vagrant; found him sleeping in the market."

His Honor looks at the poor boy for some minutes, a smile of kindliness seems lighting up his face; he says he would there were some place of refuge—a place where reformation rather than punishment might be the aim and end, where such poor creatures could be sent to, instead of confining them in cells occupied by depraved prisoners.

Mr. Sheriff Hardscrabble, always eager to get every one into jail he can, inasmuch as it pays him twenty-two cents a day clear profit on each and every person confined, says: "A hard customer. Found sleeping in the market, eh? Well, we must merge him in a tub of water, and scrub him up a little." Mr. Hardscrabble views him with an air of satisfaction, touches him with a small cane he holds in his hand, as if he were something very common. Indeed, Mr. Hardscrabble seems quite at a loss to know what species of animal he is, or whether he be really intended for any other use than filling up his cells and returning him twenty-two cents a day clear profit. "Probably an incendiary," mutters the sagacious sheriff. The helpless boy would explain how he came to sleep in the market—how he, a poor cabin-boy, walked, foot-sore and hungry, from Wilmington, in the hope of getting a ship; and being moneyless and friendless he laid down in the market to sleep. Mr. Hardscrabble, however, suggests that such stories are extremely common. His Honor thinks it not worth while to differ from this opinion, but to the end that no great legal wisdom may be thrown away, he orders the accused to be sent to the common jail for three months. This, in the opinion of Judge Sleepyhorn, is an extremely mild penalty for being found sleeping in the market.

Next there comes forward a lean, up-country Cracker, (an half-civilized native,) who commences telling his story with commendable simplicity, the Judge in the meanwhile endeavoring to suppress a smile, which the quaintness of his remarks excite. Making a tenement of his cart, as is usual with these people when they visit the city, which they do now and then for the purpose of replenishing their stock of whiskey, he had, about eleven o'clock on the previous night, been set upon by three intoxicated students, who, having driven off his mule, overturned his cart, landing him and his wife prostrate in the ditch. A great noise was the result, and the guard, with their accustomed zeal for seizing upon the innocent party, dragged up the weaker (the Cracker and his wife) and let the guilty go free. He had brought the good wife, he added, as a living evidence of the truth of what he said, and would bring the mule if his honor was not satisfied. The good wife commences a volley of what she is pleased to call voluntary testimony, praising and defending all the good qualities of her much-abused husband, without permitting any one else an opposing word. No sufficient charge being brought against the Cracker (he wisely slipped a five dollar bill into the hands of Stubbs), he joins his good wife and goes on his way rejoicing.

During this little episode between the court and the Cracker's wife, Madame Grace Ashley, arrayed in her most fashionable toilet, comes blazing into Court, bows to the Judge and a few of her most select friends of the Bar. A seat for Madame is provided near his Honor's desk. His Honor's blushes seem somewhat overtaxed; Madame, on the other hand, is not at all disconcerted; indeed, she claims an extensive acquaintance with the most distinguished of the Bar.

The Judge suggests to Mr. Stubbs that it would be as well to waive the charge against the clergyman. Somewhat the worse for his night in the guard-house, Parson Patterson comes forward and commences in the most unintelligible manner to explain the whole affair, when the Judge very blandly interrupts by inquiring if he is a member of the clergy at this moment. "Welle," returns the parson, with characteristic drawl, "can't zactly say I am." The natural seediness of the parson excites suspicion, nevertheless he is scrupulous of his white cravat, and preserves withal a strictly clerical aspect. Having paused a few moments and exchanged glances with the Judge, he continues: "I do nigger preaching on Sunday—that is (Parson Patterson corrects himself), I hold forth, here and there—we are all flesh and blood—on plantations when I have a demand for my services. Our large planters hold it good policy to encourage the piety of their property."

"You make a good thing of it?" inquires the Judge, jocosely. The parson replies, with much meekness of manner, that business is not so good as it was, planters having got it into their heads that sermons can be got at a very low figure. Here he commences to explain his singular position. He happened to meet an old and much-esteemed friend, whom he accompanied home, and while spending the evening conversing on spiritual matters—it was best not to lie—he took a little too much. On his way to the hotel he selected Beresford street as a short cut, and being near the house where he was unfortunately found when the shooting took place, he ran into it to escape the police—

"Don't believe a word he says," interrupts Madame Ashley, springing suddenly to her feet, and commencing to pour out her phials of wrath on the head of the poor parson, whom she accuses of being a suspicious and extremely unprofitable frequenter of her house, which she describes as exceedingly respectable. "Your Honor can bear me out in what I say!" pursues Madame, bowing with an air of exultation, as the sheriff demands order.

"A sorry lot, these plantation preachers! Punish him right soundly, your honor. It is not the first time he has damaged the respectability of my house!" again interrupts Madame Ashley. His Honor replies only with a blush. Mr. Snivel, who watches with quisical countenance, over the bar, enjoys the joke wonderfully.

Order being restored, the Judge turns to address the parson.

"I see, my friend—I always address my prisoners familiarly—you place but little value on the fact of your being a clergyman, on the ground that you only preach to slaves. This charge brought against you is a grave one—I assure you! And I cannot incline to the view you take of your profession. I may not be as erudite as some; however, I hold it that the ignorant and not the learned have most need of good example."

"Aye! I always told the old reprobate so," interposes Madam Ashley, with great fervor.

"A charge," resumes the Judge, "quite sufficient to warrant me in committing you to durance vile, might be preferred. You may thank my generosity that it is not. These houses, as you know, Mr. Patterson, are not only dangerous, but damaging to men of potent morality like you."

"But, your Honor knows, they are much frequented," meekly drawls the parson.

"It affords no palliation," sharply responds the Judge, his face crimsoning with blushes. "Mark ye, my friend of the clergy, these places make sad destruction of our young men. Indeed I may say with becoming sincerity and truth, that they spread a poison over the community, and act as the great enemy of our social system."

"Heigh ho!" ejaculates Madame Ashley, to the great delight of the throng assembled, "Satan has come to rebuke sin." Madame bids his Honor a very polite good morning, and takes her departure, looking disdainfully over her shoulder as she disappears out of the door.

Not a little disturbed in his equanimity, the Judge pursues his charge. "The clergy ought to keep their garments clear of such places, for being the source of all evil, the effect on the community is not good—I mean when such things are brought to light! I would address you frankly and admonish you to go no more into such places. Let your ways merit the approbation of those to whom you preach the Gospel. You can go. Henceforth, live after the ways of the virtuous."

Parson Patterson thanks his Honor, begs to assure him of his innocence, and seems only too anxious to get away. His Honor bows to Mr. Patterson, Mr. Patterson returns it, and adds another for the audience, whereupon the court adjourns, and so ends the episode. His Honor takes Mr. Snivel's arm, and together they proceed to the "most convenient" saloon, where, over a well-compounded punch, "the bench and the bar" compliment each other on the happy disposal of such vexatious cases.

CHAPTER XXVII
THE HOUSE OF THE NINE NATIONS, AND WHAT MAY BE SEEN IN IT

On the corner of Anthony street and the Points,[4] in New-York, there stands, like a grim savage, the house of the Nine Nations, a dingy wooden tenement, that for twenty years has threatened to tumble away from its more upright neighbor, and before which the stranger wayfarer is seen to stop and contemplate. In a neighborhood redolent of crime, there it stands, its vices thick upon its head, exciting in the mind of the observer its association with some dark and terrible deed. On the one side, opens that area of misery, mud and sombre walls, called "Cow Bay;" on the other a triangular plot, reeking with the garbage of the miserable cellars that flank it, and in which swarms of wasting beings seek a hiding-place, inhale pestilential air, and die. Gutters running with seething matter; homeless outcasts sitting, besotted, on crazy doorsteps; the vicious, with savage visage, and keen, watchful eye, loitering at the doors of filthy "groceries;" the sickly and neglected child crawling upon the side-pave, or seeking a crust to appease its hunger—all are found here, gasping, in rags, a breath of air by day, or seeking a shelter, at night, in dens so abject that the world can furnish no counterpart. And this forlorn picture of dilapidated houses, half-clad, squabbish women, blistered-faced men, and sickly children, the house of the Nine Nations overlooks. And yet this house, to the disgrace of an opulent people be it said, is but the sample of an hundred others standing in the same neighborhood.

With its basement-doors opening into its bottomless pit; with its continual outgoing and ingoing of sooty and cruel-visaged denizens; with its rickety old steps leading to the second story; with its battered windows, begrimed walls, demolished shutters, clapboards hanging at sixes and sevens—with its suspicious aspect;—there it stands, with its distained sign over the doors of its bottomless pit. You may read on this sign, that a gentleman from Ireland, who for convenience' sake we will call Mr. Krone, is licensed to sell imported and other liquors.

Indeed the house of the Nine Nations would seem to say within itself: "I am mother of this banquet of death you behold with your eyes." There it stands, its stream of poison hurrying its victims to the grave; its little dark passages leading to curious hiding-places; its caving roof, and its ominous-looking back platform, overlooking the dead walls of Murderers' Yard. How it mocks your philanthropy, your regal edifices, your boasted charities—your gorgeous churches! Everybody but the corporation knows the house of the Nine Nations, a haunt for wasted prostitutes, assassins, burglars, thieves—every grade of criminals known to depraved nature. The corporation would seem either to have a charming sympathy for it, or to look upon it with that good-natured indifference so happily illustrated while eating its oysters and drinking its whiskey. An empty-headed corporation is sure always to have its hands very full, which is the case with yours at this moment. Having the people's money to waste, its own ambition to serve, and its hat to fill with political waste paper—what more would you ask of it?

The man of the house of the Nine Nations, you ought to know, makes criminals by the hundred, deluges your alms houses with paupers, and makes your Potters' field reek with his victims: for this he is become rich. Mr. Krone is an intimate friend of more than one Councilman, and a man of much measure in the political world—that is, Mr. Krone is a politician-maker. When you say there exists too close an intimacy between the pugilist and the politician, Mr. Krone will bet twenty drinks with any one of his customers that he can prove such doctrines at fault. He can secure the election of his favorite candidate with the same facility that he can make an hundred paupers per week. You may well believe him a choice flower in the bouquet of the corporation; we mean the corporation that banquets and becomes jubilant while assassins stab their victims in the broad street—that becomes befogged while bands of ruffians disgrace the city with their fiendish outrages—that makes presidents and drinks whiskey when the city would seem given over to the swell-mobsman—when no security is offered to life, and wholesale harlotry, flaunting with naked arms and bared bosoms, passes along in possession of Broadway by night.

It is the night succeeding the day Lady Swiggs discovered, at the house of the Foreign Missions, the loss of her cherished donations. As this is a world of disappointments, Lady Swiggs resigns herself to this most galling of all, and with her Milton firmly grasped in her hand, may be seen in a little room at Sister Scudder's, rocking herself in the arm-chair, and wondering if Brother Spyke has captured the robber-wretch. A chilly wind howls, and a drizzling rain falls thick over the dingy dwellings of the Points, which, sullen and dark, seem in a dripping mood. A glimmering light, here and there, throws curious shadows over the liquid streets. Now the drenched form of some half-naked and homeless being is reflected, standing shivering in the entrance to some dark and narrow alley; then the half-crazed inebriate hurries into the open door of a dismal cellar, or seeks eagerly a shelter for his bewildered head, in some suspicious den. Flashing through the shadow of the police lamp, in "Cow Bay," a forlorn female is seen, a bottle held tightly under her shawl. Sailing as it were into the bottomless pit of the house of the Nine Nations, then suddenly returning with the drug, seeking the cheerless garret of her dissolute partner, and there striving to blunt her feelings against the horrors of starvation.

Two men stand, an umbrella over their heads, at the corner, in the glare of the bottomless pit, which is in a blaze of light, and crowded with savage-faced figures, of various ages and colors,—all habited in the poison-seller's uniform of rags. "I don't think you'll find him here, sir," says one, addressing the other, who is tall and slender of person, and singularly timid. "God knows I am a stranger here. To-morrow I leave for Antioch," is the reply, delivered in nervous accents. The one is Brother Syngleton Spyke, the other Mr. Detective Fitzgerald, a man of more than middle stature, with compact figure, firmly-knit limbs, and an expression of countenance rather pleasant.

"You see, sir, this Toddleworth is a harmless creature, always aims to be obliging and civil. I don't, sir—I really don't think he'll steal. But one can't tell what a man will do who is driven to such straits as the poor devils here are. We rather like Toddleworth at the station, look upon him as rather wanting in the head, and for that reason rather incline to favor him. I may say we now and then let him 'tie up' all night in the station. And for this he seems very thankful. I may say," continues Mr. Fitzgerald, touching the visor of his cap, "that he always repays with kindness any little attention we may extend to him at the station, and at times seems too anxious to make it his home. We give him a shirt and a few shillings now and then; and when we want to be rid of him we begin to talk about fashionable wives. He is sure to go then. Can't stand such a topic, I assure you, sir, and is sure to go off in a huff when Sergeant Pottle starts it."

They enter the great door of the bottomless pit; the young missionary hesitates. His countenance changes, his eyes scan steadily over the scene. A room some sixty feet by twenty opens to his astonished eyes. Its black, boarded walls, and bare beams, are enlivened here and there with extravagant pictures of notorious pugilists, show-bills, and illustrated advertisements of lascivious books, in which the murder of an unfortunate woman is the principal feature. Slippery mud covers the floor. Mr. Krone sits on an empty whiskey-barrel, his stunted features betraying the hardened avarice of his character. He smokes his black pipe, folds his arms deliberately, discoursing of the affairs of the nation to two stupefied negroes and one blear-eyed son of the Emerald Isle. Three uncouth females, with hair hanging matted over their faces, and their features hidden in distortion, stand cooling their bared limbs at a running faucet just inside the door, to the left. A group of half-naked negroes lie insensible on the floor, to the right. A little further on two prostrate females, shivering, and reeking of gin, sleep undisturbed by the profanity that is making the very air resound. "The gin gets a-many of us," is the mournful cry of many a wasting inebriate. Mr. Krone, however, will tell you he has no sympathy with such cries. You arraign, and perhaps punish, the apothecary who sells by mistake his deadly drug. With a philosophical air, Mr. Krone will tell you he deals out his poison without scruple, fills alms-houses without a pang of remorse, and proves that a politician-maker may do much to degrade society and remain in high favor with his friends of the bench of justice. On one side of the dungeon-like place stands a rickety old counter, behind which three savage-faced men stand, filling and serving incessant potions of deleterious liquor to the miserable beings, haggard and ragged, crowding to be first served. Behind the bar, or counter, rises a pyramid of dingy shelves, on which are arranged little painted kegs, labelled, and made bright by the glaring gas-light reflected upon them. On the opposite side, on rows of slab benches, sit a group of motley beings,—the young girl and the old man, the negro and the frail white,—half sleeping, half conscious; all imbibing the stifling draught.

Like revelling witches in rags, and seen through the bedimmed atmosphere at the further end of the den, are half-frantic men, women, and girls, now sitting at deal tables, playing for drinks, now jostling, jeering, and profaning in wild disorder. A girl of sixteen, wasted and deformed with dissipation, approaches Brother Spyke, extends her blanched hand, and importunes him for gin. He shudders, and shrinks from her touch, as from a reptile. A look of scorn, and she turns from him, and is lost among the grotesque crowd in the distance.

"This gin," says Mr. Fitzgerald, turning methodically to Brother Spyke, "they make do for food and clothing. We used to call this the devil's paradise. As to Krone, we used to call him the devil's bar-tender. These ragged revellers, you see, beg and steal during the day, and get gin with it at night. Krone thinks nothing of it! Lord bless your soul, sir! why, this man is reckoned a tip-top politician; on an emergency he can turn up such a lot of votes!" Mr. Fitzgerald, approaching Mr. Krone, says "you're a pretty fellow. Keeping such a place as this!" The detective playfully strikes the hat of the other, crowding it over his eyes, and inquiring if he has seen

Tom Toddleworth during the day. Mr. Toddleworth was not seen during the day. No one in the bottomless pit knows where he may be found. A dozen husky voices are heard to say, he has no home—stores himself away anywhere, and may be found everywhere.

Brother Spyke bows, and sighs. Mr. Fitzgerald says: "he is always harmless—this Toddleworth." As the two searchers are about to withdraw, the shrunken figure of a woman rushes wildly into the pit. "Devils! devils!—hideous devils of darkness! here you are—still hover—hover—hovering; turning midnight into revelling, day into horrid dreaming!" she shrieks at the top of her voice. Now she pauses suddenly, and with a demoniacal laugh sets her dull, glassy eyes on Mr. Krone, then walks round him with clenched fists and threatening gestures. The politician-maker sits unmoved. Now she throws her hair about her bare breasts, turns her eyes upward, imploringly, and approaches Brother Spyke, with hand extended. Her tale of sorrow and suffering is written in her very look. "She won't hurt you—never harms anybody;" says Mr. Fitzgerald, methodically, observing Brother Spyke's timidity.

"No, no, no," she mutters incoherently, "you are not of this place—you know, like the rich world up-town, little of these revelling devils. Cling! yes, cling to the wise one—tell him to keep you from this, and forever be your teacher. Tell him! tell him! oh! tell him!" She wrings her hands, and having sailed as it were into the further end of the pit, vaults back, and commences a series of wild gyrations round Mr. Krone.

"Poor wretch!" says Brother Spyke, complacently, "the gin has dried up her senses—made her what she is."

"Maniac Munday! Maniac Munday!" suddenly echoes and re-echoes through the pit. She turns her ear, and with a listless countenance listens attentively, then breaks out into an hysterical laugh. "Yes! ye loathsome denizens. Like me, no one seeks you, no one cares for you. I am poor, poor maniac Munday. The maniac that one fell error brought to this awful end." Again she lowers her voice, flings her hair back over her shoulders, and gives vent to her tears. Like one burdened with sorrow she commences humming an air, that even in this dark den floats sweetly through the polluted atmosphere. "Well, I am what I am," she sighs, having paused in her tune. "That one fatal step—that plighted faith! How bitter to look back." Her bony fingers wander to her lips, which she commences biting and fretting, as her countenance becomes pale and corpse-like. Again her reason takes its flight. She staggers to the drenched counter, holds forth her bottle, lays her last sixpence tauntingly upon the board, and watches with glassy eyes the drawing of the poisonous drug. Meanwhile Mr. Krone, with an imprecation, declares he has power to elect his candidate to the Senate. The man behind the counter—the man of savage face, has filled the maniac's bottle, which he pushes toward her with one hand, as with the other he sweeps her coin into a drawer. "Oh! save poor maniac Munday—save poor maniac Munday!" the woman cries, like one in despair, clutching the bottle, and reels out of the pit.

CHAPTER XXVIII
IN WHICH IS PRESENTED ANOTHER PICTURE OF THE HOUSE OF THE NINE NATIONS

Pale and hesitating, Brother Spyke says: "I have no passion for delving into such places; and having seen enough for one night, am content to leave the search for this vile old man to you." The valiant missionary addresses Mr. Fitzgerald, who stands with one foot upon the rickety old steps that lead to the second story of the House of the Nine Nations.

This morning, Brother Spyke was ready to do battle with the whole heathen world, to drag it up into light, to evangelize it. Now he quails before this heathen world, so terribly dark, at his own door.

"You have, sir," says the detective, "seen nuthin' as yet. The sights are in these 'ere upper dens; but, I may say it, a body wants nerve. Some of our Aldermen say ye can't see such sights nowhere else."

The missionary replies, holding tenaciously to his umbrella, "That may be true; but I fear they will be waiting me at home." Again he scans inquiringly into the drenched area of the Points; then bidding the officer good-night, is soon out of sight, on his way into Centre Street. Reaching the old stoop, the detective touches a spring, and the shattered door opens into a narrow, gloomy passage, along which he gropes his way, over a floor cobbled with filth, and against an atmosphere thick of disease. Now a faint light flashes through a crevice in the left wall, plays fantastically upon the black surface of the opposite, then dies away. The detective lights his lantern, stands a moment with his ear turned, as if listening to the revelry in the bottomless pit. A door opens to his touch, he enters a cave-like room — it is the one from out which the light stole so curiously, and in which all is misery and sadness. A few embers still burn in a great brick fireplace, shedding a lurid glow over the damp, filthy walls, the discolored ceiling, and the grotesque group upon the floor. "You needn't come at this time of night—we are all honest people;" speaks a massive negro, of savage visage, who (he is clothed in rags) sits at the left side of the fireplace. He coaxes the remnant of his fire to cook some coarse food he has placed in a small, black stew-pan, he watches with steady gaze. Three white females (we blush to say it), their bare, brawny arms resting on their knees, and their disfigured faces drooped into their hands, form an half circle on the opposite side.

"The world don't think nothin' of us down here—we haven't had a bite to eat to-night," gruffly resumes the negro.

"May them that have riches enjoy them, for to be supperless is no uncommon thing wid us," interrupts one of the women, gathering about her the shreds of her tattered garment, parting the matted hair over her face, and revealing her ghastly features. The detective turns his light full upon her. "If we live we live, if we die we die—nobody cares! Look you yonder, Mr. Fitzgerald," continues the negro, with a sarcastic leer. Turning his light to where the negro points, the detective casts a glance into the shadow, and there discovers the rags move. A dozen pair of glassy eyes are seen peering from out the filthy coverings, over which lean arms and blanched hands keep up an incessant motion. Here an emaciated and heart-sick Welsh girl, of thirteen (enciente) lays shivering on the broken floor; there an half-famished Scotch woman, two moaning children nestling at her heart, suffers uncovered upon a pallet of straw. The busy world without would seem not to have a care for her; the clergy have got the heathen world upon their shoulders. Hunger, like a grim tyrant, has driven her to seek shelter in this wretched abode. Despair has made her but too anxious that the grave or prison walls should close the record of her sorrows. How tightly she with her right hand presses her babe to her bosom; how appealingly with her left she asks a pittance of the detective! Will he not save from death her starving child? He has nothing to give her, turns his head, answers only with a look of pity, and moves slowly towards the door.

"You have not been long off the Island, Washington?" inquires the detective, with an air of familiarity.

"I wish," replies the negro, sullenly, "I was back. An honest man as I is, can't get on in this world. Necessity makes rascals of better men than me, Mr. Fitzgerald. Mr. Krone (he's a white man, though) makes all the politicians for the district, and charges me eight dollars a month for this hole. Just measure them two things together, Mr. Fitzgerald; then see if takin' in sixpenny, lodgers pays." Mr. Fitzgerald commences counting them. "You needn't count," pursues the negro, uncovering his stew-pan, "there's only eighteen in to-night. Have twenty, sometimes! Don't get nothin' for that poor Scotch woman an' her children. Can't get it when they hain't got it— you know that, Mr. Fitzgerald."

The detective inquires if any of them have seen Mr. Toddleworth to-day. Washington has not seen him, and makes no scruple of saying he thinks very little of him.

"Faith an' it's hard times with poor Tom," speaks up one of the women, in a deep brogue. "It was only last night—the same I'm tellin' is true, God knows—Mrs. McCarty took him to the Rookery—the divil a mouthful he'd ate durin' the day—and says, bein' a ginerous sort of body, come, take a drop, an' a bite to ate. Mister Toddleworth did that same, and thin lay the night on the floor. To-night—it's the truth, God knows—Tom Downey took him above. An' it's Tom who woundn't be the frind of the man who hadn't a shillin' in his pocket."

The detective shrugs his shoulders, and having thanked the woman, withdraws into the passage, to the end of which he cautiously picks his way, and knocks at a distained door that fronts him. A voice deep and husky bids him enter, which he does, as the lurid glare of his lantern reveals a room some twelve by sixteen feet, the plaster hanging in festoons from the black walls, and so low of ceiling that he scarce can stand upright. Four bunk-beds, a little bureau, a broken chair or two, and a few cheap pictures, hung here and there on the sombre walls, give it an air of comfort in grateful contrast with the room just left. "Who lives here?" inquires the detective, turning his light full upon each object that attracts his attention. "Shure it's only me—Mrs. Terence Murphy—and my three sisters (the youngest is scarce fourteen), and the two English sisters: all honest people, God knows," replies Mrs. Murphy, with a rapid tongue.

"It's not right of you to live this way," returns the detective, continuing to survey the prostrate forms of Mrs. Murphy, her three sisters, and the two fair-haired English girls, and the besotted beings they claim as husbands. Alarm is pictured in every countenance. A browned face withdraws under a dingy coverlid, an anxious face peers from out a pallet on the floor, a prostrate figure in the corner inquires the object of Mr. Detective Fitzgerald's visit—and Mrs. Murphy, holding it more becoming of respectable society, leaves the bed in which she had accommodated five others, and gets into one she calls her own. A second thought, and she makes up her mind not to get into bed, but to ask Mr. Fitzgerald if he will be good enough, when next he meets his Onher, the Mayor, just to say to him how Mr. Krone is bringing disgrace upon the house and every one in it, by letting rooms to negroes. Here she commences pouring out her pent-up wrath upon the head of Mr. Krone, and the colored gentleman, whom she declares has a dozen white females in his room every night. The detective encourages her by saying it is not right of Mr. Krone, who looks more at the color of his money than the skin of his tenants. "To come of a dacint family—and be brought to this!" says Mrs. Murphy, allowing her passion to rise, and swearing to have revenge of the negro in the next room.

"You drink this gin, yet—I have warned you against it," interposes the detective, pointing to some bottles on the bureau. "Faith, an' it's the gin gets a many of us," returns the woman, curtly, as she gathers about her the skirts of her garments. "Onyhow, yerself wouldn't deprive us of a drop now and then, jist to keep up the spirits." The detective shakes his head, then discloses to them the object of his search, adding, in parenthesis, that he does not think Mr. Toddleworth is the thief. A dozen tongues are ready to confirm the detective's belief. "Not a shillin' of it did the poor crature take—indeed he didn't, now, Mr. Fitzgerald. 'Onor's 'onor, all over the wurld!" says Mrs. Murphy, grasping the detective by the hand. "Stay till I tell ye all about it. Mary Maguire—indeed an' ye knows her, Mr. Fitzgerald—this same afternoon looked in to say—'how do ye do, Mrs. Murphy. See this! Mrs. Murphy,' says she, 'an' the divil a sich a pocket of money I'd see before, as she held in her right hand, jist. 'Long life to ye, Mary,' says I. 'We'll have a pint, Mrs. Murphy,' says she. 'May ye niver want the worth of it,' says I. And the pint was not long in, when Mary got a little the worse of it, and let all out about the money. 'You won't whisper it, Mrs. Murphy,' says she, 'if I'd tell ye in confidence by what manes I got the lift?'"

"'Not in the wide world, Mary,' says I; 'ye may trust me for that same.' 'Shure didn't I raise it from the pocket of an auld woman in spectacles, that watched the fool beyant dig up the corporation.' 'An' it'll not do yerself much good,' says I, liftin' the same, and cuttin' away to the house. 'You won't whisper it?' says she."

"I can confirm the truth of that same," rejoins a brusque-figured man, rising from his pallet, and speaking with regained confidence. "Mary looked in at the Blazers, and being the worse of liquor, showed a dale of ready money, and trated everybody, and gave the money to everybody, and was wilcome wid everybody. Then Mrs. McCarty got aboard of her ginerosity, and got her into the Rookery, where the Miss McCartys thought it would not be amiss to have a quart. The same was brought in, and Mary hersel' was soon like a dead woman on the floor, jist—"

"And they got the money all away?" interrupts the detective.

"Faith, an' she'll not have a blessed dollar come daylight," continues the man, resuming his pallet.

The detective bids Mrs. Murphy good night, and is soon groping his way over a rickety old floor, along a dark, narrow passage, scarce high enough to admit him, and running at right angles with the first. A door on the left opens into a grotto-like place, the sickly atmosphere of which seems hurling its poison into the very blood. "Who's here?" inquires the detective, and a voice, feeble and hollow, responds: "Lodgers!"

The damp, greasy walls; the broken ceilings; the sooty fireplace, with its shattered bricks; the decayed wainscoating—its dark, forlorn aspect, all bespeak it the fit abode of rats. And yet Mr. Krone thinks it comfortable enough (the authorities think Mr. Krone the best judge) for the accommodation of thirteen remnants of human misery, all of whom are here huddled together on the wet, broken floor, borrowing warmth of one another. The detective's light falls curiously upon the dread picture, which he stands contemplating. A pale, sickly girl, of some eleven summers, her hair falling wildly over her wan features, lays upon some rags near the fireplace, clinging to an inebriated mother. Here a father, heart-sick and prostrate with disease, seeks to keep warm his three ragged children, nestling about him. An homeless outcast, necessity forces him to send them out to prey upon the community by day, and to seek in this wretched hovel a shelter at night. Yonder the rags are thrown back, a moving mass is disclosed, and there protrudes a disfigured face, made ghostly by the shadow of the detective's lantern. At the detective's feet a prostrate girl, insensible of gin, is seized with convulsions, clutches with wasted hands at the few rags about her poor, flabby body, then with fingers grasping, and teeth firmly set, her whole frame writhes in agony. Your missionary never whispered a kind, encouraging word in her ear; his hand never pressed that blanched bone with which she now saddens your heart! Different might it have been with her had some gentle-tongued Brother Spyke sought her out, bore patiently with her waywardness, snatched her from this life of shame, and placed her high in an atmosphere of light and love.

It is here, gentle shepherds, the benighted stand most in need of your labors. Seek not to evangelize the Mahomedan world until you have worked a reform here; and when you have done it, a monument in heaven will be your reward.

"Mr. Toddleworth is not here," says the detective, withdrawing into the passage, then ascending a broken and steep stairs that lead into the third story. Nine shivering forms crouched in one dismal room; four squabbish women, and three besotted men in another; and in a third, nine ragged boys and two small girls—such are the scenes of squalid misery presented here. In a little front room, Mr. Tom Downey, his wife, and eight children, lay together upon the floor, half covered with rags. Mr. Downey startles at the appearance of the detective, rises nervously from his pallet, and after the pause of a moment, says: "Indeed, yer welcome, Mr. Fitzgerald. Indeed, I have not—an' God knows it's the truth I tell—seen Mr. Toddleworth the week;" he replies, in answer to a question from the detective.

"You took a drop with him this afternoon?" continues the detective, observing his nervousness.

"God knows it's a mistake, Mr. Fitzgerald." Mr. Downey changes the subject, by saying the foreigners in the garret are a great nuisance, and disturb him of his rest at night.

A small, crooked stair leads into "Organ-grinders' Roost," in the garret. To "Organ-grinders' Roost" the detective ascends. If, reader, you have ever pictured in your mind the cave of despair, peopled by beings human only in shape, you may form a faint idea of the wretchedness presented in "Organ-grinders' Roost," at the top of the house of the Nine Nations. Seven stalworth men shoot out from among a mass of rags on the floor, and with dark, wandering eyes, and massive, uncombed beards, commence in their native Italian a series of interrogatories, not one of which the detective can understand. They would inquire for whom he seeks at this strange hour. He (the detective) stands unmoved, as with savage gesture—he has discovered his star—they tell him they are famishing of hunger. A pretty black-eyed girl, to whose pale, but beautifully oval face an expression of sorrow lends a touching softness, lays on the bare floor, beside a mother of patriarchal aspect. Now she is seized with a sharp cough that brings blood at every paroxysm. As if forgetting herself, she lays her hand gently upon the cheek of her mother, anxious to comfort her. Ah! the hard hand of poverty has been upon her through life, and stubbornly refuses to relax its grip, even in her old age. An organ forms here and there a division between the sleepers; two grave-visaged monkeys sit chattering in the fireplace, then crouch down on the few charred sticks. A picture of the crucifix is seen conspicuous over the dingy fireplace, while from the slanting roof hang several leathern girdles. Oh, what a struggle for life is their's! Mothers, fathers, daughters, and little children, thus promiscuously grouped, and coming up in neglect and shame. There an old man, whom remorseless death is just calling into eternity, with dull, glassy eyes, white, flowing beard, bald head, sunken mouth, begrimed and deeply-wrinkled face, rises, spectre-like, from his pallet. Now he draws from his breast a small crucifix, and commences muttering to it in a guttural voice. "Peace, peace, good old man—the holy father will come soon—the holy virgin will come soon: he will receive the good spirit to his bosom," says a black-eyed daughter, patting him gently upon the head, then looking in his face solicitously, as he turns his eyes upward, and for a few moments seems invoking the mercy of the Allwise.

"Yes, father," she resumes, lightening up the mat of straw upon which he lays, "the world has been unkind to you, but you are passing from it to a better—you will be at peace soon."

"Soon, soon, soon," mumbles the old man, in a whisper; and having carefully returned the crucifix to his bosom, grasps fervently the hand of the girl and kisses it, as her eyes swim in tears.

Such, to the shame of those who live in princely palaces, and revel in luxury, are but faintly-drawn pictures of what may be seen in the house of the Nine Nations.

The detective is about to give up the search, and turns to descend the stairs, when suddenly he discerns a passage leading to the north end of the garret. Here, in a little closet-like room, on the right, the rats his only companions, lies the prostrate form of poor Toddleworth.

"Well, I persevered till I found you," says the detective, turning his light full upon the body. Another minute, and his features become as marble; he stands aghast, and his whole frame seems struggling under the effect of some violent shock. "What, what, what!" he shouts, in nervous accents, "Murder! murder! murder! some one has murdered him." Motionless the form lies, the shadow of the light revealing the ghastly spectacle. The head lies in a pool of blood, the bedimmed eyes, having taken their last look, remain fixedly set on the black roof. "He has died of a blow—of a broken skull!" says the frightened official, feeling, and feeling, and pressing the arms and hands that are fast becoming rigid. Life is gone out; a pauper's grave will soon close over what remains of this wretched outcast. The detective hastens down stairs, spreads the alarm over the neighborhood, and soon the House of the Nine Nations is the scene of great excitement.

CHAPTER XXIX
IN WHICH MAY BE SEEN A FEW
OF OUR COMMON EVILS

Leaving for a time the scenes in the House of the Nine Nations, let us return to Charleston, that we may see how matters appertaining to this history are progressing. Mr. Snivel is a popular candidate for the Senate of South Carolina; and having shot his man down in the street, the question of his fighting abilities we regard as honorably settled. Madame Montford, too, has by him been kept in a state of nervous anxiety, for he has not yet found time to search in the "Poor-house for the woman Munday." All our very first, and best-known families, have dropped Madame, who is become a wet sheet on the fashionable world. A select committee of the St. Cecilia has twice considered her expulsion, while numerous very respectable and equally active old ladies have been shaking their scandal-bags at her head. Sins have been laid at her door that would indeed damage a reputation with a fairer endorsement than New York can give.

Our city at this moment is warmed into a singular state of excitement. A Georgia editor (we regard editors as belonging to a very windy class of men), not having the mightiness of our chivalry before him, said the Union would have peace if South Carolina were shut up in a penitentiary. And for this we have invited the indiscreet gentleman to step over the border, that we may hang him, being extremely fond of such common-place amusements. What the facetious fellow meant was, that our own State would enjoy peace and prosperity were our mob-politicians all in the penitentiary. And with this sensible opinion we heartily agree.

We regard our state of civilization as extremely enviable. To-day we made a lion of the notorious Hines, the forger. Hines, fashioning after our hapless chivalry, boasts that South Carolina is his State—his political mother. He has, nevertheless, graced with his presence no few penitentiaries. We feasted him in that same prison where we degrade and starve the honest poor; we knew him guilty of an heinous crime—yet we carried him jubilantly to the "halls of justice." And while distinguished lawyers tendered their services to the "clever villain," you might have witnessed in sorrow a mock trial, and heard a mob sanction with its acclamations his release.

Oh, truth and justice! how feeble is thy existence where the god slavery reigns. And while men are heard sounding the praises of this highwayman at the street corners, extolling men who have shot down their fellow-men in the streets, and calling those "Hon. gentlemen," who have in the most cowardly manner assassinated their opponents, let us turn to a different picture. Two genteely-dressed men are seen entering the old, jail. "I have twice promised them a happy surprise," says one, whose pale, studious features, wear an expression of gentleness. The face of the other is somewhat florid, but beaming with warmth of heart. They enter, having passed up one of the long halls, a room looking into the prison-yard. Several weary-faced prisoners are seated round a deal table, playing cards; among them is the old sailor described in the early part of this history. "You don't know my friend, here?" says the young man of the studious face, addressing the prisoners, and pointing to his companion. The prisoners look inquiringly at the stranger, then shake their heads in response.

"No, you don't know me: you never knew me when I was a man," speaks the stranger, raising his hat, as a smile lights up his features. "You don't know Tom Swiggs, the miserable inebriate—"

A spontaneous shout of recognition, echoing and reechoing through the old halls, interrupts this declaration. One by one the imprisoned men grasp him by the hand, and shower upon him the warmest, the heartiest congratulations. A once fallen brother has risen to a knowledge of his own happiness. Hands that raised him from that mat of straw, when the mental man seemed lost, now welcome him restored, a purer being.

"Ah, Spunyarn," says Tom, greeting the old sailor with childlike fondness, as the tears are seen gushing into the eyes, and coursing down the browned face of the old mariner, "I owe you a debt I fear I never can pay. I have thought of you in my absence, and had hoped on my return to see you released. I am sorry you are not—"

"Well, as to that," interrupts the old sailor, his face resuming its wonted calm, "I can't—you know I can't, Tom,—sail without a clearance. I sometimes think I'm never going to get one. Two years, as you know, I've been here, now backing and then filling, in and out, just as it suits that chap with the face like a snatch-block. They call him a justice. 'Pon my soul, Tom, I begin to think justice for us poor folks is got aground. Well, give us your hand agin' (he seizes Tom by the hand); its all well wi' you, anyhows.'

"Yes, thank God," says Tom, returning his friendly shake, "I have conquered the enemy, and my thanks for it are due to those who reached my heart with kind words, and gave me a brother's hand. I was not dead to my own degradation; but imprisonment left me no hope. The sting of disappointment may pain your feelings; hope deferred may torture you here in a prison; the persecutions of enemies may madden your very soul; but when a mother turns coldly from you—No, I will not say it, for I love her still—" he hesitates, as the old sailor says, with touching simplicity, he never knew what it was to have a mother or father. Having spread before the old man and his companions sundry refreshments he had ordered brought in, and received in return their thanks, he inquires of Spunyarn how it happened that he got into prison, and how it is that he remains here a fixture.

"I'll tell you, Tom," says the old sailor, commencing his story. "We'd just come ashore—had a rough passage—and, says I to myself, here's lay up ashore awhile. So I gets a crimp, who takes me to a crib. 'It's all right here—you'll have snug quarters, Jack,' says he, introducing me to the chap who kept it. I gives him twenty dollars on stack, and gets up my chest and hammock, thinking it was all fair and square. Then I meets an old shipmate, who I took in tow, he being hard ashore for cash. 'Let us top the meetin' with a glass,' says I. 'Agreed,' says Bill, and I calls her on, the very best. 'Ten cents a glass,' says the fellow behind the counter, giving us stuff that burnt as it went. 'Mister,' says I, 'do ye want to poison a sailor?' 'If you no like him,' says he, 'go get better somewhere else.' I told him to give me back the twenty, and me dunnage.

"'You don't get him—clear out of mine 'ouse,' says he.

"'Under the peak,' says I, fetching him a but under the lug that beached him among his beer-barrels. He picked himself up, and began talking about a magistrate. And knowing what sort of navigation a fellow'd have in the hands of that sort of land-craft, I began to think about laying my course for another port. 'Hold on here,' says a big-sided land-lubber, seizing me by the fore-sheets. 'Cast off there,' says I, 'or I'll put ye on yer beam-ends.'

"'I'm a constable,' says he, pulling out a pair of irons he said must go on my hands."

"I hope he did not put them on," interrupts the young theologian, for it is he who accompanies Tom.

"Avast! I'll come to that. He said he'd only charge me five dollars for going to jail without 'em, so rather than have me calling damaged, I giv him it. It was only a trifle. 'Now, Jack,' says the fellow, as we went along, in a friendly sort of way, 'just let us pop in and see the justice. I think a ten 'll get ye a clearance.' 'No objection to that,' says I, and in we went, and there sat the justice, face as long and sharp as a marlinspike, in a dirty old hole, that looked like our forecastle. 'Bad affair this, Jack,' says he, looking up over his spectacles. 'You must be locked up for a year and a day, Jack.'

"'You'll give a sailor a hearin', won't ye?' says I. 'As to that,—well, I don't know, Jack; you musn't break the laws of South Carolina when you get ashore. You seem like a desirable sailor, and can no doubt get a ship and good wages—this is a bad affair. However, as I'm not inclined to be hard, if you are disposed to pay twenty dollars, you can go.' 'Law and justice,' says I, shaking my fist at him—'do ye take this salt-water citizen for a fool?'

"'Take him away, Mr. Stubble—lock him up!—lock him up!' says the justice, and here I am, locked up, hard up, hoping. I'd been tied up about three weeks when the justice looked in one day, and after inquiring for me, and saying, 'good morning, Jack,' and seeming a little by the head: 'about this affair of yourn, Jack,' says he, 'now, if you'll mind your eye when you get out—my trouble's worth ten dollars—and pay me, I'll discharge you, and charge the costs to the State.'

"'Charge the cost to the State!' says I. 'Do you take Spunyarn for a marine?' At this he hauled his wind, and stood out."

"You have had a hearing before the Grand Jury, have you not?" inquires Tom, evincing a deep interest in the story of his old friend.

"Not I. This South Carolina justice is a hard old craft to sail in. The Grand Jury only looks in once every six months, and then looks out again, without inquiring who's here. And just before the time it comes round, I'm shuffled out, and just after it has left, I'm shuffled in again—fees charged to the State! That's it. So here I am, a fee-making machine, bobbing in and out of jail to suit the conveniences of Mister Justice. I don't say this with any ill will—I don't." Having concluded his story, the old sailor follows his visitors to the prison gate, takes an affectionate leave of Tom Swiggs, and returns to join his companions. On the following day, Tom intercedes with Mr. Snivel, for it is he who thus harvests fees of the State by retaining the old sailor in prison, and procures his release. And here, in Mr. Snivel, you have an instrument of that debased magistracy which triumphs over the weak, that sits in ignorance and indolence, that invests the hypocritical designer with a power almost absolute, that keeps justice muzzled on her throne— the natural offspring of that demon-making institution that scruples not to brunt the intellect of millions, while dragging a pall of sloth over the land.

CHAPTER XXX
CONTAINING VARIOUS THINGS
APPERTAINING TO THIS HISTORY

Maria McArthur having, by her womanly sympathy, awakened the generous impulses of Tom Swiggs, he is resolved they shall have a new channel for their action. Her kindness touched his heart; her solicitude for his welfare gained his affections, and a recognition of that love she so long and silently cherished for him, is the natural result. The heart that does not move to woman's kindness, must indeed be hard. But there were other things which strengthened Tom's affections for Maria. The poverty of her aged father; the insults offered her by Keepum and Snivel; the manner in which they sought her ruin while harassing her father; the artlessness and lone condition of the pure-minded girl; and the almost holy affection evinced for the old man on whom she doted—all tended to bring him nearer and nearer to her, until he irresistibly found himself at her feet, pledging that faith lovers call eternal. Maria is not of that species of being the world calls beautiful; but there is about her something pure, thoughtful, even noble; and this her lone condition heightens. Love does not always bow before beauty. The singularities of human nature are most strikingly blended in woman. She can overcome physical defects; she can cultivate attractions most appreciated by those who study her worth deepest. Have you not seen those whose charms at first-sight found no place in your thoughts, but as you were drawn nearer and nearer to them, so also did your esteem quicken, and that esteem, almost unconsciously, you found ripening into affection, until in turn you were seized with an ardent passion? You have. And you have found yourself enamored of the very one against whom you had endeavored most to restrain your generous impulses. Like the fine lines upon a picture with a repulsive design, you trace them, and recur to them until your admiration is carried away captive. So it is with woman's charms. Tom Swiggs, then, the restored man, bows before the simple goodness of the daughter of the old Antiquary.

Mr. Trueman, the shipowner, gave Tom employment, and has proved a friend to him. Tom, in turn, has so far gained his confidence and respect that Mr. Trueman contemplates sending him to London, on board one of his ships. Nor has Tom forgotten to repay the old Antiquary, who gave him a shelter when he was homeless; this home is still under the roof of the old man, toward whose comfort he contributes weekly a portion of his earnings. If you could but look into that little back-parlor, you would see a picture of humble cheerfulness presented in the old man, his daughter, and Tom Swiggs, seated round the tea-table. Let us, however, turn and look into one of our gaudy saloons, that we may see how different a picture is presented there.

It is the night previous to an election for Mayor. Leaden clouds hang threatening over the city; the gas-light throws out its shadows at an early hour; and loud-talking men throng our street-corners and public resorts. Our politicians tell us that the destiny of the rich and the poor is to forever guard that institution which employs all our passions, and absorbs all our energies.

In a curtained box, at the St. Charles, sits Mr. Snivel and George Mullholland—the latter careworn and downcast of countenance. "Let us finish this champaign, my good fellow," says the politician, emptying his glass. "A man—I mean one who wants to get up in the world—must, like me, have two distinct natures. He must have a grave, moral nature—that is necessary to the affairs of State. And he must, to accommodate himself to the world (law and society, I mean), have a terribly loose nature—a perfect quicksand, into which he can drag everything that serves himself. You have seen how I can develop both these, eh?" The downcast man shakes his head, as the politician watches him with a steady gaze. "Take the advice of a friend, now, let the Judge alone—don't threaten again to shoot that girl. Threats are sometimes dragged in as testimony against a man (Mr. Snivel taps George admonishingly on the arm); and should anything of a serious nature befall her—the law is curious—why, what you have said might implicate you, though you were innocent."

"You," interrupts George, "have shot your man down in the street."

"A very different affair, George. My position in society protects me. I am a member of the Jockey-Club, a candidate for the State Senate—a Justice of the Peace—yes, a politician! You are—Well, I was going to say—nothing! We regard northerners as enemies; socially, they are nothing. Come, George, come with me. I am your best friend. You shall see the power in my hands." The two men saunter out together, pass up a narrow lane leading from King Street, and are soon groping their way up the dark stairway of an old, neglected-looking wooden building, that for several years has remained deserted by everything but rats and politicians,—one seeming to gnaw away at the bowels of the nation, the other at the bowels of the old building. Having ascended to the second floor, Mr. Snivel touches a spring, a suspicious little trap opens, and two bright eyes peer out, as a low, whispering voice inquires, "Who's there?" Mr. Snivel has exchanged the countersign, and with his companion is admitted into a dark vestibule, in which sits a brawny guardsman.

"Cribs are necessary, sir—I suppose you never looked into one before?"

George, in a voice discovering timidity, says he never has.

"You must have cribs, and crib-voters; they are necessary to get into high office—indeed, I may say, to keep up with the political spirit of the age." Mr. Snivel is interrupted by the deep, coarse voice of Milman Mingle, the vote-cribber, whose broad, savage face looks out at a small guard trap. "All right," he says, recognizing Mr. Snivel. Another minute, and a door opens into a long, sombre-looking room, redolent of the fumes of whiskey and tobacco. "The day is ours. We'll elect our candidate, and then my election is certain; naturalized thirteen rather green ones to-day—to-morrow they will be trump cards. Stubbs has attended to the little matter of the ballot-boxes." Mr. Snivel gives the vote-cribber's hand a warm shake, and turns to introduce his friend. The vote-cribber has seen him before. "There are thirteen in," he says, and two more he has in his eye, and will have in to-night, having sent trappers out for them.

Cold meats, bread, cheese, and crackers, and a bountiful supply of bad whiskey, are spread over a table in the centre of the room; while the pale light of two small lamps, suspended from the ceiling, throws a curious shadow over the repulsive features of thirteen forlorn, ragged, and half-drunken men, sitting here and there round the room, on wooden benches. You see ignorance and cruelty written in their very countenances. For nearly three weeks they have not scented the air of heaven, but have been held here in a despicable bondage. Ragged and filthy, like Falstaff's invincibles, they will be marched to the polls to-morrow, and cast their votes at the bid of the cribber. "A happy lot of fellows," says Mr. Snivel, exultingly. "I have a passion for this sort of business—am general supervisor of all these cribs, you understand. We have several of them. Some of these 'drifts' we kidnap, and some come and be locked up of their own accord—merely for the feed and drink. We use them, and then snuff them out until we want them again." Having turned from George, and complimented the vote-cribber for his skill, he bids him good-night. Together George and the politician wend their way to an obscure part of the city, and having passed up two flight of winding stairs, into a large, old-fashioned house on the Neck, are in a sort of barrack-room, fitted up with bunks and benches, and filled with a grotesque assembly, making night jubilant—eating, drinking, smoking, and singing. "A jolly set of fellows," says Mr. Snivel, with an expression of satisfaction. "This is a decoy crib—the vagabonds all belong to the party of our opponents, but don't know it. We work in this way: we catch them— they are mostly foreigners—lock them up, give them good food and drink, and make them—not the half can speak our language—believe we belong to the same party. They yield, as submissive as curs. To morrow, we—this is in confidence—drug them all, send them into a fast sleep, in which we keep them till the polls are closed, then, not wanting them longer, we kick them out for a set of drunkards. Dangerous sort of cribbing, this. I let you into the secret out of pure friendship." Mr. Snivel pauses. George has at heart something of deeper interest to him than votes and vote-cribbers. But why, he says to himself, does Mr. Snivel evince this anxiety to befriend me? This question is answered by Mr. Snivel inviting him to take a look into the Keno den.

CHAPTER XXXI
THE KENO DEN, AND WHAT MAY BE SEEN IN IT

The clock has just struck twelve. Mr. Snivel and George, passing from the scenes of our last chapter, enter a Keno den,[5] situated on Meeting street. "You must get money, George. Here you are nothing without money. Take this, try your hand, make your genius serve you." Mr. Snivel puts twenty dollars into George's hand. They are in a room some twenty by thirty feet in dimensions, dimly-lighted. Standing here and there are gambling tables, around which are seated numerous mechanics, losing, and being defrauded of that for which they have labored hard during the week. Hope, anxiety, and even desperation is pictured on the countenances of the players. Maddened and disappointed, one young man rises from a table, at which sits a craven-faced man sweeping the winnings into his pile, and with profane tongue, says he has lost his all. Another, with flushed face and bloodshot eyes, declares it the sixth time he has lost his earnings here. A third reels confusedly about the room, says a mechanic is but a dog in South Carolina; and the sooner he comes to a dog's end the better.

Mr. Snivel points George to a table, at which he is soon seated. "Blank—blank—blank!" he reiterates, as the numbers turn up, and one by one the moody bank-keeper sweeps the money into his fast-increasing heap. "Cursed fate!—it is against me," mutters the forlorn man. "Another gone, and yet another! How this deluding, this fascinating money tortures me." With hectic face and agitated nerve, he puts down his last dollar. "Luck's mysterious!" exclaims Mr. Snivel, looking on unmoved, as the man of the moody face declares a blank, and again sweeps the money into his heap. "Gone!" says George, "all's gone now." He rises from his seat, in despair.

"Don't get frantic, George—be a philosopher—try again—here's a ten. Luck 'll turn," says Mr. Snivel, patting the deluded man familiarly on the shoulder, as he resumes his seat. "Will poverty never cease torturing me? I have tried to be a man, an honest man, a respectable man. And yet, here I am, again cast upon a gambler's sea, struggling with its fearful tempests. How cold, how stone-like the faces around me!" he muses, watching with death-like gaze each number as it turns up. Again he has staked his last dollar; again fortune frowns upon him. Like a furnace of livid flame, the excitement seems burning up his brain. "I am a fool again," he says, throwing the blank number contemptuously upon the table. "Take it—take it, speechless, imperturbable man! Rake it into your pile, for my eyes are dim, and my fortune I must seek elsewhere."

A noise at the door, as of some one in distress, is heard, and there rushes frantically into the den a pale, dejected-looking woman, bearing in her arms a sick and emaciated babe. "Oh, William! William!—has it come to this?" she shrieks, casting a wild glance round the den, until, with a dark, sad expression, her eye falls upon the object of her search. It is her husband, once a happy mechanic. Enticed by degrees into this den of ruin, becoming fascinated with its games of chance, he is how an *habitue*. To-night he left his suffering family, lost his all here, and now, having drank to relieve his feelings, lies insensible on the floor. "Come home!—come home! for God's sake come home to your suffering family," cries the woman, vaulting to him and taking him by the hand, her hair floating dishevelled down her shoulders. "I sent Tommy into the street to beg—I am ashamed—and he is picked up by the watch for a thief, a vagrant!" The prostrate man remains insensible to her appeal. Two policemen, who have been quietly neglecting their duties while taking a few chances, sit unmoved. Mr. Snivel thinks the woman better be removed. "Our half-starved mechanics," he says, "are a depraved set; and these wives they bring with them from the North are a sort of cross between a lean stage-driver and a wildcat. She seems a poor, destitute creature—just what they all come to, out here." Mr. Snivel shrugs his shoulders, bids George good night, and takes his departure. "Take care of yourself, George," he says admonitiously, as the destitute man watches him take his leave. The woman, frantic at the coldness and apathy manifested for her distress, lays her babe hurriedly upon the floor, and with passion and despair darting from her very eyes, makes a lunge across the keno table at the man who sits stoically at the bank. In an instant everything is turned into uproar and confusion. Glasses, chairs, and tables, are hurled about the floor; shriek follows shriek—"help! pity me! murder!" rises above the confusion, the watch without sound the alarm, and the watch within suddenly become conscious of their duty. In the midst of all the confusion, a voice cries out: "My pocket book—my pocket book!—I have been robbed." A light flashes from a guardsman's lantern, and George Mullholland is discovered with the forlorn woman in his arms—she clings tenaciously to her babe—rushing into the street.

CHAPTER XXXII
WHICH A STATE OF SOCIETY
IS SLIGHTLY REVEALED

A week has rolled into the past since the event at the Keno den.

Madame Montford, pale, thoughtful, and abstracted, sits musing in her parlor. "Between this hope and fear—this remorse of conscience, this struggle to overcome the suspicions of society, I have no peace. I am weary of this slandering—this unforgiving world. And yet it is my own conscience that refuses to forgive me. Go where I will I see the cold finger of scorn pointed at me: I read in every countenance, 'Madame Montford, you have wronged some one—your guilty conscience betrays you!' I have sought to atone for my error—to render justice to one my heart tells me I have wronged, yet I cannot shake off the dread burden; and there seems rest for me only in the grave. Ah! there it is. The one error of my life, and the moans used to conceal it, may have brought misery upon more heads than one." She lays her hand upon her heart, and shakes her head sorrowfully. "Yes! something like a death-knell rings in my ears—'more than one have you sent, unhappy, to the grave.' Rejected by the one I fancy my own; my very touch, scorned; my motives misconstrued—all, perhaps, by—a doubt yet hangs between us—an abandoned stranger. Duty to my conscience has driven me to acts that have betrayed me to society. I cannot shake my guilt from me even for a day; and now society coldly cancels all my claims to its attentions. If I could believe her dead; if I but knew this girl was not the object of all my heart's unrest, then the wearying doubt would be buried, and my heart might find peace in some remote corner of the earth. Well, well—perhaps I am wasting all this torture on an unworthy object. I should have thought of this sooner, for now foul slander is upon every tongue, and my misery is made thrice painful by my old flatterers. I will make one more effort, then if I fail of getting a certain clue to her, I will remove to some foreign country, shake off these haunting dreams, and be no longer a victim to my own thoughts." Somewhat relieved, Madame is roused from her reverie by a gentle tap at the door. "I have waited your coming, and am glad to see you," she says, extending her hand, as a servant, in response to her command, ushers into her presence no less a person than Tom Swiggs.

"I have sent for you," she resumes, motioning him gracefully to a chair, in which she begs he will be seated, "because I feel I can confide in you—"

"Anything in my power is at your service, Madame," modestly interposes Tom, regaining confidence.

"I entrusted something of much importance to me, to Mr. Snivel—"

"We call him the Hon. Mr. Snivel now, since he has got to be a great politician," interrupts Tom.

"And he not only betrayed my Confidence," pursues Madame Montford, "but retains the amount I paid him, and forgets to render the promised service. You, I am told, can render me a service—"

"As for Mr. Snivel," pursues Tom, hastily, "he has of late had his hands full, getting a poor but good-natured fellow, by the name of George Mullholland, into trouble. His friend, Judge Sleepyhorn, and he, have for some time had a plot on hand to crush this poor fellow. A few nights ago Snivel drove him mad at a gambling den, and in his desperation he robbed a man of his pocket-book. He shared the money with a poor woman he rescued at the den, and that is the way it was discovered that he was the criminal. He is a poor, thoughtless man, and he has been goaded on from one thing to another, until he was driven to commit this act. First, his wife was got away from him—" Tom pauses and blushes, as Madame Montford says: "His wife was got away from him?"

"Yes, Madame," returns Tom, with an expression of sincerity, "The Judge got her away from him; and this morning he was arraigned before that same Judge for examination, and Mr. Snivel was a principal witness, and there was enough found against him to commit him for trial at the Sessions." Discovering that this information is exciting her emotions, Tom pauses, and contemplates her with steady gaze. She desires he will be her guide to the Poor-House, and there assist her in searching for Mag Munday, whom, report says, is confined in a cell. Tom having expressed his readiness to serve her, they are soon on their way to that establishment.

A low, squatty building, with a red, moss-covered roof, two lean chimneys peeping out, the windows blockaded with dirt, and situated in one of the by-lanes of the city, is our Poor-House, standing half hid behind a crabbed old wall, and looking very like a much-neglected Quaker church in vegetation. We boast much of our institutions, and this being a sample of them, we hold it in great reverence. You may say that nothing so forcibly illustrates a state of society as the character of its institutions for the care of those unfortunate beings whom a capricious nature has deprived of their reason. We agree with you. We see our Poor-House crumbling to the ground with decay, yet imagine it, or affect to imagine it, a very grand edifice, in every way suited to the wants of such rough ends of humanity as are found in it. Like Satan, we are brilliant believers in ourselves, not bad sophists, and singularly clever in finding apologies for all great crimes.

At the door of the Poor-House stands a dilapidated hearse, to which an old gray horse is attached. A number of buzzards have gathered about him, turn their heads suspiciously now and then, and seem meditating a descent upon his bones at no very distant day. Madame casts a glance at the hearse, and the poor old horse, and the cawing buzzards, then follows Tom, timidly, to the door. He has rung the bell, and soon there stands before them, in the damp doorway, a fussy old man, with a very broad, red face, and a very blunt nose, and two very dull, gray eyes, which he fortifies with a fair of massive-framed spectacles, that have a passion for getting upon the tip-end of his broad blunt nose.

"There, you want to see somebody! Always somebody wanted to be seen, when we have dead folks to get rid of," mutters the old man, querulously, then looking inquiringly at the visitors. Tom says they would like to go over the premises. "Yes—know you would. Ain't so dull but I can see what folks want when they look in here." The old man, his countenance wearing an expression of stupidity, runs his dingy fingers over the crown of his bald head, and seems questioning within himself whether to admit them. "I'm not in a very good humor to-day," he rather growls than speaks, "but you can come in—I'm of a good family—and I'll call Glentworthy. I'm old—I can't get about much. We'll all get old." The building seems in a very bad temper generally.

Mr. Glentworthy is called. Mr. Glentworthy, with a profane expletive, pops his head out at the top of the stairs, and inquires who wants him. The visitors have advanced into a little, narrow passage, lumbered with all sorts of rubbish, and swarming with flies. Mr. Saddlerock (for this is the old man's name) seems in a declining mood, the building seems in a declining mood, Mr. Glentworthy seems in a declining mood—everything you look at seems in a declining mood. "As if I hadn't enough to do, gettin' off this dead cribber!" interpolates Mr. Glentworthy, withdrawing his wicked face, and taking himself back into a room on the left.

"He's not so bad a man, only it doesn't come out at first," pursues Mr. Saddlerock, continuing to rub his head, and to fuss round on his toes. His mind, Madame Montford verily believes stuck in a fog. "We must wait a bit," says the old man, his face seeming to elongate. "You can look about—there's not much to be seen, and what there is—well, it's not the finest." Mr. Saddlerock shuffles his feet, and then shuffles himself into a small side room. Through the building there breathes a warm, sickly atmosphere; the effect has left its marks upon the sad, waning countenances of its unfortunate inmates.

Tom and Madame Montford set out to explore the establishment. They enter room after room, find them small, dark, and filthy beyond description. Some are crowded with half-naked, flabby females, whose careworn faces, and well-starved aspect, tells a sorrowful tale of the chivalry. An abundant supply of profane works, in yellow and red covers, would indeed seem to have been substituted for food, which, to the shame of our commissioners, be it said, is a scarce article here. Cooped up in another little room, after the fashion of wild beasts in a cage, are seven poor idiots, whose forlorn condition, sad, dull countenances, as they sit round a table, staring vacantly at one another, like mummies in contemplation, form a wild but singularly touching picture. Each countenance pales before the seeming study of its opponent, until, enraptured and amazed, they break out into a wild, hysterical laugh. And thus, poisoned, starved, and left to die, does time with these poor mortals fleet on.

The visitors ascend to the second story. A shuffling of feet in a room at the top of the stairs excites their curiosity. Mr. Glentworthy's voice grates harshly on the ear, in language we cannot insert in this history. "Our high families never look into low places—chance if the commissioner has looked in here for years," says Tom, observing Madame Montford protect her inhaling organs with her perfumed cambric. "There is a principle of economy carried out—and a very nice principle, too, in getting these poor out of the world as quick as possible." Tom pushes open a door, and, heavens! what a sight is here. He stands aghast in the doorway—Madam, on tip-toe, peers anxiously in over his shoulders. Mr. Glentworthy and two negroes—the former slightly inebriated, the latter trembling of fright—are preparing to box up a lifeless mass, lying carelessly upon the floor. The distorted features, the profusion of long, red hair, curling over a scared face, and the stalworth figure, shed some light upon the identity of the deceased. "Who is it?" ejaculates Mr. Glentworthy, in response to an inquiry from Tom. Mr. Glentworthy shrugs his shoulders, and commences whistling a tune. "That cove!" he resumes, having stopped short in his tune, "a man what don't know that cove, never had much to do with politics. Stuffed more ballot boxes, cribbed more voters, and knocked down more slip-shod citizens—that cove has, than, put 'em all together, would make a South Carolina regiment. A mighty man among politicians, he was! Now the devil has cribbed him—he'll know how good it is!" Mr. Glentworthy says this with an air of superlative satisfaction, resuming his tune. The dead man is Milman Mingle, the vote-cribber, who died of a wound he received at the hands of an antagonist, whom he was endeavoring to "block out" while going to the polls to cast his vote. "Big politician, but had no home!" says Madame, with a sigh.

Mr. Glentworthy soon had what remained of the vote-cribber—the man to whom so many were indebted for their high offices—into a deal box, and the deal box into the old hearse, and the old hearse, driven by a mischievous negro, hastening to that great crib to which we must all go. "Visitors," Mr. Glentworthy smiles, "must not question the way we do business here, I get no pay, and there's only old Saddlerock and me to do all the work. Old Saddlerock, you see, is a bit of a miser, and having a large family of small Saddlerocks to provide for, scrapes what he can into his own pocket. No one is the wiser. They can't be—they never come in." Mr. Glentworthy, in reply to a question from Madame Montford, says Mag Munday (he has some faint recollection of her) was twice in the house, which he dignifies with the title of "Institution." She never was in the "mad cells"—to his recollection. "Them what get there, mostly die there." A gift of two dollars secures Mr. Glentworthy's services, and restores him to perfect good nature. "You will remember," says Tom, "that this woman ran neglected about the streets, was much abused, and ended in becoming a maniac." Mr. Glentworthy remembers very well, but adds: "We have so many maniacs on our hands, that we can't distinctly remember them all. The clergymen take good care never to look in here. They couldn't do any good if they did, for nobody cares for the rubbish sent here; and if you tried to Christianize them, you would only get laughed at. I don't like to be laughed at. Munday's not here now, that's settled—but I'll—for curiosity's sake—show you into the 'mad cells.'" Mr. Glentworthy leads the way, down the rickety old stairs, through the lumbered passage, into an open square, and from thence into a small out-building, at the extreme end of which some dozen wet, slippery steps, led into a dark subterranean passage, on each side of which are small, dungeon-like cells. "Heavens!" exclaims Madame Montford, picking her way down the steep, slippery steps. "How chilling! how tomb-like! Can it be that mortals are confined here, and live?" she mutters, incoherently. The stifling atmosphere is redolent of disease.

"It straightens 'em down, sublimely—to put 'em in here," says Mr. Glentworthy, laconically, lighting his lamp. "I hope to get old Saddlerock in here. Give him such a mellowing!" He turns his light, and the shadows play, spectre-like, along a low, wet aisle, hung on each side with rusty bolts and locks, revealing the doors of cells. An ominous stillness is broken by the dull clank of chains, the muttering of voices, the shuffling of limbs;

then a low wail breaks upon the ear, and rises higher and higher, shriller and shriller, until in piercing shrieks it chills the very heart. Now it ceases, and the echoes, like the murmuring winds, die faintly away. "Look in here, now," says Mr. Glentworthy—"a likely wench—once she was!"

He swings open a door, and there issues from a cell about four feet six inches wide, and nine long, the hideous countenance of a poor, mulatto girl, whose shrunken body, skeleton-like arms, distended and glassy eyes, tell but too forcibly her tale of sorrow. How vivid the picture of wild idiocy is pictured in her sad, sorrowing face. No painter's touch could have added a line more perfect. Now she rushes forward, with a suddenness that makes Madame Montford shrink back, appalled—now she fixes her eyes, hangs down her head, and gives vent to her tears. "My soul is white—yes, yes, yes! I know it is white; God tells me it is white—he knows—he never tortures. He doesn't keep me here to die—no, I can't die here in the dark. I won't get to heaven if I do. Oh! yes, yes, yes, I have a white soul, but my skin is not," she rather murmurs than speaks, continuing to hold down her head, while parting her long, clustering hair over her shoulders. Notwithstanding the spectacle of horror presented in this living skeleton, there is something in her look and action which bespeaks more the abuse of long confinement than the result of natural aberration of mind. "She gets fierce now and then, and yells," says the unmoved Glentworthy, "but she won't hurt ye—" [6] "How long," inquires Madame Montford, who has been questioning within herself whether any act of her life could have brought a Human being into such a place, "has she been confined here?" Mr. Glentworthy says she tells her own tale.

"Five years,—five years,—five long, long years, I have waited for him in the dark, but he won't come," she lisps in a faltering voice, as her emotions overwhelm her. Then crouching back upon the floor, she supports her head pensively in her left hand, her elbow resting on her knee, and her right hand poised against the brick wall, "Pencele!" says Mr. Glentworthy, for such is the wretched woman's name, "cannot you sing a song for your friends?" Turning aside to Madame Montford, he adds, "she sings nicely. We shall soon get her out of the way—can't last much longer." Mr. Glentworthy, drawing a small bottle from his pocket, places it to his lips, saying he stole it from old Saddlerock, and gulps down a portion of the contents. His breath is already redolent of whiskey. "Oh, yes, yes, yes! I can sing for them, I can smother them with kisses. Good faces seldom look in here, seldom look in here," she rises to her feet, and extends her bony hand, as the tears steal down Madame Montford's cheeks. Tom stands speechless. He wishes he had power to redress the wrongs of this suffering maniac—his very soul fires up against the coldness and apathy of a people who permit such outrages against humanity. "There!—he comes! he comes! he comes!" the maniac speaks, with faltering voice, then strikes up a plaintive air, which she sings with a voice of much sweetness, to these words:

> When you find him, speed him to me,
> And this heart will cease its bleeding, &c.

The history of all this poor maniac's sufferings is told in a few simple words that fall incautiously from Mr. Glentworthy's lips: "Poor fool, she had only been married a couple of weeks, when they sold her husband down South. She thinks if she keeps mad, he'll come back."

There was something touching, something melancholy in the music of her song, as its strains verberated and reverberated through the dread vault, then, like the echo of a lover's lute on some Alpine hill, died softly away.

CHAPTER XXXIII
IN WHICH THERE IS A SINGULAR REVELATION

Madame Montford returns, unsuccessful, to her parlor. It is conscience that unlocks the guilty heart, that forces mortals to seek relief where there is no chance of finding it. It was this irresistible emotion that found her counseling Tom Swiggs, making of him a confidant in her search for the woman she felt could remove the doubt, in respect to Anna's identity, that hung so painfully in her mind. And yet, such was her position, hesitating as it were between her ambition to move in fashionable society, and her anxiety to atone for a past error, that she dare not disclose the secret of all her troubles even to him. She sought him, not that he could soften her anxiety, but that being an humble person, she could pursue her object through him, unobserved to society—in a word, that he would be a protection against the apprehensions of scandal-mongers. Such are the shifts to which the ambitious guilty have recourse. What she has beheld in the poor-house, too, only serves to quicken her thoughts of the misery she may have inflicted upon others, and to stimulate her resolution to persevere in her search for the woman. Conscious that wealth and luxury does not always bring happiness, and that without a spotless character, woman is but a feeble creature in this world, she would now sacrifice everything else for that one ennobling charm.

It may be proper here to add, that although Tom Swiggs could not enter into the repentant woman's designs, having arranged with his employer to sail for London in a few days, she learned of him something that reflected a little more light in her path. And that was, that the woman Anna Bonard, repined of her act in leaving George Mullholland, to whom she was anxious to return—that she was now held against her will; that she detested Judge Sleepyhorn, although he had provided lavishly for her comfort. Anna knew George loved her, and that love, even to an abandoned woman (if she could know it sincere), was dearer to her than all else. She learned, too, that high up on Anna's right arm, there was imprinted in blue and red ink, two hearts and a broken anchor. And this tended further to increase her anxiety. And while evolving all these things in her mind, and contemplating the next best course to pursue, her parlor is invaded by Mr. Snivel. He is no longer

Mr. Soloman, nor Mr. Snivel. He is the Hon. Mr. Snivel. It is curious to contemplate the character of the men to whose name we attach this mark of distinction. "I know you will pardon my seeming neglect, Madame," he says, grasping her hand warmly, as a smile of exultation lights up his countenance. "The fact is, we public men are so absorbed in the affairs of the nation, that we have scarce a thought to give to affairs of a private nature. We have elected our ticket. I was determined it should be so, if Jericho fell. And, more than all, I am made an honorable, by the popular sentiment of the people—"

"To be popular with the people, is truly an honor," interrupts the lady, facetiously.

"Thank you—O, thank you, for the compliment," pursues our hero. "Now, as to this unfortunate person you seek, knowing it was of little use to search for her in our institutions of charity—one never can find out anything about the wretches who get into them—I put the matter into the hands of one of our day-police—a plaguey sharp fellow—and he set about scenting her out. I gave him a large sum, and promised him more if successful. Here, then, after a long and tedious search—I have no doubt the fellow earned his money—is what he got from New York, this morning." The Hon. Mr. Snivel, fixing his eye steadily upon her, hands her a letter which reads thus:

"New York, *Dec. 14th, 18—*.

"Last night, while making search after a habitant of the Points, a odd old chip what has wandered about here for some years, some think he has bin a better sort of man once, I struck across the woman you want. She is somewhere tucked away in a Cow Bay garret, and is awful crazy; I'll keep me eye out till somethin' further. If her friends wants to give her a lift out of this place, they'd better come and see me at once.

"Yours, as ever,

"M— — Fitzgerald."

Mr. Snivel ogles Madame Montford over the page of a book he affects to read. "Guilt! deep and strong," he says within himself, as Madame, with flushed countenance and trembling hand, ponders and ponders over the paper. Then her emotions quicken, her eyes exchange glances with Mr. Snivel, and she whispers, with a sigh, "found—at last! And yet how foolish of me to give way to my feelings? The affair, at best, is none of mine." Mr. Snivel bows, and curls his Saxon mustache. "To do good for others is the natural quality of a generous nature."

Madame, somewhat relieved by this condescension of the Hon. gentleman, says, in reply, "I am curious at solving family affairs."

"And I!" says our hero, with refreshing coolness—"always ready to do a bit of a good turn."

Madame pauses, as if in doubt whether to proceed or qualify what she has already said. "A relative, whose happiness I make my own," she resumes, and again pauses, while the words tremble upon her lips. She hears the words knelling in her ears: "A guilty conscience needs no betrayer."

"You have," pursues our hero, "a certain clue; and of that I may congratulate you."

Madame says she will prepare at once to return to her home in New York, and—and here again the words hang upon her lips. She was going to say, her future proceedings would be governed by the paper she holds so nervously in her finger.

Snivel here receives a nostrum from the lady's purse. "Truly!—Madame," he says, in taking leave of her, "the St. Cecilia will regret you—we shall all regret you; you honored and graced our assemblies so. Our first families will part with you reluctantly. It may, however, be some satisfaction to know how many kind things will be said of you in your absence." Mr. Snivel makes his last bow, a sarcastic smile playing over his face, and pauses into the street.

On the following day she encloses a present of fifty dollars to Tom Swiggs, enjoins the necessity of his keeping her visit to the poor-house a secret, and takes leave of Charleston.

And here our scene changes, and we must transport the reader to New York. It is the day following the night Mr. Detective Fitzgerald discovered what remained of poor Toddleworth, in the garret of the House of the Nine Nations. The City Hall clock strikes twelve. The goodly are gathered into the House of the Foreign Missions, in which peace and respectability would seem to preside. The good-natured fat man is in his seat, pondering over letters lately received from the "dark regions" of Arabia; the somewhat lean, but very respectable-looking Secretary, is got nicely into his spectacles, and sits pondering over lusty folios of reports from Hindostan, and various other fields of missionary labor, all setting forth the various large amounts of money expended, how much more could be expended, and what a blessing it is to be enabled to announce the fact that there is now a hope of something being done. The same anxious-faced bevy of females we described in a previous chapter, are here, seated at a table, deeply interested in certain periodicals and papers; while here and there about the room, are several contemplative gentlemen in black. Brother Spyke, having deeply interested Brothers Phills and Prim with an account of his visit to the Bottomless Pit, paces up and down the room, thinking of Antioch, and the evangelization of the heathen world. "Truly, brother," speaks the good-natured fat man, "his coming seemeth long." "Eleven was the hour; but why he tarryeth I know not," returns Brother Spyke, with calm demeanor. "There is something more alarming in Sister Slocum's absence," interposes one of the ladies. The house seems in a waiting mood, when suddenly Mr. Detective Fitzgerald enters, and changes it to one of anxiety. Several voices inquire if he was successful. He shakes his head, and having recounted his adventures, the discovery of where the money went to, and the utter hopelessness of an effort to recover it; "as for the man, Toddleworth," he says, methodically, "he was found with a broken skull. The Coroner has had an inquest over him; but murders are so common. The verdict was, that he died of a broken skull, by the hands of some one to the jury unknown. Suspicions were strong against one Tom Downey, who is very like a heathen, and is mistrusted of several murders. The affair disturbed the neighborhood a little, and the Coroner tried to get something out concerning the man's history; but it all went to the wind, for the people were all so ignorant. They all knew everything about him, which turned out to be just nothing, which they were ready to swear to. One believed Father Flaherty made the Bible, another believed the Devil still chained in Columbia College—a third believed the stars were lanterns to guide priests—the only angels they know—on their way to heaven."

"Truly!" exclaims the man of the spectacles, in a moment of abstraction.

Brother Spyke says: "the Lord be merciful."

"On the body of the poor man we found this document. It was rolled carefully up in a rag, and is supposed to throw some light on his history." Mr. Fitzgerald draws leisurely from his pocket a distained and much-crumpled paper, written over in a bold, business-like hand, and passes it to the man in the spectacle, as a dozen or more anxious faces gather round, eager to explore the contents.

"He went out of the Points as mysteriously as he came in. We buried him a bit ago, and have got Downey in the Tombs: he'll be hanged, no doubt," concludes the detective, laying aside his cap, and setting himself, uninvited, into a chair. The man in the spectacles commences reading the paper, which runs as follows:

"I have been to you an unknown, and had died such an unknown, but that my conscience tells me I have a duty to perform. I have wronged no one, owe no one a penny, harbor no malice against any one; I am a victim of a broken heart, and my own melancholy. Many years ago I pursued an honorable business in this city, and was respected and esteemed. Many knew me, and fortune seemed to shed upon me her smiles. I married a lady of wealth and affluence, one I loved and doted on. Our affections seemed formed for our bond; we lived for one another; our happiness seemed complete. But alas! an evil hour came. Ambitious of admiration, she gradually became a slave to fashionable society, and then gave herself up to those flatterers who hang about it, and whose chief occupation it is to make weak-minded women vain of their own charms. Coldness, and indifference to home, soon followed. My house was invaded, my home—that home I regarded so sacredly—became the resort of men in whose society I found no pleasure, with whom I had no feeling in common. I could not remonstrate, for that would have betrayed in me a want of confidence in the fidelity of one I loved too blindly. I was not one of those who make life miserable in seeing a little and suspecting much. No! I forgave many things that wounded my feelings; and my love for her would not permit a thought to invade the sanctity of her fidelity. Business called me into a foreign country, where I remained several months, then returned—not, alas! to a home made happy by the purity of one I esteemed an angel;—not to the arms of a pure, fond wife, but to find my confidence betrayed, my home invaded—she, in whom I had treasured up my love, polluted; and slander, like a desert wind, pouring its desolating breath into my very heart. In my blindness I would have forgiven her, taken her back to my distracted bosom, and fled with her to some distant land, there still to have lived and loved her. But she sought rather to conceal her guilt than ask forgiveness. My reason fled me, my passion rose above my judgment, I sank under the burden of my sorrow, attempted to put an end to her life, and to my own misery. Failing in this, for my hand was stayed by a voice I heard calling to me, I fled the country and sought relief for my feelings in the wilds of Chili. I left nearly all to my wife, took but little with me, for my object was to bury myself from the world that had known me, and respected me. Destitution followed me; whither I went there seemed no rest, no peace of mind for me. The past floated uppermost in my mind. I was ever recurring to home, to those with whom I had associated, to an hundred things that had endeared me to my own country. Years passed—years of suffering and sorrow, and I found myself a lone wanderer, without friend or money. During this time it was reported at home, as well as chronicled in the newspapers, that I was dead. The inventor of this report had ends, I will not name them here, to serve. I was indeed dead to all who had known me happy in this world. Disguised, a mere shadow of what I was once, I wandered back to New York, heart-sick and discouraged, and buried myself among those whose destitution, worse, perhaps, than my own, afforded me a means of consolation. My life has long been a burden to me; I have many times prayed God, in his mercy, to take me away, to close the account of my misery. Do you ask my name? Ah! that is what pains me most. To live unknown, a wretched outcast, in a city where I once enjoyed a name that was respected, is what has haunted my thoughts, and tortured my feelings. But I cannot withhold it, even though it has gone down, tainted and dishonored. It is Henry Montford. And with this short record I close my history, leaving the rest for those to search out who find this paper, at my death, which cannot be long hence.

"Henry Montford.

"*New York, Nov.* —, *184-.*"

A few sighs follow the reading of the paper, but no very deep interest, no very tender emotion, is awakened in the hearts of the goodly. Nevertheless, it throws a flood of light upon the morals of a class of society vulgarly termed fashionable. The meek females hold their tears and shake their heads. Brother Spyke elongates his lean figure, draws near, and says the whole thing is very unsatisfactory. Not one word is let drop about the lost money.

Brother Phills will say this—that the romance is very cleverly got up, as the theatre people say.

The good-natured fat man, breathing somewhat freer, says: "Truly! these people have a pleasant way of passing out of the world. They die of their artful practices—seeking to devour the good and the generous."

"There's more suffers than imposes—an' there's more than's written meant in that same bit of paper. Toddleworth was as inoffensive a creature as you'd meet in a day. May God forgive him all his faults;" interposes Mr. Detective Fitzgerald, gathering up his cap and passing slowly out of the room.

And this colloquy is put an end to by the sudden appearance of Sister Slocum. A rustling silk dress, of quiet color, and set off with three modest flounces; an India shawl, loosely thrown over her shoulders; a dainty little collar, of honiton, drawn neatly about her neck, and a bonnet of buff-colored silk, tastefully set off with tart-pie work without, and lined with virtuous white satin within, so saucily poised on her head, suggests the idea that she has an eye to fashion as well as the heathen world. Her face, too, always so broad, bright, and benevolent in its changes—is chastely framed in a crape border, so nicely crimped, so nicely tucked under her benevolent chin at one end, and so nicely pinned under the virtuous white lining at the other. Goodness itself radiates from those large; earnest blue eyes, those soft, white cheeks, that large forehead, with those dashes of silvery hair crossing it so smoothly and so exactly—that well-developed, but rather broad nose, and that mouth so expressive of gentleness.

Sister Slocum, it requires no very acute observer to discover, has got something more than the heathen world at heart, for all those soft, congenial features are shadowed with sadness. Silently she takes her seat, sits abstracted for a few minutes—the house is thrown into a wondering mood—then looks wisely through her spectacles, and having folded her hands with an air of great resignation, shakes, and shakes, and shakes her head. Her eyes suddenly fill with tears, her thoughts wander, or seem to wander, she attempts to speak, her voice chokes, and the words hang upon her lips. All is consternation and excitement. Anxious faces gather round, and whispering voices inquire the cause. The lean man in the spectacles having applied his hartshorn bottle, Sister Slocum, to the great joy of all present, is so far restored as to be able to announce the singular, but no less melancholy fact, that our dear guest, Sister Swiggs, has passed from this world to a better. She retired full of sorrow, but came not in the morning. And this so troubled Sister Scudder that there was no peace until she entered her room. But she found the angel had been there before her, smoothed the pillow of the stranger, and left her to sleep in death. On earth her work was well done, and in the arms of the angel, her pure spirit now beareth witness in heaven. Sister Slocum's emotions forbid her saying more. She concludes, and buries her face in her cambric. Then an outpouring of consoling words follow. "He cometh like a thief in the night: His works are full of mystery; truly, He chasteneth; He giveth and taketh away." Such are a few of the sentiments lisped, regrettingly, for the departed.

How vain are the hopes with which we build castles in the air; how strange the motives that impel us to ill-advised acts. We leave untouched the things that call loudest for our energies, and treasure up our little that we may serve that which least concerns us. In this instance it is seen how that which came of evil went in evil; how disappointment stepped in and blew the castle down at a breath.

There could not be a doubt that the disease of which Sister Smiggs died, and which it is feared the State to which she belongs will one day die, was little dignity. Leaving her then in the arms of the House of the Foreign Mission, and her burial to the Secretary of the very excellent "Tract Society" she struggled so faithfully to serve, we close this chapter of events, the reader having, no doubt, discovered the husband of Madame Montford in the wretched man, Mr. Toddleworth.

CHAPTER XXXIV
THE TWO PICTURES

We come now to another stage of this history. Six months have glided into the past since the events recorded in the foregoing chapter. The political world of Charleston is resolved to remain in the Union a few months longer. It is a pleasant evening in early May. The western sky is golden with the setting sun, and the heavens are filled with battlements of refulgent clouds, now softening away into night. Yonder to the East, reposes a dark grove. A gentle breeze fans through its foliage, the leaves laugh and whisper, the perfumes of flowers are diffusing through the air birds make melodious with their songs, the trilling stream mingles its murmurs, and nature would seem gathering her beauties into one enchanting harmony. In the foreground of the grove, and looking as if it borrowed solitude of the deep foliage, in which it is half buried, rises a pretty villa, wherein may be seen, surrounded by luxuries the common herd might well envy, the fair, the beautiful siren, Anna Bonard. In the dingy little back parlor of the old antiquary, grim poverty looking in through every crevasse, sits the artless and pure-minded Maria McArthur. How different are the thoughts, the hopes, the emotions of these two women. Comfort would seem smiling on the one, while destitution threatens the other. To the eye that looks only upon the surface, how deceptive is the picture. The one with every wish gratified, an expression of sorrow shadowing her countenance, and that freshness and sweetness for which she was distinguished passing away, contemplates herself a submissive captive, at the mercy of one for whom she has no love, whose gold she cannot inherit, and whose roof she must some day leave for the street. The other feels poverty grasping at her, but is proud in the possession of her virtue; and though trouble would seem tracing its lines upon her features, her heart remains untouched by remorse;—she is strong in the consciousness that when all else is gone, her virtue will remain her beacon light to happiness. Anna, in the loss of that virtue, sees herself shut out from that very world that points her to the yawning chasm of her future; she feels how like a slave in the hands of one whose heart is as cold as his smiles are false, she is. Maria owes the world no hate, nor are her thoughts disturbed by such contemplations. Anna, with embittered and remorseful feelings—with dark and terrible passions agitating her bosom, looks back over her eventful life, to a period when even her own history is shut to her, only to find the tortures of her soul heightened. Maria looks back upon a life of fond attachment to her father, to her humble efforts to serve others, and to know that she has borne with Christian fortitude those ills which are incident to humble life. With her, an emotion of joy repays the contemplation. To Anna, the future is hung in dark forebodings. She recalls to mind the interview with Madame Montford, but that only tends to deepen the storm of anguish the contemplation of her parentage naturally gives rise to. With Maria, the present hangs dark and the future brightens. She thinks of the absent one she loves—of how she can best serve her aged father, and how she can make their little home cheerful until the return of Tom Swiggs, who is gone abroad. It must be here disclosed that the old man had joined their hands, and invoked a blessing on their heads, ere Tom took his departure. Maria looks forward to the day of his return with joyous emotions. That return is the day dream of her heart; in it she sees her future brightening. Such are the cherished thoughts of a pure mind. Poverty may gnaw away at the hearthstone, cares and sorrow may fall thick in your path, the rich may frown upon you, and the vicious sport with your misfortunes, but virtue gives you power to overcome them all. In Maria's ear something whispers: Woman! hold fast to thy virtue, for if once it go neither gold nor false tongues can buy it back.

Anna sees the companion of her early life, and the sharer of her sufferings, shut up in a prison, a robber, doomed to the lash. "He was sincere to me, and my only true friend—am I the cause of this?" she muses. Her heart answers, and her bosom fills with dark and stormy emotions. One small boon is now all she asks. She could bow down and worship before the throne of virgin innocence, for now its worth towers, majestic, before her. It discovers to her the falsity of her day-dream; it tells her what an empty vessel is this life of ours without it. She knows George Mullholland loves her passionately; she knows how deep will be his grief, how revengeful his feelings. It is poverty that fastens the poison in the heart of the rejected lover. The thought of this flashes through her mind. His hopeless condition, crushed out as it were to gratify him in whose company her pleasures are but transitory, and may any day end, darkens as she contemplates it. How can she acquit her conscience of having deliberately and faithlessly renounced one who was so true to her? She repines, her womanly nature revolts at the thought—the destiny her superstition pictured so dark and terrible, stares her in the face. She resolves a plan for his release, and, relieved with a hope that she can accomplish it while propitiating the friendship of the Judge, the next day seeks him in his prison cell, and with all that vehemence woman, in the outpouring of her generous impulses, can call to her aid, implores his forgiveness. But the rust of disappointment has dried up his better nature; his heart is wrung with the shafts of ingratitude—all the fierce passions of his nature, hate, scorn and revenge, rise up in the one stormy outburst of his soul. He casts upon her a look of withering scorn, the past of that life so chequered flashes vividly through his thoughts, his hate deepens, he hurls her from him, invokes a curse upon her head, and shuts her from his sight. "Mine will be the retribution!" he says, knitting his dark brow.

How is it with the Judge—that high functionary who provides thus sumptuously for his mistress? His morals, like his judgments, are excused, in the cheap quality of our social morality.

Such is gilded vice; such is humble virtue.

A few days more and the term of the Sessions commences. George is arraigned, and the honorable Mr. Snivel, who laid the plot, and furthered the crime, now appears as a principal witness. He procures the man's conviction, and listens with guilty heart to the sentence, for he is rearraigned on sentence day, and Mr. Snivel is present. And while the culprit is sentenced to two years imprisonment, and to receive eighty lashes, laid on his bare back, while at the public whipping-post, at four stated times, the man who stimulated the hand of the criminal, is honored and flattered by society. Such is the majesty of the law.

CHAPTER XXXV
IN WHICH A LITTLE LIGHT IS SHED UPON THE CHARACTER OF OUR CHIVALRY

Mr. McArthur has jogged on, in the good old way but his worldly store seems not to increase. The time, nevertheless, is arrived when he is expected to return the little amount borrowed of Keepum, through the agency of Mr. Snivel. Again and again has he been notified that he must pay or go to that place in which we lock up all our very estimable "first families," whose money has taken wings and flown away. Not content with this, the two worthy gentlemen have more than once invaded the Antiquary's back parlor, and offered, as we have described in a former chapter, improper advances to his daughter.

Mr. Keepum, dressed in a flashy coat, his sharp, mercenary face, hectic of night revels, and his small but wicked eyes wandering over Mr. McArthur's stock in trade, is seen in pursuit of his darling object. "I don't mind so much about the pay, old man! I'm up well in the world. The fact is, I am esteemed—and I am!—a public benefactor. I never forget how much we owe to the chivalric spirit of our ancestors, and in dealing with the poor—money matters and politics are different from anything else—I am too generous. I don't mind my own interests enough. There it is!" Mr. Keepum says this with an evident relief to himself. Indeed it must here be acknowledged that this very excellent member of the St. Cecilia Society, and profound dealer in lottery tickets, like our fine gentlemen who are so scrupulous of their chivalry while stabbing men behind their backs, fancies himself one of the most disinterested beings known to generous nature.

Bent and tottering, the old man recounts the value of his curiosities; which, like our chivalry, is much talked of but hard to get at. He offers in apology for the nonpayment of the debt his knowledge of the old continentals, just as we offer our chivalry in excuse for every disgraceful act—every savage law. In fine, he follows the maxims of our politicians, recapitulating a dozen or more things (wiping the sweat from his brow the while) that have no earthly connection with the subject. "They are all very well," Mr. Keepum rejoins, with an air of self-importance, dusting the ashes from his cigar. He only wishes to impress the old man with the fact that he is his very best friend.

And having somewhat relieved the Antiquary's mind of its apprehensions, for McArthur stood in great fear of duns, Mr. Keepum pops, uninvited, into the "back parlor," where he has not long been when Maria's screams for assistance break forth.

"Ah! I am old—there is not much left me now. Yes, I am old, my infirmities are upon me. Pray, good man, spare me my daughter. Nay, you must not break the peace of my house;" mutters the old man, advancing into the room, with infirm step, and looking wistfully at his daughter, as if eager to clasp her in his arms. Maria stands in a defiant attitude, her left hand poised on a chair, and her right pointing scornfully in the face of Keepum, who recoils under the look of withering scorn that darkens her countenance. "A gentleman! begone, knave! for your looks betray you. You cannot buy my ruin with your gold; you cannot deceive me with your false tongue. If hate were a noble passion, I would not vent that which now agitates my bosom on you. Nay, I would reserve it for a better purpose—"

"Indeed, indeed—now I say honestly, your daughter mistakes me. I was only being a little friendly to her," interrupts the chopfallen man. He did not think her capable of summoning so much passion to her aid.

Maria, it must be said, was one of those seemingly calm natures in which resentment takes deepest root, in which the passions are most violent when roused. Solitude does, indeed, tend to invest the passionate nature with a calm surface. A less penetrating observer than the chivalrous Keepum, might have discovered in Maria a spirit he could not so easily humble to his uses. It is the modest, thoughtful woman, you cannot make lick the dust in sorrow and tears. "Coward! you laid ruffian hands on me!" says Maria, again towering to her height, and giving vent to her feelings.

"Madam, Madam," pursues Keepum, trembling and crouching, "you asperse my honor,—my sacred honor, Madam. You see—let me say a word, now—you are letting your temper get the better of you. I never, and the public know I never did—I never did a dishonorable thing in my life." Turning to the bewildered old man, he continues: "to be called a knave, and upbraided in this manner by your daughter, when I have befriended you all these days!" His wicked eyes fall guilty to the floor.

"Out man!—out! Let your sense of right, if you have it, teach you what is friendship. Know that, like mercy, it is not poured out with hands reeking of female dishonor."

Mr. Keepum, like many more of our very fine gentlemen, had so trained his thoughts to look upon the poor as slaves created for a base use, that he neither could bring his mind to believe in the existence of such things as noble spirits under humble roofs, nor to imagine himself—even while committing the grossest outrages—doing aught to sully the high chivalric spirit he fancied he possessed. The old Antiquary, on the other hand, was not a little surprised to find his daughter displaying such extraordinary means of repulsing an enemy.

Trembling, and childlike he stands, conscious of being in the grasp of a knave, whose object was more the ruin of his daughter than the recovery of a small amount of money, the tears glistening in his eyes, and the finger of old age marked on his furrowed brow.

"Father, father!" says Maria, and the words hang upon her quivering lips, her face becomes pale as marble, her strength deserts her,—she trembles from head to foot, and sinks upon the old man's bosom, struggling to smother her sobs. Her passion has left her; her calmer nature has risen up to rebuke it. The old man leads her tenderly to the sofa, and there seeks to sooth her troubled spirit.

"As if this hub bub was always to last!" a voice speaks suddenly. It is the Hon. Mr. Snivel, who looks in at the eleventh hour, as he says, to find affairs always in a fuss. "Being a man of legal knowledge—always ready to do a bit of a good turn—especially in putting a disordered house to rights—I thought it well to look in, having a leisure minute or two (we have had a convention for dissolving the Union, and passed a vote to that end!) to give to my old friends," Mr. Snivel says, in a voice at once conciliating and insinuating. "I always think of a border feud when I come here—things that find no favor with me." Mr. Snivel, having first patted the old man on the shoulder, exchanges a significant wink with his friend Keepum, and then bestows upon him what he is pleased to call a little wholesome advice. "People misunderstand Mr. Keepum," he says, "who is one of the most generous of men, but lacks discretion, and in trying to be polite to everybody, lets his feelings have too much latitude now and then." Maria buries her face in her handkerchief, as if indifferent to the reconciliation offered.

"Now let this all be forgotten—let friendship reign among friends: that's my motto. But! I say,—this is a bad piece of news we have this morning. Clipped this from an English paper," resumes the Hon. gentleman, drawing coolly from his pocket a bit of paper, having the appearance of an extract.

"You are never without some kind of news—mostly bad!" says Keepum, flinging himself into a chair, with an air of restored confidence. Mr. Snivel bows, thanks the gentleman for the compliment, and commences to read. "This news," he adds, "may be relied upon, having come from Lloyd's List: 'Intelligence was received here (this is, you must remember, from a London paper, he says, in parentheses) this morning, of the total loss of the American ship — —, bound from this port for Charleston, U.S., near the Needles. Every soul on board, except the Captain and second mate, perished. The gale was one of the worst ever known on this coast—'"

"The worst ever known on this coast!" ejaculates Mr. Keepum, his wicked eyes steadily fixed upon Maria. "One of Trueman's ships," Mr. Snivel adds. "Unlucky fellow, that Trueman—second ship he has lost."

"By-the-bye," rejoins Keepum, as if a thought has just flashed upon him, "your old friend, Tom Swiggs, was supercargo, clerk, or whatever you may call it, aboard that ship, eh?"

It is the knave who can most naturally affect surprise and regret when it suits his purposes, and Mr. Snivel is well learned in the art. "True!" he says, "as I'm a Christian. Well, I had made a man of him—I don't regret it, for I always liked him—and this is the end of the poor fellow, eh?" Turning to McArthur, he adds, rather unconcernedly: "You know somewhat of him?" The old man sits motionless beside his daughter, the changes of whose countenance discover the inward emotions that agitate her bosom. Her eyes fill with tears; she exchanges inquiring glances, first with Keepum, then with Snivel; then a thought strikes her that she received a letter from Tom, setting forth his prospects, and his intention to return in the ship above named. It was very natural that news thus artfully manufactured, and revealed with such apparent truthfulness, should produce a deep impression in the mind of an unsuspecting girl. Indeed, it was with some effort that she bore up under it. Expressions of grief she would fain suppress before the enemy gain a mastery over her—and ere they are gone the cup flows over, and she sinks exhausted upon the sofa.

"There! good as far as it goes. You have now another mode of gaining the victory," Mr. Snivel whispers in the ear of his friend, Keepum; and the two gentlemen pass into the street.

CHAPTER XXXVI
IN WHICH A LAW IS SEEN TO SERVE BASE PURPOSES

Maria has passed a night of unhappiness. Hopes and fears are knelling in the morning, which brings nothing to relieve her anxiety for the absent one; and Mr. Snivel has taken the precaution to have the news of the lost ship find its way into the papers.

And while our city seems in a state of very general excitement; while great placards on every street corner inform the wondering stranger that a mighty Convention (presided over by the Hon. S. Snivel) for dissolving the Union, is shortly to be holden; while our political world has got the Union on its shoulders, and threatens to throw it into the nearest ditch; while our streets swarm with long, lean, and very hairy-faced delegates (all lusty of war and secession), who have dragged themselves into the city to drink no end of whiskey, and say all sorts of foolish things their savage and half-civilized constituents are expected to applaud; while our more material and conservative citizens are thinking what asses we make of ourselves; while the ship-of-war we built to fight the rest of the Union, lies an ugly lump in the harbor, and "won't go over the bar;" while the "shoe-factory" we established to supply niggerdom with soles, is snuffed out for want of energy and capacity to manage it; while some of our non-slaveholding, but most active secession merchants, are moving seriously in the great project of establishing a "Southern Candle-factory"—a thing much needed in the "up-country," while our graver statesmen (who don't get the State out of the Union fast enough for the ignorant rabble, who have nothing but their folly at stake) are pondering over the policy of spending five hundred thousand dollars for the building of another war-ship—one that "will go over the bar;" and while curiously-written letters from Generals Commander and Quattlebum, offering to bring their allied forces into the field—to blow this confederation down at a breath whenever called upon, are being published, to the great joy of all secessiondom; while saltpetre, broadswords, and the muskets made for us by Yankees to fight Yankees, and which were found to have wood instead of flint in their hammers, (and which trick of the Yankees we said was just like the Yankees,) are in great demand—and a few of our mob-politicians, who are all "Kern'ls" of regiments that never muster, prove conclusively our necessity for keeping a fighting-man in Congress; while, we assert, many of our first and best known families have sunk the assemblies of the St. Cecilia in the more important question of what order of government will best suit—in the event of our getting happily out of the Union!—our refined and very exacting state of society;—whether an Empire or a Monarchy, and whether we ought to set up a Quattlebum or Commander dynasty?—whether the Bungle family or the Jungle family (both fighting families) will have a place nearest the throne; what sort of orders will be bestowed, who will get them, and what colored liveries will best become us (all of which grave questions threaten us with a very extensive war of families)?—while all these great matters find us in a sea of trouble, there enters the curiosity-shop of the old Antiquary a suspicious-looking individual in green spectacles.

"Mr. Hardscrabble!" says the man, bowing and taking a seat, leisurely, upon the decrepit sofa. Mr. McArthur returns his salutation, contemplates him doubtingly for a minute, then resumes his fussing and brushing.

The small, lean figure; the somewhat seedy broadcloth in which it is enveloped; the well-browned and very sharp features; the straight, dark-gray hair, and the absent manner of Mr. Hardscrabble, might, with the uninitiated, cause him to be mistaken for an "up-country" clergyman of the Methodist denomination.

"Mr. Hardscrabble? Mr. Hardscrabble? Mr. Hardscrabble?" muses the Antiquary, canting his head wisely, "the Sheriff, as I'm a man of years!"

Mr. Hardscrabble comforts his eyes with his spectacles, and having glanced vacantly over the little shop, as if to take an inventory of its contents, draws from his breast-pocket a paper containing very ominous seals and scrawls.

"I'm reluctant about doing these things with an old man like you," Mr. Hardscrabble condescends to say, in a sharp, grating voice; "but I have to obey the demands of my office." Here he commences reading the paper to the trembling old man, who, having adjusted his broad-bowed spectacles, and arrayed them against the spectacles of Mr. Hardscrabble, says he thinks it contains a great many useless recapitulations.

Mr. Hardscrabble, his eyes peering eagerly through his glasses, and his lower jaw falling and exposing the inner domain of his mouth, replies with an—"Umph." The old Antiquary was never before called upon to examine a document so confusing to his mind. Not content with a surrender of his property, it demands his body into the bargain—all at the suit of one Keepum. He makes several motions to go show it to his daughter; but that,

Mr. Hardscrabble thinks, is scarce worth while. "I sympathize with you—knowing how frugal you have been through life. A list of your effects—if you have one—will save a deal of trouble. I fear (Mr. Hardscrabble works his quid) my costs will hardly come out of them."

"There's a fortune in them—if the love of things of yore—" The old man hesitates, and shakes his head dolefully.

"Yore!—a thing that would starve out our profession."

"A little time to turn, you know. There's my stock of uniforms."

"Well—I—know," Mr. Hardscrabble rejoins, with a drawl; "but I must lock up the traps. Yes, I must lock you up, and sell you out—unless you redeem before sale day; that you can't do, I suppose?"

And while the old man totters into the little back parlor, and, giving way to his emotions, throws himself upon the bosom of his fond daughter, to whom he discloses his troubles, Mr. Hardscrabble puts locks and bolts upon his curiosity-shop. This important business done, he leads the old man away, and gives him a lodging in the old jail.

CHAPTER XXXVII
A SHORT CHAPTER OF ORDINARY EVENTS

To bear up against the malice of inexorable enemies is at once the gift and the shield of a noble nature. And here it will be enough to say, that Maria bore the burden of her ills with fortitude and resignation, trusting in Him who rights the wronged, to be her deliverer. What took place when she saw her aged father led away, a prisoner; what thoughts invaded that father's mind when the prison bolt grated on his ear, and he found himself shut from all that had been dear to him through life, regard for the feelings of the reader forbids us recounting here.

Naturally intelligent, Maria had, by close application to books, acquired some knowledge of the world. Nor was she entirely ignorant of those arts designing men call to their aid when seeking to effect the ruin of the unwary female. Thus fortified, she fancied she saw in the story of the lost ship a plot against herself, while the persecution of her father was only a means to effect the object. Launched between hope and fear, then—hope that her lover still lived, and that with his return her day would brighten—fear lest the report might be founded in truth, she nerves herself for the struggle. She knew full well that to give up in despair—to cast herself upon the cold charities of a busy world, would only be to hasten her downfall. Indeed, she had already felt how cold, and how far apart were the lines that separated our rich from our poor.

The little back parlor is yet spared to Maria, and in it she may now be seen plying at her needle, early and late. It is the only means left her of succoring the parent from whom she has been so ruthlessly separated. Hoping, fearing, bright to-day and dark to-morrow, willing to work and wait—here she sits. A few days pass, and the odds and ends of the Antiquary's little shop, like the "shirts" of the gallant Fremont, whom we oppressed while poor, and essayed to flatter when a hero, are gazetted under the head of "sheriff's sale." Hope, alas! brings no comfort to Maria. Time rolls on, the month's rent falls due, her father pines and sinks in confinement, and her needle is found inadequate to the task undertaken. Necessity demands, and one by one she parts with her few cherished mementos of the past, that she may save an aged father from starvation.

The "prisoner" has given notice that he will take the benefit of the act—commonly called "an act for the relief of poor debtors." But before he can reach this boon, ten days must elapse. Generous-minded legislators, no doubt, intended well when they constructed this act, but so complex are its provisions that any legal gentleman may make it a very convenient means of oppression. And in a community where laws not only have their origin in the passions of men, but are made to serve popular prejudices—where the quality of justice obtained depends upon the position and sentiments of him who seeks it,—the weak have no chance against the powerful.

The multiplicity of notices, citations, and schedules, necessary to the setting free of this "poor debtor" (for these fussy officials must be paid), Maria finds making a heavy drain on her lean purse.

The Court is in session, and the ten days having glided away, the old man is brought into "open Court" by two officials with long tipstaffs, and faces looking as if they had been carefully pickled in strong drinks. "Surely, now, they'll set me free—I can give them no more—I am old and infirm—they have got all—and my daughter!" he muses within himself. Ah! he little knows how uncertain a thing is the law.

The Judge is engaged over a case in which two very fine old families are disputing for the blood and bones of a little "nigger" girl. The possession of this helpless slave, the Judge (he sits in easy dignity) very naturally regards of superior importance when compared with the freedom of a "poor debtor." He cannot listen to the story of destitution—precisely what was sought by Keepum—to-day, and to-morrow the Court adjourns for six months.

The Antiquary is remanded back to his cell. No one in Court cares for him; no one has a thought for the achings of that heart his release would unburden; the sorrows of that lone girl are known only to herself and the One in whom she puts her trust. She, nevertheless, seeks the old man in his prison, and there comforts him as best she can.

Five days more, and the "prisoner" is brought before the Commissioner for Special Bail, who is no less a personage than the rosy-faced Clerk of the Court, just adjourned. And here we cannot forbear to say, that however despicable the object sought, however barren of right the plea, however adverse to common humanity the spirit of the action, there is always to be found some legal gentleman, true to the lower instincts of the profession, ready to lend himself to his client's motives. And in this instance, the cunning Keepum finds an excellent instrument of furthering his ends, in one Peter Crimpton, a somewhat faded and rather disreputable member of the learned profession. It is said of Crimpton, that he is clever at managing cases where oppression rather than justice is sought, and that his present client furnishes the larger half of his practice.

And while Maria, too sensitive to face the gaze of the coarse crowd, pauses without, silent and anxious, listening one moment and hoping the next will see her old father restored to her, the adroit Crimpton rises to object to "the Schedule." To the end that he may substantiate his objections, he proposes to examine the prisoner. Having no alternative, the Commissioner grants the request.

The old Antiquary made out his schedule with the aid of the good-hearted jailer, who inserted as his effects, *"Necessary wearing apparel."* It was all he had. Like the gallant Fremont, when he offered to resign his shirts to his chivalric creditor, he could give them no more. A few questions are put; the old man answers them with childlike simplicity, then sits down, his trembling fingers wandering into his beard. Mr. Crimpton produces his paper, sets forth his objections, and asks permission to file them, that the case may come before a jury of "Special Bail."

Permission is granted. The reader will not fail to discover the object of this procedure. Keepum hopes to continue the old man in prison, that he may succeed in breaking down the proud spirit of his daughter.

The Commissioner listens attentively to the reading of the objections. The first sets forth that Mr. McArthur has a gold watch;[7] the second, that he has a valuable breastpin, said to have been worn by Lord Cornwallis; and the third, that he has one Yorick's skull. All of these, Mr. Crimpton regrets to say, are withheld from the schedule, which virtually constitutes fraud. The facile Commissioner bows; the assembled crowd look on unmoved; but the old man shakes his head and listens. He is surprised to find himself accused of fraud; but the law gives him no power to show his own innocence. The Judge of the Sessions was competent to decide the question now raised, and to have prevented this reverting to a "special jury"—this giving the vindictive plaintiff a means of torturing his infirm victim. Had he but listened to the old man's tale of poverty, he might have saved the heart of that forlorn girl many a bitter pang.

The motion granted, a day is appointed—ten days must elapse—for a hearing before the Commissioner of "Special Bail," and his special jury. The rosy-faced functionary, being a jolly and somewhat flexible sort of man, must needs give his health an airing in the country. What is the liberty of a poor white with us? Our Governor, whom we esteem singularly sagacious, said it were better all our poor were enslaved, and this opinion finds high favor with our first families. The worthy Commissioner, in addition to taking care of his health, is expected to make any number of speeches, full of wind and war, to several recently called Secession Conventions. He will find time (being a General by courtesy) to review the up-country militia, and the right and left divisions of the South Carolina army. He will be feted by some few of our most distinguished Generals, and lecture before the people of Beaufort (a very noisy town of forty-two inhabitants, all heroes), to whom he will prove the necessity of our State providing itself with an independent steam navy.

The old Antiquary is remanded back to jail—to wait the coming day. Maria, almost breathless with anxiety, runs to him as he comes tottering out of Court in advance of the official, lays her trembling hand upon his arm, and looks inquiringly in his face. "Oh! my father, my father!—released? released?" she inquires, with quivering lips and throbbing heart. A forced smile plays over his time-worn face, he looks upward, shakes his head in sorrow, and having patted her affectionately on the shoulder, throws his arms about her neck and kisses her. That mute appeal, that melancholy voucher of his sorrows, knells the painful answer in her ears, "Then you are not free to come with me? Oh, father, father!" and she wrings her hands and gives vent to her tears.

"The time will come, my daughter, when my Judge will hear me—will judge me right. My time will come soon—" And here the old man pauses, and chokes with his emotions. Maria returns the old man's kiss, and being satisfied that he is yet in the hands of his oppressors, sets about cheering up his drooping spirits. "Don't think of me, father," she says—"don't think of me! Let us put our trust in Him who can shorten the days of our tribulation." She takes the old man's arm, and like one who would forget her own troubles in her anxiety to relieve another, supports him on his way back to prison.

It is high noon. She stands before the prison gate, now glancing at the serene sky, then at the cold, frowning walls, and again at the old pile, as if contemplating the wearying hours he must pass within it. "Don't repine— nerve yourself with resolution, and all will be well!" Having said this with an air of confidence in herself, she throws her arms about the old man's neck, presses him to her bosom, kisses and kisses his wrinkled cheek, then grasps his hand warmly in her own. "Forget those who persecute you, for it is good. Look above, father—to Him who tempers the winds, who watches over the weak, and gives the victory to the right!" She pauses, as the old man holds her hand in silence. "This life is but a transient sojourn at best; full of hopes and fears, that, like a soldier's dream, pass away when the battle is ended." Again she fondly shakes his hand, lisps a sorrowing "good-bye," watches him, in silence, out of sight, then turns away in tears, and seeks her home. There is something so pure, so earnest in her solicitude for the old man, that it seems more of heaven than earth.

CHAPTER XXXVIII
A STORY WITHOUT WHICH THIS HISTORY
WOULD BE FOUND WANTING

On taking leave of her father, Maria, her heart overburdened with grief, and her mind abstracted, turned towards the Battery, and continued, slowly and sadly, until she found herself seated beneath a tree, looking out upon the calm bay. Here, scarce conscious of those who were observing her in their sallies, she mused until dusky evening, when the air seemed hushed, and the busy hum of day was dying away in the distance. The dark woodland on the opposite bank gave a bold border to the soft picture; the ships rode sluggishly upon the polished waters; the negro's touching song echoed and re-echoed along the shore; and the boatman's chorus broke upon the stilly air in strains so dulcet. And as the mellow shadows of night stole over the scene—as the heavens looked down in all their sereneness, and the stars shone out, and twinkled, and laughed, and danced upon the blue waters, and coquetted with the moonbeams—for the moon was up, and shedding a halo of mystic light over the scene—making night merry, nature seemed speaking to Maria in words of condolence. Her heart was touched, her spirits gained strength, her soul seemed in a loftier and purer atmosphere.

"Poor, but virtuous—virtue ennobles the poor. Once gone, the world never gives it back!" she muses, and is awakened from her reverie by a sweet, sympathizing voice, whispering in her ear. "Woman! you are in trouble,—linger no longer here, or you will fall into the hands of your enemies." She looks up, and there stands at her side a young female, whose beauty the angels might envy. The figure came upon her so suddenly that she hesitates for a reply to the admonition.

"Take this, it will do something toward relieving your wants (do not open it now), and with this (she places a stiletto in her hand) you can strike down the one who attempts your virtue. Nay, remember that while you cling to that, you are safe—lose it, and you are gone forever. Your troubles will soon end; mine are for a life-time. Yours find a relaxation in your innocence; mine is seared into my heart with my own shame. It is guilt—shame! that infuses into the heart that poison, for which years of rectitude afford no antidote. Go quickly—get from this lone place! You are richer than me." She slips something into Maria's hand, and suddenly disappears.

Maria rises from her seat, intending to follow the stranger, but she is out of sight. Who can this mysterious messenger, this beautiful stranger be? Maria muses. A thought flashes across her mind; it is she who sought our house at midnight, when my father revealed her dark future! "Yes," she says to herself, "it is the same lovely face; how oft it has flitted in my fancy!"

She reaches her home only to find its doors closed against her. A ruthless landlord has taken her all, and forced her into the street.

You may shut out the sterner sex without involving character or inviting insult; but with woman the case is very different. However pure her character, to turn her into the street, is to subject her to a stigma, if not to fasten upon her a disgrace. You may paint, in your imagination, the picture of a woman in distress, but you can know little of the heart-achings of the sufferer. The surface only reflects the faint gleams, standing out here and there like the lesser objects upon a dark canvas.

Maria turns reluctantly from that home of so many happy associations, to wander about the streets and by-ways of the city. The houses of the rich seem frowning upon her; her timid nature tells her they have no doors open to her. The haunts of the poor, at this moment, infuse a sanguine joyousness into her soul. How glad would she be, if they did but open to her. Is not the Allwise, through the beauties of His works, holding her up, while man only is struggling to pull her down?

And while Maria wanders homeless about the streets of Charleston, we must beg you, gentle reader, to accompany us into one of the great thoroughfares of London, where is being enacted a scene appertaining to this history.

It is well-nigh midnight, the hour when young London is most astir in his favorite haunts; when ragged and well-starved flower-girls, issuing from no one knows where, beset your path through Trafalgar and Liecester squares, and pierce your heart with their pleadings; when the Casinoes of the Haymarket and Picadilly are vomiting into the streets their frail but richly-dressed women; when gaudy supper-rooms, reeking of lobster and bad liquor, are made noisy with the demands of their flauntily-dressed customers; when little girls of thirteen are dodging in and out of mysterious courts and passages leading to and from Liecester square; when wily cabmen, ranged around the "great globe," importune you for a last fare; and when the aristocratic swell, with hectic face and maudlin laugh, saunters from his club-room to seek excitement in the revels at Vauxhall.

A brown mist hangs over the dull area of Trafalgar square. The bells of old St. Martin's church have chimed merrily out their last night peal; the sharp voice of the omnibus conductor no longer offends the ear; the tiny little fountains have ceased to give out their green water; and the lights of the Union Club on one side, and Morley's hotel on the other, throw pale shadows into the open square.

The solitary figure of a man, dressed in the garb of a gentleman, is seen sauntering past Northumberland house, then up the east side of the square. Now he halts at the corner of old St. Martin's church, turns and contemplates the scene before him. On his right is that squatty mass of freestone and smoke, Englishmen exultingly call the Royal Academy, but which Frenchmen affect contempt for, and uninitiated Americans mistake for a tomb. An equestrian statue of one of the Georges rises at the east corner; Morley's Hotel, where Americans get poor fare and enormous charges, with the privilege of fancying themselves quite as good as the queen, on the left; the dead walls of Northumberland House, with their prisonlike aspect, and the mounted lion, his tail high in air, and quite as rigid as the Duke's dignity, in front; the opening that terminates the Strand, and gives place to Parliament street, at the head of which an equestrian statue of Charles the First, much admired by Englishmen, stands, his back on Westminster; the dingy shops of Spring Garden, and the Union Club to the right; and, towering high over all, Nelson's Column, the statue looking as if it had turned its back in pity on the little fountains, to look with contempt, first upon the bronze face of the unfortunate Charles, then upon Parliament, whose parsimony in withholding justice from his daughter, he would rebuke—and the picture is complete.

The stranger turns, walks slowly past the steps of St. Martin's church, crosses to the opposite side of the street, and enters a narrow, wet, and dimly-lighted court, on the left. Having passed up a few paces, he finds himself hemmed in between the dead walls of St. Martin's "Work-house" on one side, and the Royal Academy on the other. He hesitates between fear and curiosity. The dull, sombre aspect of the court is indeed enough to excite the fears of the timid; but curiosity being the stronger impulse, he proceeds, resolved to explore it—to see whence it leads.

A short turn to the right, and he has reached the front wall of the Queen's Barracks, on his left, and the entrance to the "Work-house," on his right; the one overlooking the other, and separated by a narrow street. Leave men are seen reluctantly returning in at the night-gate; the dull tramp of the sentinel within sounds ominously on the still air; and the chilly atmosphere steals into the system. Again the stranger pauses, as if questioning the safety of his position. Suddenly a low moan grates upon his ear, he starts back, then listens. Again it rises, in a sad wail, and pierces his very heart. His first thought is, that some tortured mortal is bemoaning his bruises in a cell of the "Work-house," which he mistakes for a prison. But his eyes fall to the ground, and his apprehensions are dispelled.

The doors of the "Work-house" are fast closed; but there, huddled along the cold pavement, and lying crouched upon its doorsteps, in heaps that resemble the gatherings of a rag-seller, are four-and-thirty shivering, famishing, and homeless human beings—[8] (mostly young girls and aged women), who have sought at this "institution of charity" shelter for the night, and bread to appease their hunger.[9] Alas! its ruthless keepers have refused them bread, shut them into the street, and left them in rags scarce sufficient to cover their nakedness, to sleep upon the cold stones, a mute but terrible rebuke to those hearts that bleed over the sorrows of Africa, but have no blood to give out when the object of pity is a poor, heart-sick girl, forced to make the cold pavement her bed. The stranger shudders. "Are these heaps of human beings?" he questions within himself, doubting the reality before him. As if counting and hesitating what course to pursue for their relief, he paces up and down the grotesque mass, touching one, and gazing upon the haggard features of another, who looks up to see what it is that disturbs her. Again the low moan breaks on his ear, as the sentinel cries the first hour of morning. The figure of a female, her head resting on one of the steps, moves, a trembling hand steals from under her shawl, makes an effort to reach her head, and falls numb at her side. "Her hand is cold—her breathing like one in death—oh! God!—how terrible—what, what am I to do?" he says, taking the sufferer's hand in his own. Now he rubs it, now raises her head, makes an effort to wake a few of the miserable sleepers, and calls aloud for help. "Help! help! help!" he shouts, and the shout re-echoes through the air and along the hollow court. "A woman is dying,—dying here on the cold stones—with no one to raise a hand for her!" He seizes the exhausted woman in his arms, and with herculean strength rushes up the narrow street, in the hope of finding relief at the Gin Palace he sees at its head, in a blaze of light. But the body is seized with spasms, an hollow, hysteric wail follows, his strength gives way under the burden, and he sets the sufferer down in the shadow of a gas light. Her dress, although worn threadbare, still bears evidence of having belonged to one who has enjoyed comfort, and, perhaps, luxury. Indeed, there is something about the woman which bespeaks her not of the class generally found sleeping on the steps of St. Martin's Work-house.

"What's here to do?" gruffly inquires a policeman, coming up with an air of indifference. The stranger says the woman is dying. The policeman stoops down, lays his hand upon her temples, then mechanically feels her arms and hands.

"And I—must die—die—die in the street," whispers the woman, her head falling carelessly from the policeman's hand, in which it had rested.

"Got her a bit below, at the Work'ouse door, among them wot sleeps there, eh?"

The stranger says he did.

"A common enough thing," pursues the policeman; "this a bad lot. Anyhow, we must give her a tow to the station." He rubs his hands, and prepares to raise her from the ground.

"Hold! hold," interrupts the other, "she will die ere you get her there."

"Die,—ah! yes, yes," whispers the woman. The mention of death seems to have wrung like poison into her very soul. "Don't—don't move me—the spell is almost broken. Oh! how can I die here, a wretch. Yes, I am going now—let me rest, rest, rest," the moaning supplicant mutters in a guttural voice, grasps spasmodically at the policeman's hand, heaves a deep sigh, and sets her eyes fixedly upon the stranger. She seems recognizing in his features something that gives her strength.

"There—there—there!" she continues, incoherently, as a fit of hysterics seize upon her; "you, you, you, have—yes, you have come at the last hour, when my sufferings close. I see devils all about me—haunting me— torturing my very soul—burning me up! See them! see them!—here they come—tearing, worrying me—in a cloud of flame!" She clutches with her hands, her countenance fills with despair, and her body writhes in agony.

"Bring brandy! warm,—stimulant! anything to give her strength! Quick! quick!—go fetch it, or she is gone!" stammers out the stranger.

In another minute she calms away, and sinks exhausted upon the pavement. Policeman shakes his head, and says, "It 'ont do no good—she's done for."

The light of the "Trumpeter's Arms" still blazes into the street, while a few greasy ale-bibbers sit moody about the tap-room.

The two men raise the exhausted woman from the ground and carry her to the door. Mine host of the Trumpeter's Arms shrugs his shoulders and says, "She can't come in here." He fears she will damage the respectability of his house. "The Work-house is the place for her," he continues, gruffly.

A sight at the stranger's well-filled purse, however, and a few shillings slipped into the host's hand, secures his generosity and the woman's admittance. "Indeed," says the host, bowing most servilely, "gentlemen, the whole Trumpeter's Arms is at your service." The woman is carried into a lonely, little back room, and laid upon a cot, which, with two wooden chairs, constitutes its furniture. And while the policeman goes in search of medical aid, the host of the Trumpeter's bestirs himself right manfully in the forthcoming of a stimulant. The stranger, meanwhile, lends himself to the care of the forlorn sufferer with the gentleness of a woman. He smoothes her pillow, arranges her dress tenderly, and administers the stimulant with a hand accustomed to the sick.

A few minutes pass, and the woman seems to revive and brighten up. Mine host has set a light on the chair, at the side of the cot, and left her alone with the stranger. Slowly she opens her eyes, and with increasing anxiety sets them full upon him. Their recognition is mutual. "Madame Flamingo!" ejaculates the man, grasping her hand.

"Tom Swiggs!" exclaims the woman, burying her face for a second, then pressing his hand to her lips, and kissing it with the fondness of a child, as her eyes swim in tears. "How strange to find you thus—" continues Tom, for truly it is he who sits by the forlorn woman.

"More strange," mutters the woman, shaking her head sorrowfully, "that I should be brought to this terrible end. I am dying—I cannot last long—the fever has left me only to die a neglected wretch. Hear me—hear me, while I tell you the tale of my troubles, that others may take warning. And may God give me strength. And you—if I have wronged you, forgive me—it is all I can ask in this world." Here Tom administers another draught of warm brandy and water, the influence of which is soon perceptible in the regaining strength of the patient.

CHAPTER XXXIX
A STORY WITH MANY COUNTERPARTS

A very common story is this of Madame Flamingo's troubles. It has counterparts enough, and though they may be traced to a class of society less notorious than that with which she moved, are generally kept in the dark chamber of hidden thoughts. We are indeed fast gaining an unenviable fame for snobbery, for affecting to be what we never can be, and for our sad imitation of foreign flunkydom, which, finding us rivals in the realm of its tinsil, begins to button up its coat and look contemptuously at us over the left shoulder. If, albeit, the result of that passion for titles and plush (things which the empty-headed of the old world would seem to have consigned to the empty-headed of the new), which has of late so singularly discovered itself among our "best-known families," could be told, it would unfold many a tale of misery and betrayal. Pardon this digression, generous reader, and proceed with us to the story of Madame Flamingo.

"And now," says the forlorn woman, in a faint, hollow voice, "when my ambition seemed served—I was ambitious, perhaps vain—I found myself the victim of an intrigue. I ask forgiveness of Him who only can forgive the wicked; but how can I expect to gain it?" She presses Tom's hand, and pauses for a second. "Yes, I was ambitious," she continues, "and there was something I wanted. I had money enough to live in comfort, but the thought that it was got of vice and the ruin of others, weighed me down. I wanted the respect of the world. To die a forgotten wretch; to have the grave close over me, and if remembered at all, only with execration, caused me many a dark thought." Here she struggles to suppress her emotions. "I sought to change my condition; that, you see, has brought me here. I married one to whom I intrusted my all, in whose rank, as represented to me by Mr. Snivel, and confirmed by his friend, the Judge, I confided. I hoped to move with him to a foreign country, where the past would all be wiped out, and where the associations of respectable society would be the reward of future virtue.

"In London, where I now reap the fruits of my vanity, we enjoyed good society for a time, were sought after, and heaped with attentions. But I met those who had known me; it got out who I was; I was represented much worse than I was, and even those who had flattered me in one sphere, did not know me. In Paris it was the same. And there my husband said it would not do to be known by his titles, for, being an exile, it might be the means of his being recognized and kidnapped, and carried back a prisoner to his own dear Poland. In this I acquiesced, as I did in everything else that lightened his cares. Gradually he grew cold and morose towards me, left me for days at a time, and returned only to abuse and treat me cruelly. He had possession of all my money, which I soon found he was gambling away, without gaining an entrée for me into society.

"From Paris we travelled, as if without any settled purpose, into Italy, and from thence to Vienna, where I discovered that instead of being a prince, my husband was an impostor, and I his dupe. He had formerly been a crafty shoemaker; was known to the police as a notorious character, who, instead of having been engaged in the political struggles of his countrymen, had fled the country to escape the penalty of being the confederate of a desperate gang of coiners and counterfeiters. We had only been two days in Vienna when I found he had disappeared, and left me destitute of money or friends. My connection with him only rendered my condition more deplorable, for the police would not credit my story; and while he eluded its vigilance, I was suspected of being a spy in the confidence of a felon, and ruthlessly ordered to leave the country."

"Did not your passport protect you?" interrupts Tom, with evident feeling.

"No one paid it the least regard," resumes Madame Flamingo, becoming weaker and weaker. "No one at our legations evinced sympathy for me. Indeed, they all refused to believe my story. I wandered back from city to city, selling my wardrobe and the few jewels I had left, and confidently expecting to find in each place I entered, some one I had known, who would listen to my story, and supply me with means to reach my home. I could soon have repaid it, but my friends had gone with my money; no one dare venture to trust me—no one had confidence in me—every one to whom I appealed had an excuse that betrayed their suspicion of me. Almost destitute, I found myself back in London—how I got here, I scarce know— where I could make myself understood. My hopes now brightened, I felt that some generous-hearted captain would give me a passage to New York, and once home, my troubles would end. But being worn down with fatigue, and my strength prostrated, a fever set in, and I was forced to seek refuge in a miserable garret in Drury-Lane, and where I parted with all but what now remains on my back, to procure nourishment. I had begun to recover somewhat, but the malady left me broken down, and when all was gone, I was turned into the street. Yes, yes, yes, (she whispers,) they gave me to the streets; for twenty-four hours I have wandered without nourishment, or a place to lay my head. I sought shelter in a dark court, and there laid down to die; and when my eyes were dim, and all before me seemed mysterious and dark with curious visions, a hand touched me, and I felt myself borne away." Here her voice chokes, she sinks back upon the pillow, and closes her eyes as her hands fall careless at her side. "She breathes! she breathes yet!" says Tom, advancing his ear to the pale, quivering lips of the wretched woman. Now he bathes her temples with the vinegar from a bottle in the hand of the host, who is just entered, and stands looking on, his countenance full of alarm.

"If she deys in my 'ouse, good sir, w'oat then?"

"You mean the expense?"

"Just so—it'll be nae trifle, ye kno'!" The host shakes his head, doubtingly. Tom begs he will not be troubled about that, and gives another assurance from his purse that quite relieves the host's apprehensions. A low, heavy breathing, followed by a return of spasms, bespeaks the sinking condition of the sufferer. The policeman returns, preceded by a physician—the only one to be got at, he says—in very dilapidated broadcloth, and whose breath is rather strong of gin. "An' whereabutes did ye pick the woman up,—an, an, wha's teu stond the bill?" he inquires, in a deep Scotch brogue, then ordering the little window opened, feels clumsily the almost pulseless hand. Encouraged on the matter of his bill, he turns first to the host, then to Tom, and says, "the wuman's nae much, for she's amast dede wi' exhaustion." And while he is ordering a nostrum he knows can do no good, the woman makes a violent struggle, opens her eyes, and seems casting a last glance round the dark room. Now she sets them fixedly upon the ceiling, her lips pale, and her countenance becomes spectre-like—a low, gurgling sound is heard, the messenger of retribution is come—Madame Flamingo is dead!

CHAPTER XL
IN WHICH THE LAW IS SEEN TO CONFLICT WITH OUR CHERISHED CHIVALRY

"What could the woman mean, when on taking leave of me she said, 'you are far richer than me?'" questions Maria McArthur to herself, when, finding she is alone and homeless in the street, she opens the packet the woman Anna slipped so mysteriously into her hand, and finds it contains two twenty-dollar gold pieces. And while evolving in her mind whether she shall appropriate them to the relief of her destitute condition, her conscience smites her. It is the gold got of vice. Her heart shares the impulse that prompted the act, but her pure spirit recoils from the acceptance of such charity. "You are far richer than me!" knells in her ears, and reveals to her the heart-burnings of the woman who lives in licentious splendor. "I have no home, no friend near me, and nowhere to lay my head; and yet I am richer than her;" she says, gazing at the moon, and the stars, and the serene heavens. And the contemplation brings to her consolation and strength. She wanders back to the gate of the old prison, resolved to return the gold in the morning, and, was the night not so far spent, ask admittance into the cell her father occupies. But she reflects, and turns away; well knowing how much more painful will be the smart of his troubles does she disclose to him what has befallen her.

She continues sauntering up a narrow by-lane in the outskirts of the city. A light suddenly flashes across her path, glimmers from the window of a little cabin, and inspires her with new hopes. She quickens her steps, reaches the door, meets a welcome reception, and is made comfortable for the night by the mulatto woman who is its solitary tenant. The woman, having given Maria of her humble cheer, seems only too anxious to disclose the fact that she is the slave and cast-off mistress of Judge Sleepyhorn, on whose head she invokes no few curses. It does not touch her pride so much that he has abandoned her, as that he has taken to himself one of another color. She is tall and straight of figure, with prominent features, long, silky black hair, and a rich olive complexion; and though somewhat faded of age, it is clear that she possessed in youth charms of great value in the flesh market.

Maria discloses to her how she came in possession of the money, as also her resolve to return it in the morning. Undine (for such is her name) applauds this with great gusto. "Now, thar!" she says, "that's the spirit I likes." And straightway she volunteers to be the medium of returning the money, adding that she will show the hussy her contempt of her by throwing it at her feet, and "letting her see a *slave* knows all about it."

Maria fully appreciates the kindness, as well as sympathizes with the wounded pride of this slave daughter; nevertheless, there is an humiliation in being driven to seek shelter in a negro cabin that touches her feelings. For a white female to seek shelter under the roof of a negro's cabin, is a deep disgrace in the eyes of our very refined society; and having subjected herself to the humiliation, she knows full well that it may be used against her—in fine, made a means to defame her character.

Night passes away, and the morning ushers in soft and sunny, but brings with it nothing to relieve her situation. She, however, returns the gold to Anna through a channel less objectionable than that Undine would have supplied, and sallies out to seek lodgings. In a house occupied by a poor German family, she seeks and obtains a little room, wherein she continues plying at her needle.

The day set apart for the trial before a jury of "special bail" arrives. The rosy-faced commissioner is in his seat, a very good-natured jury is impanelled, and the feeble old man is again brought into court. Maria saunters, thoughtful, and anxious for the result, at the outer door. Peter Crimpton rises, addresses the jury at great length, sets forth the evident intention of fraud on the part of the applicant, and the enormity of the crime. He will now prove his objections by competent witnesses. The proceedings being in accordance with what Mr. Snivel facetiously terms the strict rules of special pleading, the old man's lips are closed. Several very respectable witnesses are called, and aver they saw the old Antiquary with a gold watch mounted, at a recent date; witnesses quite as dependable aver they have known him for many years, but never mounted with anything so extravagant as a gold watch. So much for the validity of testimony! It is very clear that the very respectable witnesses have confounded some one else with the prisoner.

The Antiquary openly confesses to the possession of a pin, and the curious skull (neither of which are valuable beyond their associations), but declares it more an oversight than an intention that they were left out of the schedule. For the virtue of the schedule, Mr. Crimpton is singularly scrupulous; nor does it soften his aspersions that the old man offers to resign them for the benefit of the State. Mr. Crimpton gives his case to the jury, expressing his belief that a verdict will be rendered in his favor. A verdict of guilty (for so it is rendered in our courts) will indeed give the prisoner to him for an indefinite period. In truth, the only drawback is that the plaintiff will be required to pay thirty cents a day to Mr. Hardscrabble, who will starve him rightly soundly.

The jury, very much to Mr. Crimpton's chagrin, remain seated, and declare the prisoner not guilty. Was this sufficient—all the law demanded? No. Although justice might have been satisfied, the law had other ends to serve, and in the hands of an instrument like Crimpton, could be turned to uses delicacy forbids our transcribing here. The old man's persecutors were not satisfied; the verdict of the jury was with him, but the law gave his enemies power to retain him six months longer. Mr. Crimpton demands a writ of appeal to the sessions. The Commissioner has no alternative, notwithstanding the character of the pretext upon which it is demanded is patent on its face. Such is but a feeble description of one of the many laws South Carolina retains on her statute book to oppress the poor and give power to the rich. If we would but purge ourselves of this distemper of chivalry and secession, that so blinds our eyes to the sufferings of the poor, while driving our politicians mad over the country (we verily believe them all coming to the gallows or insane hospital), how much higher and nobler would be our claim to the respect of the world!

Again the old man is separated from his daughter, placed in the hands of a bailiff, and remanded back to prison, there to hope, fear, and while away the time, waiting six, perhaps eight months, for the sitting of the Court of Appeals. The "Appeal Court," you must know, would seem to have inherited the aristocracy of our ancestors, for, having a great aversion to business pursuits, it sits at very long intervals, and gets through very little business.

When the news of her father's remand reaches Maria, it overwhelms her with grief. Varied are her thoughts of how she shall provide for the future; dark and sad are the pictures of trouble that rise up before her. Look whichever way she will, her ruin seems sealed. The health of her aged father is fast breaking—her own is gradually declining under the pressure of her troubles. Rapidly forced from one extreme to another, she appeals to a few acquaintances who have expressed friendship for her father; but their friendship took wings when grim poverty looked in. Southern hospitality, though bountifully bestowed upon the rich, rarely condescends to shed its bright rays over the needy poor.

Maria advertises for a situation, in some of our first families, as private seamstress. Our first families having slaves for such offices, have no need of "poor white trash." She applies personally to several ladies of "eminent standing," and who busy themselves in getting up donations for northern Tract Societies. They have no sympathy to waste upon her. Her appeal only enlists coldness and indifference. The "Church Home" had lent an ear to her story, but that her address is very unsatisfactory, and it is got out that she is living a very suspicious life. The "Church Home," so virtuous and pious, can do nothing for her until she improves her mode of living. Necessity pinches Maria at every turn. "To be poor in a slave atmosphere, is truly a crime," she says to herself, musing over her hard lot, while sitting in her chamber one evening. "But I am the richer! I will rise above all!" She has just prepared to carry some nourishment to her father, when Keepum enters, his face flushed, and his features darkened with a savage scowl. "I have said you were a fool—all women are fools!—and now I know I was not mistaken!" This Mr. Keepum says while throwing his hat sullenly upon the floor. "Well," he pursues, having seated himself in a chair, looked designingly at the candle, then contorted his narrow face, and frisked his fingers through his bright red hair, "as to this here wincing and mincing— its all humbuggery of a woman like you. Affecting such morals! Don't go down here; tell you that, my spunky girl. Loose morals is what takes in poor folks."

Maria answers him only with a look of scorn. She advances to the door to find it locked.

"It was me—I locked it. Best to be private about the matter," says Keepum, a forced smile playing over his countenance.

Unresolved whether to give vent to her passion, or make an effort to inspire his better nature, she stands a few moments, as if immersed in deep thought, then suddenly falls upon her knees at his feet, and implores him to save her this last step to her ruin. "Hear me, oh, hear me, and let your heart give out its pity for one who has only her virtue left her in this world;" she appeals to him with earnest voice, and eyes swimming in tears. "Save my father, for you have power. Give him his liberty, that I, his child, his only comfort in his old age, may make him happy. Yes! yes!—he will die where he is. Will you, can you—you have a heart—see me struggle against the rude buffets of an unthinking world! Will you not save me from the Poor-house—from the shame that awaits me with greedy clutches, and receive in return the blessing of a friendless woman! Oh!—you will, you will—release my father!—give him back to me and make me happy. Ah, ha!—I see, I see, you have feelings, better feelings—feelings that are not seared. You will have pity on me; you will forgive, relent—you cannot see a wretch suffer and not be moved to lighten her pain!" The calm, pensive expression that lights up her countenance is indeed enough to inspire the tender impulses of a heart in which every sense of generosity is not dried up.

Her appeal, nevertheless, falls ineffectual. Mr. Keepum has no generous impulses to bestow upon beings so sensitive of their virtue. With him, it is a ware of very little value, inasmuch as the moral standard fixed by a better class of people is quite loose. He rises from his chair with an air of self-confidence, seizes her by the hand, and attempts to drag her upon his knee, saying, "you know I can and will make you a lady. Upon the honor of a gentleman, I love you—always have loved you; but what stands in the way, and is just enough to make any gentleman of my standing mad, is this here squeamishness—"

"No! no! go from me. Attempt not again to lay your cruel hands upon me!" The goaded woman struggles from his grasp, and shrieks for help at the very top of her voice. And as the neighbors come rushing up stairs, Mr. Keepum valorously betakes himself into the street. Maddened with disappointment, and swearing to have revenge, he seeks his home, and there muses over the "curious woman's" unswerving resolution. "Cruelty!" he says to himself—"she charges me with cruelty! Well," (here he sighs) "it's only because she lacks a bringing up that can appreciate a gentleman." (Keepum could never condescend to believe himself less than a very fine gentleman.) "As sure as the world the creature is somewhat out in the head. She fancies all sorts of things—shame, disgrace, and ruin!—only because she don't understand the quality of our morality—that's all! There's no harm, after all, in these little enjoyments—if the girl would only understand them so. Our society is free from pedantry; and there—no damage can result where no one's the wiser. It's like stealing a blush from the cheek of beauty—nobody misses it, and the cheek continues as beautiful as ever." Thus philosophizes the chivalric gentleman, until he falls into a fast sleep.

CHAPTER XLI
IN WHICH JUSTICE IS SEEN TO BE VERY ACCOMMODATING

A few days have elapsed, Maria has just paid a visit to her father, still in prison, and may be seen looking in at Mr. Keepum's office, in Broad street. "I come not to ask a favor, sir; but, at my father's request, to say to you that, having given up all he has in the world, it can do no good to any one to continue him in durance, and to ask of you—in whom the sole power rests—that you will grant him his release ere he dies?" She addresses Mr. Keepum, who seems not in a very good temper this morning, inasmuch as several of his best negroes, without regard to their value to him, got a passion for freedom into their heads, and have taken themselves away. In addition to this, he is much put out, as he says, at being compelled to forego the pleasure held out on the previous night, of tarring and feathering two northerners suspected of entertaining sentiments not exactly straight on the "peculiar question." A glorious time was expected, and a great deal of very strong patriotism wasted; but the two unfortunate individuals, by some means not yet discovered, got the vigilance committee, to whose care they were entrusted, very much intoxicated, and were not to be found when called for. Free knives, and not free speech, is our motto. And this Mr. Keepum is one of the most zealous in carrying out.

Mr. Keepum sits, his hair fretted back over his lean forehead, before a table covered with papers, all indicating an immense business in lottery and other speculations. Now he deposits his feet upon it; leans back in his chair, puffs his cigar, and says, with an air of indifference to the speaker: "I shall not be able to attend to any business of yours to-day, Madam!" His clerk, a man of sturdy figure, with a broad, red face, and dressed in rather dilapidated broadcloth, is passing in and out of the front office, bearing in his fingers documents that require a signature or mark of approval.

"I only come, sir, to tell you that we are destitute—" Maria pauses, and stands trembling in the doorway.

"That's a very common cry," interrupts Keepum, relieving his mouth of the cigar. "The affair is entirely out of my hands. Go to my attorney, Peter Crimpton, Esq.,—what he does for you will receive my sanction. I must not be interrupted to-day. I might express a thousand regrets; yes, pass an opinion on your foolish pride, but what good would it do."

And while Maria stands silent and hesitating, there enters the office abruptly a man in the garb of a mechanic. "I have come," speaks the man, in a tone of no very good humor, "for the last time. I asks of you—you professes to be a gentleman—my honest rights. If the law don't give it to me, I mean to take it with this erehand." (He shakes his hand at Keepum.) "I am a poor man who ain't thought much of because I works for a living; you have got what I had worked hard for, and lain up to make my little family comfortable. I ask a settlement and my own—what is due from one honest man to another!" He now approaches the table, strikes his hand upon it, and pauses for a reply.

Mr. Keepum coolly looks up, and with an insidious leer, says, "There, take yourself into the street. When next you enter a gentleman's office, learn to deport yourself with good manners."

"Pshaw! pshaw!" interrupts the man. "What mockery! When men like you—yes, I say men like you—that has brought ruin on so many poor families, can claim to be gentlemen, rogues may get a patent for their order." The man turns to take his departure, when the infuriated Keepum, who, as we have before described, gets exceedingly put out if any one doubts his honor, seizes an iron bar, and stealing up behind, fetches him a blow over the head that fells him lifeless to the floor.

Maria shrieks, and vaults into the street. The mass upon the floor fetches a last agonizing shrug, and a low moan, and is dead. The murderer stands over him, exultant, as the blood streams from the deep fracture. In fine, the blood of his victim would seem rather to increase his satisfaction at the deed, than excite a regret.

Call you this murder? Truly, the man has outraged God's law. And the lover of law and order, of social good, and moral honesty, would find reasons for designating the perpetrator an assassin. For has he not first distressed a family, and then left it bereft of its protector? You may think of it and designate it as you please. Nevertheless we, in our fancied mightiness, cannot condescend to such vulgar considerations. We esteem it extremely courageous of Mr. Keepum, to defend himself "to the death" against the insults of one of the common herd. Our first families applaud the act, our sensitive press say it was "an unfortunate affair," and by way of admonition, add that it were better working people be more careful how they approach gentlemen. Mr. Snivel will call this, the sublime quality of our chivalry. What say the jury of inquest?

Duly weighing the high position of Mr. Keepum, and the very low condition of the deceased, the good-natured jury return a verdict that the man met his death in consequence of an accidental blow, administered with an iron instrument, in the hands of one Keepum. From the testimony— Keepum's clerk—it is believed the act was committed in self-defence.

Mr. Keepum, as is customary with our fine gentlemen, and like a hero (we will not content ourselves with making him one jot less), magnanimously surrenders himself to the authorities. The majesty of our laws is not easily offended by gentlemen of standing. Only the poor and the helpless slave can call forth the terrible majesty of the law, and quicken to action its sensitive quality. The city is shocked that Mr. Keepum is subjected to a night in jail, notwithstanding he has the jailer's best parlor, and a barricade of champaign bottles are strewn at his feet by flattering friends, who make night jubilant with their carousal.

Southern society asks no repentance of him whose hands reek with the blood of his poor victim; southern society has no pittance for that family Keepum has made lick the dust in tears and sorrow. Even while we write— while the corpse of the murdered man, followed by a few brother craftsmen, is being borne to its last resting-place, the perpetrator, released on a paltry bail, is being regaled at a festive board. Such is our civilization! How had the case stood with a poor man! Could he have stood up against the chivalry of South Carolina, scoffed at the law, or bid good-natured justice close her eyes? No. He had been dragged to a close cell, and long months had passed ere the tardy movements of the law reached his case. Even then, popular opinion would have turned upon him, pre-judged him, and held him up as dangerous to the peace of the people. Yes, pliant justice would have affected great virtue, and getting on her high throne, never ceased her demands until he had expiated his crime at the gallows.

A few weeks pass: Keepum's reputation for courage is fully endorsed, the Attorney-General finds nothing in the act to justify him in bringing it before a Grand Jury, the law is satisfied (or ought to be satisfied), and the rich murderer sleeps without a pang of remorse.

CHAPTER XLII
IN WHICH SOME LIGHT IS THROWN
ON THE PLOT OF THIS HISTORY

June, July, and August are past away, and September, with all its autumnal beauties, ushers in, without bringing anything to lighten the cares of that girl whose father yet pines in prison. She looks forward, hoping against hope, to the return of her lover (something tells her he still lives), only to feel more keenly the pangs of hope deferred.

And now, once more, New York, we are in thy busy streets. It is a pleasant evening in early September. The soft rays of an autumn sun are tinging the western sky, and night is fast drawing her sable mantle over the scene. In Washington Square, near where the tiny fountain jets its stream into a round, grassy-bordered basin, there sits a man of middle stature, apparently in deep study. His dress is plain, and might be taken for that of either a working man, or a somewhat faded inspector of customs. Heedless of those passing to and fro, he sits until night fairly sets in, then rises, and faces towards the East. Through the trunks of trees he sees, and seems contemplating the gray walls of the University, and the bold, sombre front of the very aristocratic church of the Reformed Dutch.

"Well!" he mutters to himself, resuming his seat, and again facing to the west, "this ere business of ourn is a great book of life—'tis that! Finds us in queer places; now and then mixed up curiously." He rises a second time, advances to a gas-light, draws a letter from his pocket, and scans, with an air of evident satisfaction, over the contents. "Umph!" he resumes, and shrugs his shoulders, "I was right on the address—ought to have known it without looking." Having resumed his seat, he returns the letter to his pocket, sits with his elbow upon his knee, and his head rested thoughtfully in his right hand. The picture before him, so calm and soft, has no attractions for him. The dusky hues of night, for slowly the scene darkens, seem lending a softness and calmness to the foliage. The weeping branches of the willow, interspersed here and there, as if to invest the picture with a touching melancholy, sway gently to and fro; the leaves of the silvery poplar tremble and reflect their shadows on the fresh waters; and the flitting gaslights mingle their gleams, play and sport over the rippled surface, coquet with the tripping star-beams, then throw fantastic lights over the swaying foliage; and from beneath the massive branches of trees, there shines out, in bold relief, the marble porticoes and lintels of stately-looking mansions. Such is the calm grandeur of the scene, that one could imagine some Thalia investing it with a poetic charm the gods might muse over.

"It is not quite time yet," says the man, starting suddenly to his feet. He again approaches a gas-light, looks attentively at his watch, then saunters to the corner of Fourth and Thompson streets. An old, dilapidated wooden building, which some friend has whitewashed into respectability, and looking as if it had a strong inclination to tumble either upon the sidewalk, or against the great trunk of a hoary-headed tree at the corner, arrests his attention. "Well," he says, having paused before it, and scanned its crooked front, "this surely is the house where the woman lived when she was given the child. Practice, and putting two things together to find what one means, is the great thing in our profession. Like its old tenant, the house has got down a deal. It's on its last legs." Again he consults his watch, and with a quickened step recrosses the Square, and enters —— Avenue. Now he halts before a spacious mansion, the front of which is high and bold, and deep, and of brown freestone. The fluted columns; the elegantly-chiselled lintels; the broad, scrolled window-frames; the exactly-moulded arches; the massive steps leading to the deep, vaulted entrance, with its doors of sombre and highly-polished walnut; and its bold style of architecture, so grand in its outlines,—all invest it with a regal air. The man casts a glance along the broad avenue, then into the sombre entrance of the mansion. Now he seems questioning within himself whether to enter or retrace his steps. One-half of the outer door, which is in the Italian style, with heavy fluted mouldings, stands ajar; while from out the lace curtains of the inner, there steals a faint light. The man rests his elbow on the great stone scroll of the guard-rail, and here we leave him for a few moments.

The mansion, it may be well to add here, remains closed the greater part of the year; and when opened seems visited by few persons, and those not of the very highest standing in society. A broken-down politician, a seedy hanger-on of some "literary club," presided over by a rich, but very stupid tailor, and now and then a lady about whose skirts something not exactly straight hangs, and who has been elbowed out of fashionable society for her too ardent love of opera-singers, and handsome actors, may be seen dodging in now and then. Otherwise, the mansion would seem very generally deserted by the neighborhood.

Everybody will tell you, and everybody is an individual so extremely busy in other people's affairs, that he ought to know, that there is something that hangs so like a rain-cloud about the magnificent skirts of those who live so secluded "in that fine old pile," (mansion,) that the virtuous satin of the Avenue never can be got to "mix in." Indeed, the Avenue generally seems to have set its face against those who reside in it. They enjoy none of those very grand assemblies, balls, and receptions, for which the Avenue is become celebrated, and yet they luxuriate in wealth and splendor.

Though the head of the house seems banished by society, society makes her the subject of many evil reports and mysterious whisperings. The lady of the mansion, however, as if to retort upon her traducers, makes it known that she is very popular abroad, every now and then during her absence honoring them with mysterious clippings from foreign journals—all setting forth the admiration her appearance called forth at a grand reception given by the Earl and Countess of — —.

Society is made of inexorable metal, she thinks, for the prejudices of the neighborhood have not relaxed one iota with time. That she has been presented to kings, queens, and emperors; that she has enjoyed the hospitalities of foreign embassies; that she has (and she makes no little ado that she has) shone in the assemblies of prime ministers; that she has been invited to court concerts, and been the flattered of no end of fashionable *coteries*, serves her nothing at home. They are events, it must be admitted, much discussed, much wondered at, much regretted by those who wind themselves up in a robe of stern morality. In a few instances they are lamented, lest the morals and manners of those who make it a point to represent us abroad should reflect only the brown side of our society.

As if with regained confidence, the man, whom we left at the door scroll, is seen slowly ascending the broad steps. He enters the vaulted vestibule, and having touched the great, silver bell-knob of the inner door, stands listening to the tinkling chimes within. A pause of several minutes, and the door swings cautiously open. There stands before him the broad figure of a fussy servant man, wedged into a livery quite like that worn by the servants of an English tallow-chandler, but which, it must be said, and said to be regretted, is much in fashion with our aristocracy, who, in consequence of its brightness, believe it the exact style of some celebrated lord. The servant receives a card from the visitor, and with a bow, inquires if he will wait an answer.

"I will wait the lady's pleasure—I came by appointment," returns the man. And as the servant disappears up the hall, he takes a seat, uninvited, upon a large settee, in carved walnut. "Something mysterious about this whole affair!" he muses, scanning along the spacious hall, into the conservatory of statuary and rare plants, seen opening away at the extreme end. The high, vaulted roof; the bright, tesselated floor; the taste with which the frescoes decorating the walls are designed; the great winding stairs, so richly carpeted—all enhanced in beauty by the soft light reflected upon them from a massive chandelier of stained glass, inspire him with a feeling of awe. The stillness, and the air of grandeur pervading each object that meets his eye, reminds him of the halls of those mediæval castles he has read of in his youth. The servant returns, and makes his bow. "My leady," he says, in a strong Lincolnshire brogue, "'as weated ye an 'our or more."

The visitor, evincing some nervousness, rises quickly to his feet, follows the servant up the hall, and is ushered into a parlor of regal dimensions, on the right. His eye falls upon one solitary occupant, who rises from a lounge of oriental richness, and advances towards him with an air of familiarity their conditions seem not to warrant. Having greeted the visitor, and bid him be seated (he takes his seat, shyly, beside the door), the lady resumes her seat in a magnificent chair. For a moment the visitor scans over the great parlor, as if moved by the taste and elegance of everything that meets his eye. The hand of art has indeed been lavishly laid on the decorations of this chamber, which presents a scene of luxury princes might revel in. And though the soft wind of whispering silks seemed lending its aid to make complete the enjoyment of the occupant, it might be said, in the words of Crabbe:

"But oh, what storm was in that mind!"

The person of the lady is in harmony with the splendor of the apartment. Rather tall and graceful of figure, her complexion pale, yet soft and delicate, her features as fine and regular as ever sculptor chiselled, her manner gentle and womanly. In her face, nevertheless, there is an expression of thoughtfulness, perhaps melancholy, to which her large, earnest black eyes, and finely-arched brows, fringed with dark lashes, lend a peculiar charm. While over all there plays a shadow of languor, increased perhaps by the tinge of age, or a mind and heart overtaxed with cares.

"I received your note, which I hastened to answer. Of course you received my answer. I rejoice that you have persevered, and succeeded in finding the object I have so long sought. Not hearing from you for so many weeks, I had begun to fear she had gone forever," says the lady, in a soft, musical voice, raising her white, delicate hand to her cheek, which is suffused with blushes.

"I had myself almost given her over, for she disappeared from the Points, and no clue could be got of her," returns the man, pausing for a moment, then resuming his story. "A week ago yesterday she turned up again, and I got wind that she was in a place we call 'Black-beetle Hole'—"

"Black-beetle Hole!" ejaculates the lady, whom the reader will have discovered is no less a person than Madame Montford. Mr. Detective Fitzgerald is the visitor.

"Yes, there's where she's got, and it isn't much of a place, to say the best. But when a poor creature has no other place to get a stretch down, she stretches down there—"

"Proceed to how you found her, and what you have got from her concerning the child," the lady interrupts, with a deep sigh.

"Well," proceeds the detective, "I meets—havin' an eye out all the while—Sergeant Dobbs one morning—Dobbs knows every roost in the Points better than me!—and says he, 'Fitzgerald, that are woman, that crazy woman, you've been in tow of so long, has turned up. There was a row in Black-beetle Hole last night. I got a force and descended into the place, found it crammed with them half-dead kind of women and men, and three thieves, what wanted to have a fuss with the hag that keeps it. One on 'em was thrashing the poor crazy woman. They had torn all the rags off her back. Hows-ever, if you wants to fish her out, you'd better be spry about it—'"

The lady interrupts by saying she will disguise, and with his assistance, go bring her from the place—save her! Mr. Fitzgerald begs she will take the matter practically. She could not breathe the air of the place, he says.

"'Thank you Dobbs,' says I," he resumes, "and when it got a bit dark I went incog. to Black-beetle's Hole—"

"And where is this curious place?" she questions, with an air of anxiety.

"As to that, Madame—well, you wouldn't know it was lived in, because its underground, and one not up to the entrance never would think it led to a place where human beings crawled in at night. I don't wonder so many of 'em does things what get 'em into the Station, and after that treated to a short luxury on the Island. As I was goin' on to say, I got myself fortified, started out into the Points, and walked—we take these things practically— down and up the east sidewalk, then stopped in front of the old rotten house that Black-beetle Hole is under. Then I looks down the wet little stone steps, that ain't wide enough for a big man to get down, and what lead into the cellar. Some call it Black-beetle Hole, and then again some call it the Hole of the Black-beetles. 'Yer after no good, Mr. Fitzgerald,' says Mrs. McQuade, whose husband keeps the junk-shop over the Hole, putting her malicious face out of the window.

"'You're the woman I want, Mrs. McQuade,' says I. 'Don't be puttin' your foot in the house,' says she. And when I got her temper a little down by telling her I only wanted to know who lived in the Hole, she swore by all the saints it had niver a soul in it, and was hard closed up. Being well up to the dodges of the Points folks, I descended the steps, and gettin' underground, knocked at the Hole door, and then sent it smash in. 'Well! who's here?' says I. 'It's me,' says Mrs. Lynch, a knot of an old woman, who has kept the Hole for many years, and says she has no fear of the devil."

Madame Montford listens with increasing anxiety; Mr. Detective Fitzgerald proceeds: "'Get a light here, then;' says I. You couldn't see nothing, it was so dark, but you could hear 'em move, and breathe. And then the place was so hot and sickly. Had to stand it best way I could. There was no standing straight in the dismal place, which was wet and nasty under foot, and not more nor twelve by fourteen. The old woman said she had only a dozen lodgers in; when she made out to get a light for me I found she had twenty-three, tucked away here and there, under straw and stuff. Well, it was curious to see 'em (here the detective wipes his forehead with his handkerchief) rise up, one after another, all round you, you know, like fiends that had been buried for a time, then come to life merely to get something to eat.'"

"And did you find the woman—and was she one of them?"

"That's what I'm comin' at. Well, I caught a sight at the woman; knew her at the glance. I got a sight at her one night in the Pit at the House of the Nine Nations. 'Here! I wants you,' says I, takin' what there was left of her by the arm. She shrieked, and crouched down, and begged me not to hurt her, and looked wilder than a tiger at me. And then the whole den got into a fright, and young women, and boys, and men—they were all huddled together—set up such a screaming. 'Munday!' says I, 'you don't go to the Tombs—here! I've got good news for you.' This quieted her some, and then I picked her up—she was nearly naked—and seeing she wanted scrubbing up, carried her out of the Hole, and made her follow me to my house, where we got her into some clothes, and seeing that she was got right in her mind, I thought it would be a good time to question her."

"If you will hasten the result of your search, it will, my good sir, relieve my feelings much!" again interposes the lady, drawing her chair nearer the detective.

"'You've had.' I says to her, 'a hard enough time in this world, and now here's the man what's going to be a friend to ye—understand that!' says I, and she looked at me bewildered. We gave her something to eat, and a pledge that no one would harm her, and she tamed down, and began to look up a bit. 'Your name wasn't always Munday?' says I, in a way that she couldn't tell what I was after. She said she had taken several names, but Munday was her right name. Then she corrected herself—she was weak and hoarse—and said it was her husband's name. 'You've a good memory, Mrs. Munday,' says I; 'now, just think as far back as you can, and tell us where you lived as long back as you can think.' She shook her head, and began to bury her face in her hands I tried for several minutes, but could get nothing more out of her. Then she quickened up, shrieked out that she had just got out of the devil's regions, and made a rush for the door."

CHAPTER XLIII
IN WHICH IS REVEALED THE ONE ERROR THAT BROUGHT SO MUCH SUFFERING UPON MANY

Mr. Fitzgerald sees that his last remark is having no very good effect on Madame Montford, and hastens to qualify, ere it overcome her. "That, I may say, Madame, was not the last of her. My wife and me, seeing how her mind was going wrong again, got her in bed for the night, and took what care of her we could. Well, you see, she got rational in the morning, and, thinking it a chance, I 'plied a heap of kindness to her, and got her to tell all she knew of herself. She went on to tell where she lived—I followed your directions in questioning her—at the time you noted down. She described the house exactly. I have been to it to-night; knew it at a sight, from her description. Some few practical questions I put to her about the child you wanted to get at, I found frightened her so that she kept shut—for fear, I take it, that it was a crime she may be punished for at some time. I says, 'You was trusted with a child once, wasn't you?' 'The Lord forgive me,' she says, 'I know I'm guilty—but I've been punished enough in this world haven't I?' And she burst out into tears, and hung down her head, and got into the corner, as if wantin' nobody to see her. She only wanted a little good care, and a little kindness, to bring her to. This we did as well as we could, and made her understand that no one thought of punishing her, but wanted to be her friends. Well, the poor wretch began to pick up, as I said before, and in three days was such another woman that nobody could have told that she was the poor crazy thing that ran about the lanes and alleys of the Points. And now, Madame, doing as you bid me, I thought it more practical to come to you, knowing you could get of her all you wanted. She is made comfortable. Perhaps you wouldn't like to have her brought here—I may say I don't think it would be good policy. If you would condescend to come to our house, you can see her alone. I hope you are satisfied with my services." The detective pauses, and again wipes his face.

"My gratitude for your perseverance I can never fully express to you. I owe you a debt I never can repay. To-morrow, at ten o'clock, I will meet you at your house; and then, if you can leave me alone with her—"

"Certainly, certainly, everything will be at your service, Madame," returns the detective, rising from his seat and thanking the lady, who rewards him bountifully from her purse, and bids him good night. The servant escorts him to the door, while Madame Montford buries her face in her hands, and gives vent to her emotions.

On the morning following, a neatly-caparisoned carriage is seen driving to the door of a little brick house in Crosby street. From it Madame Montford alights, and passes in at the front door, while in another minute it rolls away up the street and is lost to sight. A few moments' consultation, and the detective, who has ushered the lady into his humbly-furnished little parlor, withdraws to give place to the pale and emaciated figure of the woman Munday, who advances with faltering step and downcast countenance. "Oh! forgive me, forgive me! have mercy upon me! forgive me this crime!" she shrieks. Suddenly she raises her eyes, and rushing forward throws herself at Madame Montford's feet, in an imploring attitude. Dark and varied fancies crowd confusedly on Madame Montford's mind at this moment.

"Nay, nay, my poor sufferer, rather I might ask forgiveness of you." She takes the woman by the hand, and, with an air of regained calmness, raises her from the floor. With her, the outer life seems preparing the inner for what is to come. "But I have long sought you—sought you in obedience to the demands of my conscience, which I would the world gave me power to purify; and now I have found you, and with you some rest for my aching heart. Come, sit down; forget what you have suffered; tell me what befell you, and what has become of the child; tell me all, and remember that I will provide for you a comfortable home for the rest of your life." Madame motions her to a chair, struggling the while to suppress her own feelings.

"I loved the child you intrusted to my care; yes, God knows I loved it, and watched over it for two years, as carefully as a mother. But I was poor, and the brother, in whose hands you intrusted the amount for its support (this, the reader must here know, was not a brother, but the paramour of Madame Montford), failed, and gave me nothing after the first six months. I never saw him, and when I found you had gone abroad—" The woman hesitates, and, with weeping eyes and trembling voice, again implores forgiveness. "My husband gave himself up to drink, lost his situation, and then he got to hating the child, and abusing me for taking it, and embarrassing our scanty means of living. Night and day, I was harassed and abused, despised and neglected. I was discouraged, and gave up in despair. I clung to the child as long as I could. I struggled, and struggled, and struggled—" Here the woman pauses, and with a submissive look, again hangs down her head and sobs.

"Be calm, be calm," says Madame Montford, drawing nearer to her, and making an effort to inspirit her. "Throw off all your fears, forget what you have suffered, for I, too, have suffered. And you parted with the child?"

"Necessity forced me," pursues the woman, shaking her head. "I saw only the street before me on one side, and felt only the cold pinchings of poverty on the other. You had gone abroad—"

"It was my intention to have adopted the child as my own when I returned," interrupts Madame Montford, still clinging to that flattering hope in which the criminal sees a chance of escape.

"And I," resumes the woman, "left the husband who neglected me, and who treated me cruelly, and gave myself,—perhaps I was to blame for it,—up to one who befriended me. He was the only one who seemed to care for me, or to have any sympathy for me. But he, like myself, was poor; and, being compelled to flee from our home, and to live in obscurity, where my husband could not find me out, the child was an incumbrance I had no means of supporting. I parted with her—yes, yes, I parted with her to Mother Bridges, who kept a stand at a corner in West street—"

"And then what became of her?" again interposes Madame Montford. The woman assumes a sullenness, and it is some time before she can be got to proceed.

"My conscience rebuked me," she resumes, as if indifferent about answering the question, "for I loved the child as my own; and the friend I lived with, and who followed the sea, printed on its right arm two hearts and a broken anchor, which remain there now. My husband died of the cholera, and the friend I had taken to, and who treated me kindly, also died, and I soon found myself an abandoned woman, an outcast—yes, ruined forever, and in the streets, leading a life that my own feelings revolted at, but from which starvation only seemed the alternative. My conscience rebuked me again and again, and something—I cannot tell what it was—impelled me with an irresistible force to watch over the fortunes of the child I knew must come to the same degraded life necessity—perhaps it was my own false step—had forced upon me. I watched her a child running neglected about the streets, then I saw her sold to Hag Zogbaum, who lived in Pell street; I never lost sight of her—no, I never lost sight of her, but fear of criminating myself kept me from making myself known to her. When I had got old in vice, and years had gone past, and she was on the first step to the vice she had been educated to, we shared the same roof. Then she was known as Anna Bonard—"

"Anna Bonard!" exclaims Madame Montford. "Then truly it is she who now lives in Charleston! There is no longer a doubt. I may seek and claim her, and return her to at least a life of comfort."

"There you will find her. Ah, many times have I looked upon her, and thought if I could only save her, how happy I could die. I shared the same roof with her in Charleston, and when I got sick she was kind to me, and watched over me, and was full of gentleness, and wept over her condition. She has sighed many a time, and said how she wished she knew how she came into the world, to be forced to live despised by the world. But I got down, down, down, from one step to another, one step to another, as I had gone up from one step to another in the splendor of vice, until I found myself, tortured in mind and body, a poor neglected wretch in the Charleston Poor-house. In it I was treated worse than a slave, left, sick and heart-broken, and uncared-for, to the preying of a fever that destroyed my mind. And as if that were not enough, I was carried into the dungeons—the 'mad cells,'—and chained. And this struck such a feeling of terror into my soul that my reason, as they said, was gone forever. But I got word to Anna, and she came to me, and gave me clothes and many little things to comfort me, and got me out, and gave me money to get back to New York, where I have been ever since, haunted from place to place, with scarce a place to lay my head. Surely I have suffered. Shall I be forgiven?" Her voice here falters, she becomes weak, and seems sinking under the burden of her emotions. "If,—if—if," she mutters, incoherently, "you can save me, and forgive me, you will have the prayers of one who has drank deep of the bitter cup." She looks up with a sad, melancholy countenance, again implores forgiveness, and bursts into loud sobs.

"Mine is the guilty part—it is me who needs forgiveness!" speaks Madame Montford, pressing the hand of the forlorn woman, as the tears stream down her cheeks. She has unburdened her emotions, but such is the irresistible power of a guilty conscience that she finds her crushed heart and smitten frame sinking under the shock—that she feels the very fever of remorse mounting to her brain.

"Be calm, be calm—for you have suffered, wandered through the dark abyss—truly you have been chastened enough in this world. But while your heart is only bruised and sore, mine is stung deep and lacerated. The image of that child now rises up before me. I see her looking back over her chequered life, and pining to know her birthright. Mine is the task of seeking her out, reconciling her, saving her from this life of shame. I must sacrifice the secrets of my own heart, go boldly in pursuit of her—" She pauses a moment. There is yet a thin veil between her and society. Society only founds its suspicions upon the mystery involved in the separation from her husband, and the doubtful character of her long residence in Europe. Society knows nothing of the birth of the child. The scandal leveled at her in Charleston, was only the result of her own indiscretion. "Yes," she whispers, attempting at the same time to soothe the feelings of the poor disconsolate woman, "I must go, and go quickly—I must drag her from the terrible life she is leading;—but, ah! I must do it so as to shield myself. Yes, I must shield myself!" And she puts into the woman's hand several pieces of gold, saying: "take this!—to-morrow you will be better provided for. Be silent. Speak to no one of what has passed between us, nor make the acquaintance of any one outside the home I shall provide for you." Thus saying, she recalls Mr. Detective Fitzgerald, rewards him with a nostrum from her purse, and charges him to make the woman comfortable at her expense.

"Her mind, now I do believe," says the detective, with an approving toss of the head, "her faculties'll come right again,—they only wants a little care and kindness, mum." The detective thanks her again and again, then puts the money methodically into his pocket.

The carriage having returned, Madame Montford vaults into it as quickly as she alighted, and is rolled away to her mansion.

CHAPTER XLIV
IN WHICH IS RECORDED EVENTS THE READER MAY NOT HAVE EXPECTED

While the events we have recorded in the foregoing chapter, confused, hurried, and curious, are being enacted in New York, let us once more turn to Charleston.

You must know that, notwithstanding our high state of civilization, we yet maintain in practice two of the most loathsome relics of barbarism—we lash helpless women, and we scourge, at the public whipping-post, the bare backs of men.

George Mullholland has twice been dragged to the whipping-post, twice stripped before a crowd in the market-place, twice lashed, maddened to desperation, and twice degraded in the eyes of the very negroes we teach to yield entire submission to the white man, however humble his grade. Hate, scorn, remorse—every dark passion his nature can summon—rises up in one torturing tempest, and fills his bosom with a mad longing for revenge. "Death!" he says, while looking out from his cell upon the bright landscape without, "what is death to me? The burnings of an outraged soul subdue the thought of death."

The woman through whom this dread finale was brought upon him, and who now repines, unable to shake off the smarts old associations crowd upon her heart, has a second and third time crept noiselessly to his cell, and sought in vain his forgiveness. Yea, she has opened the door gently, but drew back in terror before his dark frown, his sardonic scorn, his frenzied rush at her. Had he not loved her fondly, his hate had not taken such deep root in his bosom.

Two or three days pass, he has armed himself "to the death," and is resolved to make his escape, and seek revenge of his enemies. It is evening. Dark festoons of clouds hang over the city, lambent lightning plays along the heavens in the south. Now it flashes across the city, the dull panorama lights up, the tall, gaunt steeples gleam out, and the surface of the Bay flashes out in a phosphoric blaze. Patiently and diligently has he filed, and filed, and filed, until he has removed the bar that will give egress to his body. The window of his cell overlooks the ditch, beyond which is the prison wall. Noiselessly he arranges the rope, for he is in the third story, then paces his cell, silent and thoughtful. "Must it be?" he questions within himself, "must I stain these hands with the blood of the woman I love? Revenge, revenge—I will have revenge. I will destroy both of them, for to-morrow I am to be dragged a third time to the whipping-post." Now he casts a glance round the dark cell, now he pauses at the window, now the lightning courses along the high wall, then reflects back the deep ditch. Another moment, and he has commenced his descent. Down, down, down, he lowers himself. Now he holds on tenaciously, the lightning reflects his dangling figure, a prisoner in a lower cell gives the alarm, he hears the watchword of his discovery pass from cell to cell, the clashing of the keeper's door grates upon his ear like thunder—he has reached the end of his rope, and yet hangs suspended in the air. A heavy fall is heard, he has reached the ditch, bounds up its side to the wall, seizes a pole, and places against it, and, with one vault, is over into the open street. Not a moment is to be lost. Uproar and confusion reigns throughout the prison, his keepers have taken the alarm, and will soon be on his track, pursuing him with ferocious hounds. Burning for revenge, and yet bewildered, he sets off at full speed, through back lanes, over fields, passing in his course the astonished guardmen. He looks neither to the right nor the left, but speeds on toward the grove. Now he reaches the bridge that crosses the millpond, pauses for breath, then proceeds on. Suddenly a light from the villa Anna occupies flashes out. He has crossed the bridge, bounds over the little hedge-grown avenue, through the garden, and in another minute stands before her, a pistol pointed at her breast, and all the terrible passions of an enraged fiend darkening his countenance. Her implorings for mercy bring an old servant rushing into the room, the report of a pistol rings out upon the still air, shriek after shriek follows, mingled with piercing moans, and death-struggles. "Ha, ha!" says the avenger, looking on with a sardonic smile upon his face, and a curl of hate upon his lip, "I have taken the life to which I gave my own—yes, I have taken it—I have taken it!" And she writhes her body, and sets her eyes fixedly upon him, as he hastens out of the room.

"Quick! quick!" he says to himself. "There, then! I am pursued!" He recrosses the millpond over another bridge, and in his confusion turns a short angle into a lane leading to the city. The yelping of dogs, the deep, dull tramp of hoofs, the echoing of voices, the ominous baying and scenting of blood-hounds—all break upon his ear in one terrible chaos. Not a moment is to be lost. The sight at the villa will attract the attention of his pursuers, and give him time to make a distance! The thought of what he has done, and the terrible death that awaits him, crowds upon his mind, and rises up before him like a fierce monster of retribution. He rushes at full speed down the lane, vaults across a field into the main road, only to find his pursuers close upon him. The patrol along the streets have caught the alarm, which he finds spreading with lightning-speed. The clank of side-arms, the scenting and baying of the hounds, coming louder and louder, nearer and nearer, warns him of the approaching danger. A gate at the head of a wharf stands open, the hounds are fast gaining upon him, a few jumps more and they will have him fast in their ferocious grasp. He rushes through the gate, down the wharf, the tumultuous cry of his pursuers striking terror into his very heart. Another instant and the hounds are at his feet, he stands on the capsill at the end, gives one wild, despairing look into the abyss beneath—"I die revenged," he shouts, discharges a pistol into his breast, and with one wild plunge, is buried forever in the water beneath. The dark stream of an unhappy life has run out. Upon whom does the responsibility of this terrible closing rest? In the words of Thomson, the avenger left behind him only "Gaunt Beggary, and Scorn, with many hell-hounds more."

When the gray dawn of morning streamed in through the windows of the little villa, and upon the parlor table, that had so often been adorned with caskets and fresh-plucked flowers, there, in their stead, lay the lifeless form of the unhappy Anna, her features pale as marble, but beautiful even in death. There, rolled in a mystic shroud, calm as a sleeper in repose, she lay, watched over by two faithful slaves.

The Judge and Mr. Snivel have found it convenient to make a trip of pleasure into the country. And though the affair creates some little comment in fashionable society, it would be exceedingly unpopular to pry too deeply into the private affairs of men high in office. We are not encumbered with scrutinizing morality. Being an "unfortunate woman," the law cannot condescend to deal with her case. Indeed, were it brought before a judge, and the judge to find himself sitting in judgment upon a judge, his feelings would find some means of defrauding his judgment, while society would carefully close the shutter of its sanctity.

At high noon there comes a man of the name of Moon, commonly called Mr. Moon, the good-natured Coroner. In truth, a better-humored man than Mr. Moon cannot be found; and what is more, he has the happiest way in the world of disposing of such cases, and getting verdicts of his jury exactly suited to circumstances. Mr. Moon never proceeds to business without regaling his jury with good brandy and high-flavored cigars. In this instance he has bustled about and got together six very solemn and seriously-disposed gentlemen, who proceed to deliberate. "A mystery hangs over the case," says one. A second shakes his head, and views the body as if anxious to get away. A third says, reprovingly, that "such cases are coming too frequent." Mr. Moon explains the attendant circumstances, and puts a changed face on the whole affair. One juryman chalks, and another juryman chalks, and Mr. Moon says, by way of bringing the matter to a settled point, "It is a bad ending to a wretched life." A solemn stillness ensues, and then follows the verdict. The body being identified as that of one Anna Bonard, a woman celebrated for her beauty, but of notorious reputation, the jury are of opinion (having duly weighed the circumstances) that she came to her melancholy death by the hands of one George Mullholland, who was prompted to commit the act for some cause to the jury unknown. And the jury, in passing the case over to the authorities, recommend that the said Mullholland be brought to justice. This done, Mr. Moon orders her burial, and the jury hasten home, fully confident of having performed their duty unswerved.

When night came, when all was hushed without, and the silence within was broken only by the cricket's chirp, when the lone watcher, the faithful old slave, sat beside the cold, shrouded figure, when the dim light of the chamber of death seemed mingling with the shadows of departed souls, there appeared in the room, like a vision, the tall figure of a female, wrapped in a dark mantle. Slowly and noiselessly she stole to the side of the deceased, stood motionless and statue-like for several minutes, her eyes fixed in mute contemplation on the face of the corpse. The watcher looked and started back, still the figure remained motionless. Raising her right hand to her chin, pensively, she lifted her eyes heavenward, and in that silent appeal, in those dewy tears that glistened in her great orbs, in those words that seemed freezing to her quivering lips, the fierce struggle waging in that bosom was told. She heard the words, "You cannot redeem me now!" knelling in her ears, her thoughts flashed back over years of remorse, to the day of her error, and she saw rising up as it were before her, like a spectre from the tomb, seeking retribution, the image of the child she had sacrificed to her vanity. She pressed and pressed the cold hand, so delicate, so like her own; she unbared the round, snowy arm, and there beheld the imprinted hearts, and the broken anchor! Her pent-up grief then burst its bounds, the tears rolled down her cheeks, her lips quivered, her hand trembled, and her very blood seemed as ice in her veins. She cast a hurried glance round the room, a calm and serene smile seemed lighting up the features of the lifeless woman, and she bent over her, and kissed and kissed her cold, marble-like brow, and bathed it with her burning tears. It was a last sad offering; and having bestowed it, she turned slowly away, and disappeared. It was Madame Montford, who came a day too late to save the storm-tossed girl, but returned to think of the hereafter of her own soul.

CHAPTER XLV
ANOTHER SHADE OF THE PICTURE

While the earth of Potter's Field is closing over all that remains of Anna Bonard, Maria McArthur may be seen, snatching a moment of rest, as it were, seated under the shade of a tree on the Battery, musing, as is her wont. The ships sail by cheerily, there is a touching beauty about the landscape before her, all nature seems glad. Even the heavens smile serenely; and a genial warmth breathes through the soft air. "Truly the Allwise," she says within herself, "will be my protector, and is chastising me while consecrating something to my good. Mr. Keepum has made my father's release the condition of my ruin. But he is but flesh and blood, and I—no, I am not yet a slave! The virtue of the poor, truly, doth hang by tender threads; but I am resolved to die struggling to preserve it." And a light, as of some future joy, rises up in her fancy, and gives her new strength.

The German family have removed from the house in which she occupies a room, and in its place are come two women of doubtful character. Still, necessity compels her to remain in it; for though it is a means resorted to by Keepum to effect his purpose, she cannot remove without being followed, and harassed by him. Strong in the consciousness of her own purity, and doubly incensed at the proof of what extremes the designer will condescend to, she nerves herself for the struggle she sees before her. True, she was under the same roof with them; she was subjected to many inconveniencies by their presence; but not all their flattering inducements could change her resolution. Nevertheless, the resolution of a helpless female does not protect her from the insults of heartless men. She returns home to find that Mother Rumor, with her thousand tongues, is circulating all kinds of evil reports about her. It is even asserted that she has become an abandoned woman, and is the occupant of a house of doubtful repute. And this, instead of enlisting the sympathies of some kind heart, rather increases the prejudice and coldness of those upon whom she has depended for work. It is seldom the story of suffering innocence finds listeners. The sufferer is too frequently required to qualify in crime, before she becomes an object of sympathy.

She returns, one day, some work just finished for one of our high old families, the lady of which makes it a boast that she is always engaged in "laudable pursuits of a humane kind." The lady sends her servant to the door with the pittance due, and begs to say she is sorry to hear of the life Miss McArthur is leading, and requests she will not show herself at the house again. Mortified in her feelings, Maria begs an interview; but the servant soon returns an answer that her Missus cannot descend to anything of the kind. Our high old families despise working people, and wall themselves up against the poor, whose virtue they regard as an exceedingly cheap commodity. Our high old families choose rather to charge guilt, and deny the right to prove innocence.

With the four shillings, Maria, weeping, turns from the door, procures some bread and coffee, and wends her way to the old prison. But the chords of her resolution are shaken, the cold repulse has gone like poison to her heart. The ray of joy that was lighting up her future, seems passing away; whilst fainter and fainter comes the hope of once more greeting her lover. She sees vice pampered by the rich, and poor virtue begging at their doors. She sees a price set upon her own ruin; she sees men in high places waiting with eager passion the moment when the thread of her resolution will give out. The cloud of her night does, indeed, seem darkening again.

But she gains the prison, and falters as she enters the cell where the old Antiquary, his brow furrowed deep of age, sleeps calmly upon his cot. Near his hand, which he has raised over his head, lays a letter, with the envelope broken. Maria's quick eye flashes over the superscription, and recognizes in it the hand of Tom Swiggs. A transport of joy fills her bosom with emotions she has no power to constrain. She trembles from head to foot; fancies mingled with joys and fears crowd rapidly upon her thoughts. She grasps it with feelings frantic of joy, and holds it in her shaking hand; the shock has nigh overcome her. The hope in which she has so long found comfort and strength—that has so long buoyed her up, and carried her safely through trials, has truly been her beacon light. "Truly," she says within herself, "the dawn of my morning is brightening now." She opens the envelope, and finds a letter enclosed to her. "Oh! yes, yes, yes! it is him—it is from him!" she stammers, in the exuberance of her wild joy. And now the words, "You are richer than me," flash through her thoughts with revealed significance.

Maria grasps the old man's hand. He starts and wakes, as if unconscious of his situation, then fixes his eyes upon her with a steady, vacant gaze. Then, with childlike fervor, he presses her hand to his lips, and kisses it. "It was a pleasant dream—ah! yes, I was dreaming all things went so well!" Again a change comes over his countenance, and he glances round the room, with a wild and confused look. "Am I yet in prison?—well, it was only a dream. If death were like dreaming, I would crave it to take me to its peace, that my mind might no longer be harassed with the troubles of this life. Ah! there, there!"—(the old man starts suddenly, as if a thought has flashed upon him)—"there is the letter, and from poor Tom, too! I only broke the envelope. I have not opened it."

"It is safe, father; I have it," resumes Maria, holding it before him, unopened, as the words tremble upon her lips. One moment she fears it may convey bad news, and in the next she is overjoyed with the hope that it brings tidings of the safety and return of him for whose welfare she breathed many a prayer. Pale and agitated, she hesitates a moment, then proceeds to open it.

"Father, father! heaven has shielded me—heaven has shielded me! Ha! ha! ha! yes, yes, yes! He is safe! he is safe!" And she breaks out into one wild exclamation of joy, presses the letter to her lips, and kisses it, and moistens it with her tears, "It was all a plot—a dark plot set for my ruin!" she mutters, and sinks back, overcome with her emotions. The old man fondles her to his bosom, his white beard flowing over her suffused cheeks, and his tears mingling with hers. And here she remains, until the anguish of her joy runs out, and her mind resumes its wonted calm.

Having broken the spell, she reads the letter to the enraptured old man. Tom has arrived in New York; explains the cause of his long absence; speaks of several letters he has transmitted by post, (which she never received;) and his readiness to proceed to Charleston, by steamer, in a few days. His letter is warm with love and constancy; he recurs to old associations; he recounts his remembrance of the many kindnesses he received at the hands of her father, when homeless; of the care, to which he owes his reform, bestowed upon him by herself, and his burning anxiety to clasp her to his bosom.

A second thought flashes upon her fevered brain. Am I not the subject of slander! Am I not contaminated by associations? Has not society sought to clothe me with shame? Truth bends before falsehood, and virtue withers under the rust of slandering tongues. Again a storm rises up before her, and she feels the poisoned arrow piercing deep into her heart. Am I not living under the very roof that will confirm the slanders of mine enemies? she asks herself. And the answer rings back in confirmation upon her too sensitive ears, and fastens itself in her feelings like a reptile with deadly fangs. No; she is not yet free from her enemies. They have the power of falsifying her to her lover. The thought fills her bosom with sad emotions. Strong in the consciousness of her virtue, she feels how weak she is in the walks of the worldly. Her persecutors are guilty, but being all-powerful may seek in still further damaging her character, a means of shielding themselves from merited retribution. It is the natural expedient of bad men in power to fasten crime upon the weak they have injured.

Only a few days have to elapse, then, and Maria will be face to face with him in whom her fondest hopes have found refuge: but even in those few days it will be our duty to show how much injury may be inflicted upon the weak by the powerful.

The old Antiquary observes the change that has come so suddenly over Maria's feelings, but his entreaties fail to elicit the cause. Shall she return to the house made doubtful by its frail occupants; or shall she crave the jailer's permission to let her remain and share her father's cell? Ah! solicitude for her father settles the question. The alternative may increase his apprehensions, and with them his sufferings. Night comes on; she kisses him, bids him a fond adieu, and with an aching heart returns to the house that has brought so much scandal upon her.

On reaching the door she finds the house turned into a bivouac of revelry; her own chamber is invaded, and young men and women are making night jubilant over Champagne and cigars. Mr. Keepum and the Hon. Mr. Snivel are prominent among the carousers; and both are hectic of dissipation. Shall she flee back to the prison? Shall she go cast herself at the mercy of the keeper? As she is about following the thought with the act, she is seized rudely by the arms, dragged into the scene of carousal, and made the object of coarse jokes. One insists that she must come forward and drink; another holds an effervescing glass to her lips; a third says he regards her modesty out of place, and demands that she drown it with mellowing drinks. The almost helpless girl shrieks, and struggles to free herself from the grasp of her enemies. Mr. Snivel, thinking it highly improper that such cries go free, catches her in his arms, and places his hand over her mouth. "Caught among queer birds at last," he says, throwing an insidious wink at Keepum. "Will flock together, eh?"

As if suddenly invested with herculean strength, Maria hurls the ruffian from her, and lays him prostrate on the floor. In his fall the table is overset, and bottles, decanters and sundry cut glass accompaniments, are spread in a confused mass on the floor. Suddenly Mr. Keepum extinguishes the lights. This is the signal for a scene of uproar and confusion we leave the reader to picture in his imagination. The cry of "murder" is followed quickly by the cry of "watch, watch!" and when the guardmen appear, which they are not long in doing, it is seen that the very chivalric gentlemen have taken themselves off—left, as a prey for the guard, only Maria and three frail females.

Cries, entreaties, and explanations, are all useless with such men as our guard is composed of. Her clothes are torn, and she is found rioting in disreputable company. The sergeant of the guard says, "Being thus disagreeably caught, she must abide the penalty. It may teach you how to model your morals," he adds; and straightway, at midnight, she is dragged to the guard-house, and in spite of her entreaties, locked up in a cell with the outcast women. "Will you not hear me? will you not allow an innocent woman to speak in her own behalf? Do, I beg, I beseech, I implore you— listen but for a minute—render me justice, and save me from this last step of shame and disgrace," she appeals to the sergeant, as the cell door closes upon her.

Mr. Sergeant Stubble, for such is his name, shakes his head in doubt. "Always just so," he says, with a shrug of the shoulders: "every one's innocent what comes here 'specially women of your sort. The worst rioters 'come the greatest sentimentalists, and repents most when they gets locked up—does! You'll find it a righteous place for reflection, in there." Mr. Sergeant Stubble shuts the door, and smothers her cries.

CHAPTER XLVI
GAINING STRENGTH FROM PERSECUTION

You know it is Bulwer who says, and says truly: "There is in calumny a rank poison that, even when the character throws off the slander, the heart remains diseased beneath the effect." The force of this on Maria's thoughts and feelings, surrounded as she was by the vile influences of a Charleston cell, came with strange effect as she contemplated her friendless condition. There is one witness who can bear testimony to her innocence, and in Him she still puts her trust. But the charitable have closed their ears to her; and the outside world is too busy to listen to her story. Those words of the poor woman who said, "You are still richer than me," again ring their sweet music in her ear, and give strength to her weary soul. They come to her like the voice of a merciful Providence, speaking through the hushed air of midnight, and breathing the sweet spirit of love into the dusky figures who tenant that dreary cell. To Maria it is the last spark of hope, that rarely goes out in woman's heart, and has come to tell her that to-morrow her star may brighten. And now, reader, turn with us to another scene of hope and anxiety.

The steamer which bears Tom to Charleston is off Cape Romaine. He has already heard of the fate of the old man McArthur. But, he asks himself, may not truth and justice yet triumph? He paces and repaces the deck, now gazing vacantly in the direction the ship is steering, then walking to the stern and watching the long train of phosphoric light playing on the toppling waves.

There was something evasive in the manner of the man who communicated to him the intelligence concerning McArthur. "May I ask another question of you, sir?" he inquires, approaching the man who, like himself, sauntered restlessly along the deck.

The man hesitates, lights a fresh cigar. "You desire me to be frank with you, of course," rejoins the man. "But I observe you are agitated. I will answer your question, if it carry no personal wound. Speak, my friend."

"You know Maria?"

"Well."

"You know what has become of her, or where she resides?"

Again the man hesitates—then says, "These are delicate matters to discover."

"You are not responsible for my feelings," interrupts the impatient man.

"If, then, I must be plain,—she is leading the life of an outcast. Yes, sir, the story is that she has fallen, and from necessity. I will say this, though," he adds, by way of relief, "that I know nothing of it myself." The words fall like a death-knell on his thoughts and feelings. He stammers out a few words, but his tongue refuses to give utterance to his thoughts. His whole nature seems changed; his emotions have filled the cup of his sorrow; an abyss, deep, dark, and terrible, has opened to his excited imagination. All the dark scenes of his life, all the struggles he has had to gain his manliness, rise up before him like a gloomy panorama, and pointing him back to that goal of dissipation in which his mind had once found relief. He seeks his stateroom in silence, and there invokes the aid of Him who never refuses to protect the right. And here again we must return to another scene.

Morning has come, the guard-roll has been called, and Judge Sleepyhorn is about to hold high court. Maria and the companions of her cell are arraigned, some black, others white, all before so august a judge. His eye rests on a pale and dejected woman inwardly resolved to meet her fate, calm and resolute. It is to her the last struggle of an eventful life, and she is resolved to meet it with womanly fortitude.

The Judge takes his seat, looks very grave, and condescends to say there is a big docket to be disposed of this morning. "Crime seems to increase in the city," he says, bowing to Mr. Seargent Stubbs.

"If your Honor will look at that," Mr. Stubbs says, smiling,—"most on em's bin up afore. All hard cases, they is."

"If yeer Onher plases, might a woman o' my standin' say a woord in her own difince? Sure its only a woord, Judge, an' beein a dacent gintleman ye'd not refuse me the likes."

"Silence, there!" ejaculates Mr. Seargent Stubbs; "you must keep quiet in court."

"Faith its not the likes o' you'd keep me aisy, Mr. Stubbs. Do yee see that now?" returns the woman, menacingly. She is a turbulent daughter of the Emerald Isle, full five feet nine inches, of broad bare feet, with a very black eye, and much in want of raiment.

"The most corrigible case what comes to this court," says Mr. Stubbs, bowing knowingly to the judge. "Rather likes a prison, yer Honor. Bin up nine times a month. A dear customer to the state."

The Judge, looking grave, and casting his eye learnedly over the pages of a ponderous statute book, inquires of Mr. Seargent Stubbs what the charge is.

"Disturbed the hole neighborhood. A fight atween the Donahues, yer Honor."

"Dorn't believe a woord of it, yeer Onher. Sure, din't Donahue black the eye o' me, and sphil the whisky too? Bad luck to Donahue, says I. You don't say that to me, says he. I'd say it to the divil, says I. Take that! says Donahue." Here Mrs. Donahue points to her eye, and brings down even the dignity of the court.

"In order to preserve peace between you and Donahue," says his Honor, good naturedly, "I shall fine you ten dollars, or twenty days."

"Let it go at twenty days," replies Mrs. Donahue, complimenting his Honor's high character, "fir a divil o' ten dollars have I." And Mrs. Donahue resigns herself to the tender mercies of Mr. Seargent Stubbs, who removes her out of court.

A dozen or more delinquent negroes, for being out after hours without passes, are sentenced thirty stripes apiece, and removed, to the evident delight of the Court, who is resolved that the majesty of the law shall be maintained.

It is Maria's turn now. Pale and trembling she approaches the circular railing, assisted by Mr. Seargent Stubbs. She first looks imploringly at the judge, then hangs down her head, and covers her face with her hands.

"What is the charge?" inquires the Judge, turning to the loquacious Stubbs. Mr. Stubbs says: "Disorderly conduct—and in a house of bad repute."

"I am innocent—I have committed no crime," interrupts the injured woman. "You have dragged me here to shame me." Suddenly her face becomes pale as marble, her limbs tremble, and the court is thrown into a state of confusion by her falling to the floor in a swoon.

"Its all over with her now," says Mr. Stubbs, standing back in fear.

Crime has not dried up all the kinder impulses of Judge Sleepyhorn's heart. Leaving the bench he comes quickly to the relief of the unfortunate girl, holds her cold trembling hand in his own, and tenderly bathes her temples. "Sorry the poor girl," he says, sympathizingly, "should have got down so. Knew her poor old father when he was comfortably off, and all Charleston liked him." His Honor adjourns court, and ten minutes pass before the sufferer is restored to consciousness. Then with a wild despairing look she scans those around her, rests her head on her hand despondingly, and gives vent to her tears. The cup of her sorrow has indeed overrun.

"It was wrong to arrest you, young woman, and I sympathize with you. No charge has been preferred, and so you are free. A carriage waits at the door, and I have ordered you to be driven home," says the judge, relaxing into sympathy.

"I have no home now," she returns, the tears coursing down her wet cheeks. "Slaves have homes, but I have none now."

"When you want a friend, you'll find a friend in me. Keep up your spirits, and remember that virtue is its own reward." Having said this, the Judge raises her gently to her feet, supports her to the carriage, and sees her comfortably seated. "Remember, you know, where to find a friend if you want one," he says, and bids her good-morning. In another minute the carriage is rolling her back to the home from whence she was taken. She has no better home now.

CHAPTER XLVII
AN EXCITEMENT

A bright fire burned that night in Keepum's best parlor, furnished with all the luxuries modern taste could invent. Keepum, restless, paces the carpet, contemplating his own importance, for he has just been made a Major of Militia, and we have a rare love for the feather. Now he pauses at a window and looks impatiently out, then frisks his fingers through his crispy hair and resumes his pacing. He expects some one, whose coming he awaits with evident anxiety. "The time is already up," he says, drawing his watch from his pocket. The door-bell rings just then, his countenance brightens, and a servant ushers Mr. Snivel in. "The time is already up, my good fellow," says Keepum, extending his hand familiarly,—Mr. Snivel saying, "I've so many demands on my time, you know. We're in good time, you know. Must bring the thing to a head to-night." A short conversation carried on in whispers, and they sally out, and soon disappear down Broad street.

Just rounding the frowning walls of fort Sumter, a fort the restless people never had any particular love for, is a big red light of the steamer cutting through the sea like a monster of smoke and flame, on her way up the harbor. Another hour, and she will be safely moored at her landing. Tom stands on the upper deck, looking intently towards the city, his anxiety increasing as the ship approaches the end of her voyage, and his eager eye catching each familiar object only to remind him more forceably of the time when he seemed on the downward road of life. Hope had already begun to dispel his fears, and the belief that what the man had told him was founded only in slander, became stronger the more he pondered over it.

St. Michael's clock has just struck ten, and the mounted guard are distributing into their different beats. Maria, contemplating what may come to-morrow, sits at the window of her lonely chamber like one whom the world had forgotten. The dull vibrating sound of the clock still murmurs on the air as she is startled from her reverie by the sound of voices under the window. She feels her very soul desponding. It does indeed seem as if that moment has come when nature in her last struggle with hope must yield up the treasure of woman's life, and sink into a life of remorse and shame. The talking becomes more distinct; then there is a pause, succeeded by Keepum and Snivel silently entering her room, the one drawing a chair by her side, the other taking a seat near the door. "Come as friends, you know," says Keepum, exchanging glances with Snivel, then fixing his eyes wickedly on the woman. "Don't seem to enjoy our company, eh? Poor folks is got to puttin' on airs right big, now-a-days. Don't 'mount to much, anyhow; ain't much better than niggers, only can't sell 'em." "Poor folks must keep up appearances, eh," interposes Mr. Snivel. They are waiting an opportunity for seizing and overpowering the unprotected girl. We put our chivalry to strange uses at times.

But the steamer has reached her wharf; the roaring of her escaping steam disturbs the city, and reëchoes far away down the bay. Again familiar scenes open to the impatient man's view; old friends pass and repass him unrecognized; but only one thought impels him, and that is fixed on Maria. He springs ashore, dashes through the crowd of spectators, and hurries on, scarcely knowing which way he is going.

At length he pauses on the corner of King and Market streets, and glances up to read the name by the glare of gas-light. An old negro wends his way homeward. "Daddy," says he, "how long have you lived in Charleston?"

"Never was out on em, Mas'r," replies the negro, looking inquisitively into the anxious man's face. "Why, lor's me, if dis are bin't Mas'r Tom, what used t' be dis old nigger's young Mas'r."

"Is it you, Uncle Cato?" Their recognition was warm, hearty, and true. "God bless you, my boy; I've need of your services now," says Tom, still holding the hard hand of the old negro firmly grasped in his own, and discovering the object of his mission.

"Jus' tote a'ter old Cato, Mas'r Tom. Maria's down da, at Undine's cabin, yander. Ain't no better gal libin dan Miss Maria," replies Cato, enlarging on Maria's virtues. There is no time to be lost. They hurry forward, Tom following the old negro, and turning into a narrow lane to the right, leading to Undine's cabin. But here they are doomed to disappointment. They reach Undine's cabin, but Maria is not there. Undine comes to the door, and points away down the lane, in the direction of a bright light. "You will find her dare" says Undine; "and if she ain't dare, I don' know where she be." They thank her, repay her with a piece of silver, and hurry away in the direction of the light, which seems to burn dimmer and dimmer as they approach. It suddenly disappears, and, having reached the house, a rickety wooden tenement, a cry of "Save me, save me! Heaven save me!" rings out on the still air, and falls on the ear of the already excited man, like a solemn warning.

"Up dar! Mas'r Tom, up dar!" shouts Cato, pointing to a stairs leading on the outside. Up Tom vaults, and recognizing Maria's voice, supplicating for mercy, thunders at the door, which gives away before his strength. "It is me, Maria! it is me!" he proclaims. "Who is this that has dared to abuse or insult you?" and she runs and throws herself into his arms. "A light! a light, bring a light, Cato!" he demands, and the old negro hastens to obey.

In the confusion of the movement, Keepum reaches the street in safety and hastens to his home, leaving his companion to take care of himself.

A pale gleam of light streams into the open door, discovering a tall dusky figure moving noiselessly towards it. "Why, if here bin't Mas'r Snivel!" ejaculates old Cato, who returns bearing a candle, the light of which falls on the tall figure of Mr. Snivel.

"What, villain! is it you who has brought all this distress upon a friendless girl?" — —

"Glad to see you back, Tom. Don't make so much of it, my good fellow—only a bit of a lark, you know. 'Pon my honor, there was nothing wrong meant. Ready to do you a bit of a good turn, any time," interrupts Mr. Snivel, blandly, and extending his hand.

"You! villain, do me a friendly act? Never. You poisoned the mind of my mother against me, robbed her of her property, and then sought to destroy the happiness and blast forever the reputation of one who is dearer to me than a sister. You have lived a miscreant long enough. You must die now." Quickly the excited man draws a pistol, the report rings sharply on the ear, and the tall figure of Mr. Snivel staggers against the door, then falls to the ground,—dead. His day of reckoning has come, and with it a terrible retribution.

"Now Maria, here," says Tom, picking up a packet of letters that had dropped from the pocket of the man, as he fell, "is the proof of his guilt and my sincerity." They were the letters written by him to Maria, and intercepted by Mr. Snivel, through the aid of a clerk in the post-office. "He has paid the penalty of his misdeeds, and I have no regrets to offer. To-morrow I will give myself up and ask only justice."

Then clasping Maria in his arms he bids old Cato follow him, and proceeds with her to a place of safety for the night, as an anxious throng gather about the house, eager to know the cause of the shooting. "Ah, Mas'r Snivel," says old Cato, pausing to take a last look of the prostrate form, "you's did a heap o' badness. Gone now. Nobody'll say he care."

CHAPTER XLIX
ALL'S WELL

Two months have passed since the events recorded in the preceding chapter. Tom has been arraigned before a jury of his peers, and honorably acquitted, although strong efforts were made to procure a conviction, for Mr. Snivel had many friends in Charleston who considered his death a loss. But the people said it was a righteous verdict, and justified it by their applause.

And now, the dark clouds of sorrow and trial having passed away, the happy dawn of a new life is come. How powerfully the truth of the words uttered by the woman, Undine, impresses itself on her mind now,—"You are still richer than me." It is a bright sunny morning in early April. Birds are making the air melodious with their songs; flowers blooming by the roadside, are distilling their perfumes; a bright and serene sky, tinged in the East with soft, azure clouds, gives a clear, delicate outline to the foliage, so luxuriant and brilliant of color, skirting the western edge of the harbor, and reflecting itself in the calm, glassy water. A soft whispering wind comes fragrant from the west; it does indeed seem as if nature were blending her beauties to make the harmony perfect.

A grotesque group, chiefly negroes, old and young, may be seen gathered about the door of a quaint old personage near the millpond. Their curiosity is excited to the highest pitch, and they wait with evident impatience the coming of the object that has called them together. Chief among the group is old Cato, in his best clothes, consisting of a tall drab hat, a faded blue coat, the tail extending nearly to the ground, striped pantaloons, a scarlet vest, an extravagant shirt collar, tied at the neck with a piece of white cotton, and his bare feet. Cato moves up and down, evidently feeling himself an important figure of the event, and admonishing his young "brudren," who are much inclined to mischief, not a few having perched on the pickets of the parsonage, to keep on their best behavior. Then he discourses with great volubility of his long acquaintance with Mas'r Tom and Miss Maria.

As if to add another prominent picture to the scene, there appears at the door of the parsonage, every few minutes, a magnificently got-up negro, portly, grey hair, and venerable, dressed in unsullied black, a spotless white cravat, and gloves. This is Uncle Pomp, who considers himself an essential part of the parsonage, and is regarded with awe for his Bible knowledge by all the colored people of the neighborhood. Pomp glances up, then down the street, advances a few steps, admonishes the young negroes, and exchanges bows with Cato, whom he regards as quite a common brought-up negro compared with himself. Now he disappears, Cato remarking to his companions that if he had Pomp's knowledge and learning he would not thank anybody to make him a white man.

Presently there is a stir in the group: all eyes are turned up the road, and the cry is, "Dare da comes." Two carriages approach at a rapid speed, and haul up at the gate, to the evident delight and relief of the younger members of the group, who close in and begin scattering sprigs of laurel and flowers along the path, as two couple, in bridal dress, alight, trip quickly through the garden, and disappear, Pomp bowing them into the parsonage. Tom and Maria are the central figures of the interesting ceremony about to be performed. Old Cato received a warm press of the hand from Tom as he passed, and Cato returned the recognition, with "God bress Mas'r Tom." A shadow of disappointment deepened in his face as he saw the door closed, and it occurred to him that he was not to be a witness of the ceremony. But the door again opened, and Pomp relieved his wounded feelings by motioning with his finger, and, when Cato had reached the porch, bowing him into the house.

And now we have reached the last scene in the picture. There, kneeling before the altar in the parlor of that quaint old parsonage, are the happy couple and their companions. The clergyman, in his surplice, reads the touching service in a clear and impressive voice, while Pomp, in a pair of antique spectacles, ejaculates the responses in a voice peculiar to his race. Old Cato, kneeling before a chair near the door, follows with a loud — Amen. There is something supremely simple, touching, and impressive in the picture. As the closing words of the benediction fall from the clergyman's lips, Maria, her pale oval face shadowed with that sweetness and gentleness an innocent heart only can reflect, raises her eyes upwards as if to return thanks to the Giver of all good for his mercy and protection. As she did this a ray of light stole in at the window and played softly over her features, like a messenger of love come to announce a happy future. Just then the cup of her joy became full, and tears, like gems of purest water, glistened in her eyes, then moistened her pallid cheeks. Truly the woman spoke right when she said,

"You are still still richer than me."

FOOTNOTES

[1] See Senator Sumner's speech in Congress on Plantation manners.

[2] An election bully, the ugliest man in Charleston, and the deadly foe of Mingle.

[3] Now called Baxter street

[4] Now Worth street and Mission Place.

[5] A gambling den.

[6] Can it be possible that such things as are here pictured have an existence among a people laying any claim to a state of civilization? the reader may ask. The author would here say that to the end of fortifying himself against the charge of exaggeration, he submitted the MS. of this chapter to a gentleman of the highest respectability in Charleston, whose unqualified approval it received, as well as enlisting his sympathies in behalf of the unfortunate lunatics found in the cells described. Four years have passed since that time. He subsequently sent the author the following, from the "Charleston Courier," which speaks for itself.

"FROM THE REPORTS OF COUNCIL.

"January 4th, 1843

"*The following communication was received from William M. Lawton, Esq., Chairman of the Commissioners of the Poor-house.*

"'Charleston, Dec. 17th, 1852.

"'To the Honorable, the City Council of Charleston:

"'By a resolution of the Board of Commissioners of this City, I have been instructed to communicate with your honorable body in relation to the insane paupers now in Poor-house', (the insane in a poor-house!) 'and to request that you will adopt the necessary provision for sending them to the Lunatic Asylum at Columbia. * * * * There are twelve on the list, many of whom, it is feared, have already remained too long in an institution quite unsuited to their unfortunate situation.

"'With great respect, your very obedient servant,
"'(Signed) WM. M. LAWTON,
"'Chairman of the Board of Commissioners.'"

[7] Our Charleston readers will recognize the case here described, without any further key.

[8] An institution for the relief of the destitute.

[9] This sight may be seen at any time.